Peter Woolf was a career criminal and drug addict. He is now married and lives in Norfolk. His transformation came after a meeting with two of his victims. The project was pioneered by the Justice Research Consortium and its founders, Professor Lawrence Sherman and Sir Charles Pollard, in trials to test out the impact of face-to-face meetings between offenders and their victims.

Peter now works with Charles Pollard in his not-for-profit organization Restorative Solutions CIC, giving lectures to police forces and other groups up and down the country; and with the Metropolitan Police, helping to turn prolific and priority offenders away from crime in North London.

www.rbooks.co.uk

THE DAMAGE DONE

Peter Woolf
with Humphrey Price

BANTAM BOOKS

LONDON • TORONTO • SYDNEY • AUCKLAND • JOHANNESBURG

TRANSWORLD PUBLISHERS
61–63 Uxbridge Road, London W5 5SA
A Random House Group Company
www.rbooks.co.uk

THE DAMAGE DONE
A BANTAM BOOK: 9780553819335

First published in Great Britain
in 2008 by Bantam Press
a division of Transworld Publishers
Bantam edition published 2009

This book is a work of non-fiction based on the life, experiences and
recollections of the author. In some cases names of people, places, dates,
sequences or the detail of events have been changed solely to protect the
privacy of others. The author has stated to the publishers that, except in such
respects not affecting the substantial accuracy of the work, the contents of this
book are true.

Every effort has been made to obtain the necessary permissions with reference
to copyright material, both illustrative and quoted. We apologize for any
omissions in this respect and will be pleased to make the appropriate
acknowledgements in any future edition.

A CIP catalogue record for this book
is available from the British Library.

Addresses for Random House Group Ltd companies outside the UK
can be found at: www.randomhouse.co.uk
The Random House Group Ltd Reg. No. 954009

The Random House Group Limited supports The Forest Stewardship
Council (FSC®), the leading international forest certification organisation.
Our books carrying the FSC label are printed on FSC® certified paper.
FSC is the only forest certification scheme endorsed by the leading
environmental organisations, including Greenpeace. Our
paper procurement policy can be found at
www.randomhouse.co.uk/environment

MIX
Paper from
responsible sources
FSC® C016897

Typeset in 11.5/15pt Sabon by Falcon Oast Graphic Art Ltd.
Printed in Great Britain by Clays Ltd, St Ives plc

2 4 6 8 10 9 7 5 3

Contents

Acknowledgements
for 'The Damage Done'

This book is for all the nameless, faceless people who have been victims of crime.

My special thanks go to the following people; without them there would not be me.

My friend Kim Smith and all of his family, Will Riley and family, the Doctor, Tony and Val, Steve, Kelvin, Neil, Deric and Michelle, Irene and Arthur, all Bill W's friends and Bill himself.

Rehabilitation of Addicted Prisoners Trust (RAPT).

Restorative justice consortium.

Sir Charles Pollard, Nigel Whiskin, Brian Dowling and all at Restorative Solutions CIC.

Helen Orros, Kevin Straughan, Gordon, Karen, and all at the Grove.

Alice, Roy, Laura and Roy, and all the rest of those that I have left behind.

Michael and Alice (my in-laws) and all of the family, who supported me through thick and thin.

Humphrey and Sara (nice one).

Most of all, I want to say thank you to my wife Louise; without you I would never have done any of this. I love you and the children with all my heart.

Prologue

The Day I Died

It had been a good day. Sophie had done well, begging outside Sainsbury's, and Phil hadn't done badly either, collecting tips from helping people into cabs with their shopping. I'd done best of all, nicking purses as I walked about, stuff like that; I must have got about £100 in all. Normally it was Phil who did best. Phil, who like me had let drink, drugs and crime ruin his life, was known as a getter, which meant that he got people's drugs for them, and then took a little for doing the job. Sometimes he'd just run off with all the drugs, but mostly he did it to get paid too. Phil was a funny-looking bloke; the best way I can describe him is to say that he was a good-looking Herman Munster. Sophie was . . . well, Sophie made her money begging, but that wasn't what she was known for. She had started out in prostitution early on, as a teenager in Soho, but the drugs had done for her too, and as she'd do anything for money her notoriety came because she shagged a dog for some porn film. An Alsatian it was.

I wasn't any better than them. I might have looked all right – my clothes were top of the range, smart shoes and jackets and strides – but I never washed, and because of the drugs and the drink I stank, stank so badly that my own family wouldn't let me in the house if I went round to see them. Of course they also wouldn't let me in because I'd nick stuff from them. The only times I went round was when I'd been skip-diving and had found a beat-up old video recorder, or whatever. I'd spit on a sleeve and wipe it down, then take it round to one of their houses and plead with them to buy it so I could buy more drugs. I'd stand on the doorstep and they'd give me £20 just to go away. They didn't want me around them any more. I didn't even get a cuppa. Why they did it I don't know, but they always bought the rubbish I took round, perhaps hoping I might stop one day. Or die.

Certainly that's how I felt. I knew I was going so fast, all the way to the end, that I had no chance of stopping, not now. I was going to crash and die; I couldn't stop. I had nothing in my life but that need, that empty space I could only fill with more drugs, and more drink. So that was my aim: steal by day, get wasted by night.

I wasn't happy, mind. It wasn't like I wanted to be doing this.

Me and Phil and Sophie – those two were pretty

much the only people who'd speak to me by 2002; everyone else had given up on me – would buy some heroin and some crack and, if we'd had a day as good as this one, some beers too, and go back to their flat, and that would be all we'd do for the night. It was easy to get the drugs. If you had the money it always was, wherever you were. We'd make a phone call and someone would show up, hand them over. There was a guy who'd printed up business cards, called himself Deals on Wheels; maybe it was him who came round. I don't remember. I wasn't interested in who came over. So long as they had the drugs they were welcome.

I don't remember eating then, not ever; we used all our money for drugs. I suppose I picked up food as I walked about, literally picked it up – half-eaten burgers, that kind of thing. I was so far gone there was no hope for me. I'd walk around during the day – Phil and Sophie's flat was so disgusting you just had to get out of it – on the verge of tears, because everything about my life frightened me. I was beyond being unable to cope. I was a dead man, walking around.

The flat was a one-bedroom place over in Clapton, east London. It was a flat no human being should have lived in. The floor was knee-deep in litter: beer cans, bottles, wrappers, strips of foil, papers, clothes too filthy or torn to be worn; there were used syringes, dried blood inside them, on every surface; broken glass, thousands of fag-ends and rotten food lay everywhere.

We'd long given up on the toilet, which was all blocked; we'd shit in the bath. It stank so bad in the bathroom you'd want to throw up, so we'd run in and piss down the sink. If you coughed your lungs up – which we all did; the drugs fucked you up – then you spat where you were sitting. There was nowhere else for it to go, so you'd spit against the wall. Everything had something else on top of it. Even the dust had grime on top, and grease on top of that. There was filth everywhere. But it was better than the streets, or so we told ourselves.

I'd found an old mattress in an alleyway somewhere and dragged it in, and I used their front room as my bedroom. My blanket was a thin curtain I'd found chucked out – it was pretty tatty when I got it – and when it got properly cold I'd pull my coat over me. At least it was safe, though, which is what made it so much better than being on the outside. And when you're shooting up, that counts for a lot.

I had trouble shooting up then. I'd hit just about every vein in my body, in the arms, legs, groin, between the toes. Most of my veins were now broken or gone (I used to call prison my vein rejuvenation holiday), so I had only one place left to inject, which was in my neck.

I lived for nothing except drugs. I owed money to almost everyone I knew. I'd even robbed beggars and *Big Issue* sellers. I felt alone, totally alone, and every moment I was awake and not high I spent paralysed with fear. I was frightened of walking down the street in case I bumped into someone I owed money to; I was too frightened to go into a shop; I was too frightened to ask for help; I was even too frightened of telling anyone that I was frightened. I was always on my guard.

It's obvious to me now, though I didn't know it then, that I was insane at this point in my life but somehow kept soldiering on, to keep funding the heroin habit that was crippling me. It's a funny disease, this addiction thing: it's the only one that lets you think you're all right while you keep getting worse. I'd stand by the cracked mirror in Phil and Sophie's and I'd look like shit. My hair was all different lengths, and greasy with muck; my skin was almost yellow; I'd have filthy, broken fingernails; and the backs of my hands would be as dry as paper, and dirt would have filled the cracks, like a baked-up riverbed. I'd been in hospital a couple of times that year already, once with suspected TB, once with pneumonia, and on top of that I had contracted hepatitis C from a dirty needle. I'd had blood dripping from my rectum, pain like I'd never known in my kidney region, and a complete lack of energy; even walking was an effort. Yet I'd look at myself in the mirror, smooth down my hair as best I could with my hands and think, 'Yeah, you've still got it, Peter, you warrior, you outlaw, you stud.'

Pathetic, really, what addiction does to you.

Some time on the last morning I spent at that flat I woke up cold and shivering. Invariably I would sleep in my clothes, so my routine was to get up, wash my face in the kitchen sink, sometimes brush my teeth, flatten my hair down, then get out on the streets, looking for victims. It had been another bad night, with mice and who knows what running all over me. I needed a fix as soon as I came to – more than a drink, more than food. I'd always try to save just enough heroin from the night before so as to stop myself from clucking, or withdrawing, because it's hard to get going when you're clucking. The amount I'd have left was usually small, just enough to stop the sweats and the retching and the involuntary bowel movements. But we hadn't had enough the night before, so although I would have stayed hiding in that flat if I could have rather than step out into the street outside, I had no choice: outdoors I had to go, to find something, anything, to get me through the day, and into the night, which was when I could have what I needed.

As it was Sophie's birthday, we had a quick couple of beers to celebrate, then I set off with Phil towards Islington, where he was going to see his ex-wife.

I walked everywhere, mostly of course because I had no money for a bus – I stank too much to get on one anyway – but also because it's when you're out walking that you can see what there is to nick. I walked, too, because it gave me something to do. Being tired was nothing, I was tired all the time, walking didn't make any difference to that. What it did change was the hunger, the command to fill the void. If I was walking,

I could ignore the voice inside me, demanding more, telling me what to do, reminding me that I needed to score. I would scrounge a couple of quid from anyone I could, and check out the slots in phone boxes in case there was any change (you'd be surprised how many people forget to take their change).

I had a woman who used to buy saucepans off me. Don't really know what she did with them all, didn't really care as long as she bought them. I would walk into a big store, pick up a set of saucepans and walk out like they were mine. Then I would sell them, phone a dealer, and get a joey. In the smack world a joey is a £10 bag, but it depends where you come from. I've heard them called wraps, cockle bags and bagels, but to me it was a joey. Once I had injected it was back to work, prowling the streets looking for anything that would get me more drugs.

I always had a can of lager if I could afford it. One day, a really bad summer's day, I'd been walking round the Tottenham Court Road area for hours trying to make money but was really struggling. I'd had enough tackle to keep the cluck away, and as I wandered around the streets I saw there were unfinished drinks both inside and outside pubs, so I was finishing them off. I got well pissed doing this; I suppose it was my big night out, sort of. Then I picked this lager bottle up that I spotted in one doorway and took a big gulp . . . and spat it out right away, gagging. It was piss.

Some dirty bastard had pissed in it and I drank it. Didn't put me off though. I still went back and found another glass to drink from.

I walked with Phil all the way from Clapton to Islington. Not that far as the crow flies, but then the crow's not a starving junkie, is he? It was far enough for me. When I got there I thought about trying to see the family, but decided against it; there wasn't anything more they'd do for me now. I decided that I needed to do a little bit more than nick purses that day. This wasn't a deliberate 'cry for help' thing because I was too scared, too far gone, to ask for help. I think it was just another way for me to get out, to do something desperate so that I could maybe get back to the one place where I felt truly safe: prison.

It took me another half an hour to walk to Canonbury Square. I walked all round the square and looked at each house as I went past. Eventually I stopped by one and thought, 'I wonder . . .' I walked up to the big front door, clean and painted black, and pushed on it at the top and the bottom to see how many locks it had. It wobbled a bit. Just the one, then, in the middle. Easy.

I turned back to the street, leaned as casually as I could against the door, then pushed quickly and hard. It opened. I was in fast, before anyone passing by could look up and wonder what I was doing, and shut the door behind me. I went straight up the stairs. After seeing one or two empty rooms – I mean, they had beds and stuff in them but nothing I wanted to steal – I found another door shut against me. I broke that open, went in, and saw straight away that this room was full of things I could steal. Little bits and pieces, things I could sell quickly, the kind of stuff I could tell myself (if I'd given it a moment's thought, which I never did) that no one would really miss.

Then for some reason I didn't leave. I sat down on the bed and started picking things up, examining them, looking at them as if it was the very first time I'd ever seen things like this. A pair of slippers; a lamp; a suit jacket. I stared at each item, slowly turning them in my hands. I don't know why; it was as if I was dreaming. I should have gone right away, but I stayed instead. I was in that place far longer than I'd ever been inside anywhere on a job. Normally, top whack would be five minutes – get in, find the stuff I wanted, get out. This time I was probably in there for over half an hour. In the wardrobe there were these nice shoes, and I took them out and thought, 'Wouldn't it be nice if they fitted me?' But they didn't.

All of a sudden I hear a voice: 'Who are you?'

I look up, and there's this young guy, a big guy, athletic-looking, standing there.

'What are you doing in my house?' he demands.

My reply is an on-the-spot lie, a totally absurd excuse, an answer born out of fear: 'Oh, I live over the road and I was watching out of my window and I saw a person in this room acting suspiciously and I'm here to make sure he hasn't taken anything.'

'Oh yeah? What number do you live at?'

'I live at number two,' I reply, but the man knows I'm lying and I know that he knows.

This is it.

'Get out of my way,' I say, 'I'm going.'

I'm not frightened of him, but it turns out he's not frightened of me either. 'No, no, no,' he says, and as I move to go past him he grabs me and there's some pushing and shoving. He's shouting, I'm shouting, though I don't remember anything about what we said.

We force each other out into the hall, and we're swinging away at each other. It's like a proper John Wayne fight, with punches thrown and everything. I pull away and race down the stairs, into the kitchen, where I make as if to grab something from the top of the counter.

'Keep away, I've got a knife!'

But he doesn't keep away. Instead he lowers his head and comes at me. I don't know, if I really had got a knife in my hand, whether I'd have done anything with it, but I do pick up a big metal griddle sitting on the hob on the oven and hit him over the head with it. There's a horrible crack but he doesn't stop. We're still rolling around and hitting each other and fighting with anything that comes to hand. Then I pick up a big old flowerpot – a nice, stylish one, big it was – and crack that over his head as well. It's a horrible thing to look back and see something comical in something so bad, but I remember that for a split-second it was like a cartoon, the flower and the earth stuck on his head, shards of pot all around him.

I nearly make it out the door but he charges after me and grabs me. We get outside and we're still punching and hitting out at each other. He's now shouting out for help. I manage to get on to the street and pull away from him, but just as I do so and start to run off to Canonbury Road, two fellas who I guess were walking past and heard him shouting get hold of me and pull me down, kicking me, roughing me up, until finally the police show up. Someone – I don't know who – must have called them.

I'm bashed up and bruised a bit, there's a couple of cuts to my face, but I don't care. The handcuffs go on and I'm shoved into the back of the police van.

'What's your name, mate?' asks a young copper as he sits down opposite me in the back.

Now at this point I'm a bit stupid and give him something back like 'What d'you think my name is?'

'Well, I don't know, that's why I'm asking,' he replies.

I was under the illusion that everyone in Islington knew my name. Perhaps fifteen years earlier every policeman who worked that area would've known who I was. Back then I was Park Lane; now I'm under a park bench. That's what the drugs have done for me. I'm nobody now.

So we get to the station, and I'm taken before the duty sergeant to get booked in. I'm an old hand at this. I know the usual form. I should ask for a doctor before I do anything or say anything or answer any questions, even before I ask for my solicitor, as the doctor would have to come out and I'd give him the spiel about being an addict, how I can't be locked up for the night without something to get me through it, and he'd have to give me DF118 – codeine – which acts as a morphine substitute, and two blue 10ml Valium to take the edge off everything, and then I could lie back and chill out for the night. Only this time I don't do that.

'Do you want anything?' he asks.

'Yeah, I'm starving. Can I get some food? I'm so hungry, can I get two dinners?' I haven't eaten for days.

He's surprised, as the clothes I'm wearing are really good ones – like I said, a nice pair of strides, a nice pair of shoes, a £600 jacket and everything. 'Oh yeah? Would you like two desserts as well?' he asks. And he means it, he isn't being funny with me or anything. I'm bone-weary, everything looks as if it's approaching the end for me, and I'm really grateful to him. He doesn't look at me and think, 'Scummy druggy, he deserves to be hungry'; instead he looks after me. I get my two dinners and my two desserts. Once I've eaten I'm ready to answer their questions.

Really, I just wanted to go back to prison; I wanted to skip the bit in the middle – court and everything. I knew when I was arrested that I would be going to prison because I'd been on parole and had skipped away from my probation officer down on the south coast to come back to London, so I knew I'd be going straight back to jail even as they got ready to take me to court for breaking into that house. All of it, everything, just made me tired. Going to court was such an inconvenience. Like, when you had to leave your cell to go to court, you might find they'd moved someone in while you were out, and what used to be yours wasn't yours any longer. I just wanted to skip all that bollocks. 'Just send me down,' I thought. 'I can be safe in prison. I won't be frightened there.'

Once, back in Pentonville – I can't remember what I was in for – I was doing a bit of rail, as it's called, where you lean on the railings on the landing and look about, man-watching, and saw below me the fraggles. The fraggles are what the mental ones are called, not just by us but also by the screws, the ones who are so out of it they're kept dosed with drugs. They live in their cells all the time, and only come out when they have to. The fraggles would shuffle out, zombie-like, head for a chair and slump down, drooling, not to move again. The screws'd give them their Largactil injections, and dose them up with Mellaril tablets, and mong them right out.

I looked over that rail at those fraggles shuffling out

of their cells, moving like they were in treacle, and slumping into their armchairs. Nothing seemed to be going on with them, either inside or outside. And you know what? I didn't despise them, I envied them. I wanted to be one of them. I wanted that to be me, all the pain and fear and effort gone. I wanted someone to take it all away and leave me to rot, slowly, in a chair. It was just like that back on the outside: sometimes I'd see people begging in the streets, and for a fleeting moment I found that kind of attractive – no hassles, no responsibilities. Only a moment, but it's there.

In the magistrates' court the next day I interrupted proceedings and asked that they accept my guilty plea, even though they didn't want me to plead then; everyone knew I was a serial offender and that I would have to wait to go to crown court. I had told my solicitor what I was doing, and she went along with it. I just wanted it all to end; I wanted to stop everything, and rest. I was tired, tired of everything, tired of living. I wanted to go far away from people, just be on my own somewhere in a cell where I could get fed and bother no one and have no one bother me.

I was forty-four years old. I'd been committing crimes since I was six or seven. I'd been on the booze since I was a kid. I'd been on Class A drugs since before I left school. I'd been bad and dangerous and scary, only now it was me who was frightened. I just wanted everything to stop.

I didn't want to be me any more.

One

Some Kind of Childhood

There were three things that ruled my childhood: crime, drink, and violence. And all this before I even made it to school.

There's a photo of me somewhere, stuck in my pram, and I've got my hands clasped tight round a bottle, the teat stuck in my mouth. Only it isn't a bottle of milk, it's a bottle of Guinness, because Guinness is good for you, right? I can't remember a time when I didn't know what drink was. I used to love a whisky and Tizer. My family told me I was a right bad baby and wouldn't settle easily, so they used to give me teaspoons of whisky to get me to kip. When Christmas came round, they'd put a bit of whisky into some Tizer, and give me a glass of that to drink. When no one was looking I'd help myself to some more, even when I was five years old.

And the violence. I've faced some horrible men in my time, been in some bad fights, but the day I thought I was going to be beaten to death was when I was nearly five years old.

Our next-door neighbour's outside toilet was joined to ours, and I liked to sit on the tin roof out there and dream my life away. Lorraine, our neighbour's daughter, would often sit at her bedroom window, which overlooked the toilet, and talk to me. She must have been in her late teens, and she had a boyfriend named Richard, who drove a steamroller for the council, which at the time we small boys thought was well cool. In fact, it made him halfway to being a superhero.

One day Lorraine and Richard were having a really heated argument which I listened to; it was funny to a boy like me who didn't understand what it meant. Anyway, he called her a 'slag', and she laughed, saying, 'Yeah, and I'm proud of it.' Me being so young, I misunderstood 'you slag' as a compliment.

Mum – Lizzie was her name – liked a drink. I'm not sure if she was an alcoholic or not, but she used to drink often and would invariably be a bit worse for wear. One night I had come in from playing outside. I was a bit dirty so she got a bowl of water and a flannel to wash me down and stood me in front of the fire in my underpants. Lizzie was moaning and groaning about the state I was in, how she was having to kneel down to wash me. I remembered that Richard had called Lorraine 'a slag', and Lorraine had laughed, so I did likewise to Lizzie.

'Shut up, you slag,' I said.

'What d'you bloody call me, you little git?'

Lizzie was fuming. She picked up the iron poker from the fireplace and began to hit me with it. Blow after blow rained down on me. All I could do was roll up into a ball, howl with the pain, yell at her to stop, shield my head with my arms and take it. In my underpants, I had no other protection. The poker fell heavily on me, tearing skin and bruising bones. Luckily my sisters, Carol and Alice, were there and they managed to pull her off before she killed me. Yeah, that's right, killed me. I honestly believe that if they had not been there my own mother would have beaten me to death.

That episode left me black and blue all over and my head really swollen. I wasn't allowed out of the house for quite a while, not until the swelling and bruising went down. Even though I loved Lizzie – in fact I still do love her, even though she has been dead for nearly thirty years now – I never really forgave her for doing that to me.

My family think this story is hilarious, which of course just makes it worse for me – that they think that nothing funnier happened to me in my childhood. Right up to this day my sister Carol tells the story like you would a joke, thinking the whole thing was one big laugh. 'Oh Pete, d'you remember when you was walloped?' she'd say, already starting to get tears in her eyes from the thought of how funny it was. And Carol would make Alice laugh, just remembering it. But what about my pain? The agony, the humiliation of it? The outrage of this woman beating a little naked boy with a poker! Nowadays you'd be on the front page of the *Sun* for doing something like that, and hounded out of your home. But no, not me and my family. It's all a little joke. What a laugh it was when Peter was young and nearly got beaten to death.

There's a twist to this story, though. The woman who hit me wasn't my mother, nor were those two women who pulled her off me my sisters. I found this out one day many years later while sitting in the back of a police car, being carted back to prison. You see, when I called Lizzie 'Mum' earlier, at the time I thought she was my mother, but she wasn't – she was my nan. The women I thought were my sisters were in fact my mother (Alice) and my aunt (Carol). To this day Carol won't acknowledge this; she still talks about me like I'm her brother. No joke – that's what my family's like. Keeping a secret like that, one that even now my aunt won't credit as true.

Starting like that, it's no surprise I ended up a mess.

The family have a fund of stories they like to tell about me. Never mind that they can see I don't find them funny, they still cackle away over them. Like the time, before that day Lizzie beat me, when I was just four, I was at home with Alice and Carol. They thought it would be amusing to paint my face with make-up, dress me in knickers and a bra, put a suspender belt on me (they attached it to my socks) and throw me out on the street. They locked me out and laughed at me through the window. I remember this like it was yesterday, crying and pleading with them to let me in while they sat there laughing at me. So when they bring it up now, and wipe away tears of laughter at the recollection, I'm sitting there feeling something totally different. Another time, Carol chased me around the house with a saucepan full of boiling water, because I had been winding her up. When Carol was younger, she'd punch and clump you if she wanted to. She could be spiteful then, she could be vicious. Most things in our house ended in violence. Or drink.

One time I walked into our kitchen and found Lizzie on her knees with her head in the oven, attempting suicide. I asked her what she was up to. I was five at the time and had no idea what she was doing, but I knew that it didn't look right. She must have been depressed. Maybe it was the drink, maybe it was her marriage. Fred – my granddad, the man I was brought up to think was my father – would drink and fight with her. He'd beat her up most weekends after they got home from the pub. She'd fight back, though. They'd give each other a good hiding.

Fred was a bit of a hard man. He liked to fight and

he liked to drink, so along with his gambling and womanizing I suppose he would best be described as a man's man. But the thing I remember him for most is for beating up Lizzie nearly every weekend, and always at Christmas. It was the same old story every time. They would leave the house happy as you like, walk down the street arm in arm and into the pub. Once there they would set about pouring as much booze down their throats as they could, then they'd come home, smash the life out of each other and wreck the house. Christmas Days, or more precisely Christmas dinners, were almost always spoiled by a drunken brawl.

Some things about my Christmases were like other people's – we'd have a tree, and the presents would be wrapped and put under it – but not much else. I remember one year, again when I was five, when Fred found and spent the Christmas money Lizzie had saved all year and hidden away from him. He went out and spent it all on booze. He came home with a dead rabbit in his hand – God knows where he found that – flung it on the table and declared loudly, 'There's your Christmas dinner, a nice bit of rabbit to cook.' Lizzie went mad. She picked up the rabbit and knocked him about the head with it, chasing him all over the house, till the rabbit's guts were all over the place.

One day a boy called Tommy hit me. I went back across the road and into our house, crying and blubbering about how Tommy had done this, that and the other, but instead of putting his arm round me to make me feel better, Fred gave me one almighty clump round the back of the head and told me to get out and hit Tommy back with something.

I got a hammer. That's how I learned violence.

Crime was taught to me the same way. I was probably seven years old when I nicked three half-crowns off the mantelpiece. I wanted to get a Dalek and some Sugar Puffs, stuff like that. Fred accused me, I said I hadn't touched the money, and he punched me in the mouth, pushing my teeth through the skin below my bottom lip. The scar's still there to remind me, but I don't remember the punch, or the pain. What I remember is what he said to me after I told him through my sobs that I had done it.

'Why'd you take the money, son?' he asked.

'Well, I wanted toys, and sweets, and . . .' Sob, sob, sob.

Fred wasn't having any of it. 'When I was your age,' he told me, 'if I wanted something I'd go and kick the shop window in and take it.'

So from then on that's what I did. Although I usually threw something through the window to break it first.

This was my childhood, full of crooked people, violence and booze. The type of people who came to our house were all into crime in one way or another: bank robbers, burglars, pick-pockets and ponces, some at the top of their trade, others just getting by. When I was growing up, John McVicar, the armed robber who became public enemy number one for a while, was a friend of the family. He taught me to box, which he did by kneeling down on the floor and telling me to hit him as hard as I could. 'Give it your best shot,' he'd say, and I'd swing my arm and land a punch on his chin. Thing is, I couldn't hit very hard at all, and then it was his turn. He wasn't trying to hurt me, just trying to teach me how to fight, but what to him was a playful wallop would send my head ringing. He was going out with Carol at the time. He had a great car, a white Mini with tinted windows and – how glamorous was this? – a record player that we could play our 45rpm records on. Carol was very much in love with John McVicar, but when he went to jail it all came out that there was another woman, which drove her mad and in my opinion made her bitter and twisted over the years.

As I said, when my family sits round telling these stories of mayhem and violence with much fondness, they think it's all perfectly normal and funny, acceptable behaviour for the times. I find it painful. It makes me angry when they tell the stories with such gusto and enthusiasm. I love my family, but I've given up trying to get them to understand me, or to change them. I know that they did their best, and I don't blame anyone. They didn't know, and I don't hold any resentments against anyone, I really don't. But I wish it had been different.

It's like the half-empty-glass thing: some people see a half-empty glass, some see a half-full one. My family thought they did a good job bringing me up; I don't. Neither of us is more right than the other, it's just the way we look at things.

I was born in 1957. We lived in a prefab at 69 Newton Grove. A lorry crashed through it one day; took the corner right off, right where I'd been sitting a few moments earlier. Luckily I'd been arguing with someone, probably Fred, and I'd got the hump with him and stomped out the house, so that saved my life. They strung up some canvas and a couple of Acros to cover the room and we all lived like that for six months. But with a hole that size in the wall – or what was once a wall – anything that trickled and everything that scuttled could and did come through. It was cold, and damp, and I'd lie in bed while rats ran about on the floor. I'd shiver just listening to them. Still, that didn't bother Fred. What worried him was someone coming in unwanted. We had a little black and white TV, the kind you had to put a tanner in the back to get working, and we didn't have a licence for it, so Fred would cover it up. There we were, a big hole in the side of the house, canvas for walls, and Fred's covering up a TV with a tea-towel so he doesn't get nicked for not having a licence.

Then we moved to the other end of Hoxton market,

3 Bianca House, Crondall Street. That move changed my life. All of a sudden I was in with all the chaps, as the top villains liked to call themselves, because where we now lived meant we were surrounded by criminals of all sorts. All the villains of the day were round that end of Hoxton then.

Freddy Davies lived across the road from us. He was a bank robber extraordinaire who bit the heads off live eels for a party trick. He once walked into the Basing House pub down the Kingsland Road, where he was barred, and said, 'Gissa drink.'

'No, you're barred,' they said.

'Gissa drink or I'll drink this.' He lifted up a goldfish bowl on the counter, with two goldfish in it.

'No, you're still barred,' they said, and everyone laughed.

So he drank it, fish and all. He was bonkers.

He was caught robbing banks, of course, and was sent to Wormwood Scrubs prison. He got cancer of the face and the doctors took out his jawbone. Then they took out his tongue and replaced it with a bit of skin taken off his forehead, only they took it from too close to his hairline so he had hair growing out of his mouth. He was dying, but the authorities wouldn't let him out on compassionate grounds as they knew he'd just rob banks again – which was true, he would have done. So he wrapped himself up in his mattress and set himself alight; his intention was to try and kill all the nonces in the Scrubs as well. But it didn't work, and as a result of the burns he developed this problem that turned his skin black. When he came out, the doctors told him not to drink, but he went straight back on the booze and that's what killed him.

Lovely man. Hard to picture it, I know, but he was.

We had family all over the area. My grandmother, Nanny Browning we called her – years later, of course, I realized that she must have been my great-grandmother – was born during the Boer War. She was very Victorian. Her name was Alice, too. I used to hate going round there for Saturday dinner – every single Saturday, whether I liked it or not. Meat pie and beans, every week. Because of those meals I can't eat meat pies that are square. Round ones are OK, but not square; I can't touch them. I had to eat everything, see, and sometimes they were all gristly, and you had to eat the gristle because she'd give you a clump if you didn't. And we'd have a cup of coffee, from a bottle, with sterilized milk. And you had to sit and have it; you had no say in the matter. Then she'd give you a tanner.

We'd eat in silence, and when we finished we had to get up and go over to the Hop Pole, an Irish pub in Hoxton Square, on the corner with Pitfield Street and Coronet Street. It's not there now. It was the pub Fred used to go to all the time as he had a spraying shop opposite; he did second-hand office furniture and stuff like that. He'd play the piano in the pub, and the squeezebox (as we called the accordion). He used to sing Tony Bennett songs. He liked them.

Fred was half Jewish, so I had Jewish uncles with names like Uncle Reuben, Uncle Ginger and Uncle Siddy. Uncle Siddy Stiff he was known as, because he had a stiff leg he was born with. Good old Jewish boys, all of them. Then there was Auntie Beryl, and Auntie Lil Paul, and Auntie Lil, who was married to Uncle Tom. He was a carpenter and we'd go out to see him working sometimes. He'd be sawing away with one hand, the other holding the wood down, and he'd have a fag firmly clamped in his mouth all the time. He'd let the fag burn down and none of the ash would come off. It was only when he got to the very end that he'd turn his head, spit it out, then immediately light another one.

And there was my cousin, Susan Barber, who got nicked for killing her husband with poisoned gravy, cos he was a nonce – or so the rumour went. She did sixteen years of her life sentence, then had an affair with the guv'nor who was giving her driving lessons.

These were the people who brought me up. Perhaps that's why I was always out and about, wandering away from home. As a child of five and six I spent a lot of my time on my own. I even had a pretend friend. We would roam the streets of Hoxton together. To say I was a lonely child who had no mates and was incapable of interacting with others would be misleading, but this was to be a pattern for the rest of my life. I have been alone through so much of my life, mostly by choice. I suppose it was because I received no love at home. I can never remember getting cuddles, or a hug, or anything like that. Maybe that toughened me up; maybe that made me feel excluded from everyone else.

But I did have friends, as long as the parents of the friends could be in the pubs with Fred and Lizzie. Billy Wood, Johnny Smith, Tommy Boniface and me would piss around outside the Sir John Franklin or the Carpenter's Arms in Bridport Place while the mums and dads were inside having a drink. The kids would get an orange, but all of a sudden the door would open and I'd get a Pale Ale. Pale Ale, like Guinness and Mackeson's, was good for you. I even got drunk on a case of Babycham once, but I can't remember it. It's one of the stories the family likes to tell about me. I don't know where I found it.

Life for me as a kid revolved around pubs; everything was done in pubs. If I wanted to see Fred, I knew he'd be in the Hop Pole or the Vulture, both in Pitfield Street. If he and Lizzie were out, then, in order, they'd go to the Carpenter's first, then up to the Franklin. Then they'd come home and smash the life out of each other. The Green Man in Hoxton was also big in our life, and the Queen's Head. The Black Man's – really known as the White Horse; haven't got a clue why it was called the Black Man's – was in Hoxton too.

Everything involved a pub. All the photos from even before I was born are of pubs: charabancs to country pubs in Kent, standing around outside the Unicorn in Hoxton Market, always standing around in groups outside pubs. I never knew much else except pubs, and all the business I needed to do later in life was done in pubs. If I wanted to get drugs, that was done in pubs. Pubs were where I spent my days when I wasn't in jail, or out thieving.

There used to be thirteen pubs in Hoxton Street alone. We used to try and drink in them all as kids. In the nineteenth century, alongside the pubs there were three mental asylums. Hoxton has always been an alcoholic place, a dysfunctional place. The Kray twins came out of Hoxton; so too did one of the Wembley Bank robbers. It's an area that's always been steeped in alcoholism, criminality and, in later years, drug addiction. And it'll always be like that. Nice and fancy in the Hoxton Square and Old Street end, but nothing's ever going to change at the other end, near the canal – a pisshole.

The first time I ever stole anything was an Oxo cube from a shop in Hoxton market, and I was not even six. Someone in the shop had made a big pyramid of Oxo cubes and I really, really wanted one, only I was told I couldn't have it. So I waited till the moment when Lizzie wasn't looking – I can still remember my heart pounding – and then I reached up, took one from the corner of the pile, slid the precious thing into my pocket and made it out of the shop and into hiding. It tasted delicious, much nicer than the ones at home. And so my life of crime began. It's hard to believe that a mere Oxo cube could be the foundation of such misery. I expect I got my head rubbed and my hair tousled with a 'Good boy' thrown in for good measure. That's what I learned from my family.

I had my tonsils and my adenoids out when I was small – something to do with my ears and some mastoid problem. They tried this first before a more serious operation, and it worked: my ears stopped pouring gunge. I remember sitting in hospital reading the *Sporting Life* – I was only little, remember – and picking the winner for the Grand National. I had half a crown each way and I won. I grew up reading the *Sporting Life*; it's how I learned to read. And I wasn't bad at calculating odds, either.

I went to school round the corner from where we lived, at Whitmore Primary School. It was at the bottom of Hoxton, where the leisure centre is now, and the only teacher I can remember is Miss (or Mrs) Wood; I can't remember the head teacher's name or anything else about the school. Miss Wood had blonde hair and wore a tartan skirt. She seemed really old to me, as grown up as any of the adults I knew, but she was probably no more than twenty-five. If you were naughty, she'd make you stand on a chair and take your trousers down, or lift your shorts up; then she'd smack you on the tops of your bare legs with a ruler. I used to sit next to Patrick Grant, little Paddy. He shit himself one day. He had diarrhoea, and he kept putting his hand up to go to the toilet and she wouldn't let him, and all of a sudden there was this smell. It had all come out through his shorts, all over his chair. He got whacked for that, and all the kids, as kids do, ribbed him terribly.

I liked academic stuff, but of the solving-problems kind, not studying – things like those adverts on the Tube that challenged you to understand a code. I learned chess, too, and I got to be pretty good at it. Alice's husband Roy taught me chess – well, I wouldn't swear to it, but I think he did. When I was ten he took me to the Alex, a club in Stoke Newington, to play the game. The club was owned by his older brother, George Nash. There was a Pole who was a proper Grandmaster and he'd sit in the corner and wait to be challenged – he'd never challenge you – and take your money off you. I never beat him.

What I remember best about Whitmore Primary School is that it was where I learned the value of money. At least I learned what money can do for you, especially if you've got none. Having money was never a problem for me: there was always money around our house. People would give me money, and if that wasn't enough I'd help myself, careful not to let Fred find out. I'd take the money with me to school. It didn't have to be much. I'd have a threepenny bit, or a tanner bit, and

I'd get the kids lined up and say, 'First one up and down the playground,' and the kids would all line up and run for threepence, or sixpence, and I'd give them their winnings when they finished. Money has a lot of power – that's what I learned back then. People do things for money.

People like Edward, a big black kid with an African warrior's build who lived over Phillipp Street way. He was big for his age. I used to tease him, racist taunts, things like that, though I had no idea I was being racist. I'd pay him to do things. If I wanted someone beaten up, I'd say to Edward, 'Go and beat him up.' Sometimes I did that not because I wanted someone beaten up, but because I just wanted to watch Edward in action.

After school, I'd usually avoid going home for as long as I could. It wasn't any fun there, and it would usually end up in a fight, or with me getting hit. I would go instead to the playcentre, to play football. One of the adults there, Steve, who taught us football, was my hero because he had the hardest shot I'd ever seen. I used to think he was as good as Jimmy Greaves. He'd dare us to go in goal and try to save one of his shots. I had great expectations of becoming a footballer. Me and another kid would spend hours and hours practising. We hung a car tyre from the bar of a goal on the pitch at Rosemary Park and would shoot from different positions in an attempt to get the football through the middle of the tyre. Even hitting it was a big deal at first, but eventually we were both able to hit the target consistently.

Football was the thing I liked best of all. Fred took me to see Arsenal when I was six. They were playing against Nottingham Forest, and although it was only a 0–0 draw in the end, I was hooked. I can remember Ian Ure, the big Scots defender in the centre, and 'Geordie' Armstrong running up and down the wing. I wanted to be just like him. After that I went to Highbury on my own as it was only up the road. I'd stand in what was then the schoolboys' enclosure, and when the fans got going we'd get songs echoing round the stadium like 'You'll Never Take the North Bank'. We started – well, it was probably me who kicked everything off – a great big fight one day, and the North Bank sang 'You'll Never Take the Schoolboys'. I loved it.

Violence was just part of everyday life; I saw nothing odd in it at all. I saw my first dead body when I was six. Me and a few kids were messing about down the canal and I fished a plastic bag out of the water. We ripped it open, and inside was a dead baby. We poked and prodded it with sticks until it split apart, then we all ran off, leaving the stinking, rotten piece of meat on the path.

Then there was the old lady in the shop. Me and Gary Clark, a friend from school, broke into a shop one Sunday afternoon. We nicked the sweets and then went back for the drinks. The next day we went to have a look at the shop, and lo and behold it was still shut. I climbed the wall and saw that the door we had kicked in was still as we'd left it the previous day, so we decided to go in and nick all the fags and anything else we could carry. Then I said to Gary, 'Hang on, I'm gonna go upstairs and see what's up there.' On tip-toes I went as quietly as I could up the stairs, every sound like an explosion to me I was so tense. The bedroom door was shut and very, very slowly I pushed the handle of the door down. A funny smell unlike any I'd smelled before floated into my nostrils, and I knew that whatever it was it sure wasn't good. I peeped round the door. This old lady was lying there in bed, dead as a doornail, her skin a strange colour. I ran as fast as I could down those stairs, out the back door, over the wall and home.

What all this was doing to me, I don't know. What I do know is that I felt driven to be better than everyone around me. I had to be on top. It was no good being on the bottom, or in the middle, I had to be on the top, all the time. I had to be captain of the football team. Even my dog had to be the best dog, the best fighting dog. Mick was his name, half Staffordshire bull terrier, half English bulldog. I'd square Mick up to other dogs and kick him up the arse to make him bully other dogs. I was seven. Mick was killed one night. I came down in the morning and found him in the front garden. He'd had a knife stuck in him and been ripped wide open. I was really upset, he was a good old dog he was. I think I know who did it too. I'm pretty sure it was Fred who killed Mick, because Mick protected me from getting a clump from him. I can't categorically prove this but I believe it to be true. If it was Fred . . . what a fucking wanker. A dog. What a thing to do.

And what did I do? Nothing. There was nothing I could do. I'd learned not to show my emotions. You didn't have emotions; they weren't allowed. It was all about pride: it was important not to lose face. You don't cry and you don't show fear – that's what I learned in my home. To show a weakness was not the done thing. If I had shown Fred how upset I was that he'd killed my dog, he'd have jeered at me, made me more angry. I realized then that it wasn't only money that was a powerful tool; violence, and putting fear into people, was another. I learned to employ violence and fear as much as I did money, and for the same reasons.

I think I detached myself from the human race about that time, because I wasn't interested in all the bollocks. I thought there was more to life. I just couldn't work out other people so I didn't bother. Money was the guv'nor; it got people to do what I wanted. I just wasn't interested in what other people seemed to be interested in – except, of course, the boys from my school I hung about with, among them Johnny Bagshaw, Barry Jones, Billy Robinson (all in the year above me), Gary Clark, Gary Roney and Peter Tobin (from my class). I used to go round to Peter's house. His mum was called Dixie and his dad Alf. Underneath them lived Sylvie and her husband. Sylvie was a strange one, not a tooth in her head, probably about thirty-five, ugly as sin. When I was about eight or nine she asked if she could give me a blow-job. I don't know why.

Ginger was one of our little gang too. He died when he was fourteen. He OD'd on morphine sulphate. We went over to see him one day and his nan said he'd not been up yet. We went to his room and he was lying there, half the stuff shoved up his nose. It was hard but . . . Oh well, we thought.

Johnny Smith was another friend. When I was seven, Johnny and I saw a flying saucer. It was early evening, and it was hovering around Whitmore Primary School. We were in Pitfield Street, but by the time we ran round to Grange Street it had vanished. It had lights all over it but no colours. No one believed us, but I know what we saw. Also in our gang was Pudsy, Brymer, Oishi (Leonard was his real name), Binsey, the Wing – so-called because he only had one arm – and Dennis, who had an Afro and played the guitar. I'd say let's play chess, they'd say no, let's go and earn ourselves a few bob, so I'd say OK then, and we would. It was always easier to do what the gang wanted, and they weren't as interested in chess as me.

I must have got too much for Fred and Lizzie to handle around this time because I came home from

Whitmore Primary School one day, opened the door and Fred was standing there with some boxes by the door with all my bits and pieces in them. 'Don't want you here no more, you're going to live with Alice' was the greeting he gave me. And that was it. I was moved, with no say in the matter or anything.

So I went to live in Islington with Alice, the woman I thought was my sister, only she was my mother. Her husband, Roy, was away 'shaving the hairs off coconuts' – at least that's what they always told me. One day I'm watching telly and there's something on the news about men escaping from prison, and up comes Roy's face on the screen – and the penny drops. So that's where he is! Roy had gone down for seven years for armed robbery. After that, whenever I was in jail I always thought of myself as shaving the hairs off coconuts.

Alice was always out – she was a gangster's moll now. Roy's brothers always made sure she was looked after. She was only in her early twenties, so she was out clubbing and having a good time, and I was left in charge of a neighbour's kid as his mother used to go out with Alice. I used to like looking after Little Ted. I'd change his nappies – and proper cloth ones they were; none of your disposable ones then. I'd have to boil up the dirty ones, get them out with tongs and put them through the mangle.

Once Little Ted was able to go out, that was it, we

were off. I'd go back now and again to Crondall Street, to see the boys. Sometimes I was round there so much it was as if I'd never left – at least that's what Lizzie used to say to me. As a gang, we were pack animals. There was always someone who came over from the City who didn't know what they were getting into. Take an example. The Hoxton market toilets were known to be a cruising place for men, and we would have fun with them in there. We'd go quietly into the cubicles, where holes had been punched through the sides for men to stick their erections through. We'd wait until we heard someone step into the cubicle next to us, then one of us would put a shoe on the ground – usually me, because I had the biggest feet. The form was to put your foot under the partition so they'd tap it, and you knew it was on. Well, as soon as we saw the dick push through the hole, we'd raise our booted feet and stamp on it. One time our horrible gang followed a bloke in a smart three-piece suit. He went down into the toilets and we waited a few moments before going down after him. We knocked on his cubicle door and he opened it – completely naked. 'Can we have a light, mate?' He gave us his lighter – a nice Dunhill gold one it was – and we ran off with it. Well, he couldn't chase us, could he?

Sometimes the joke was on one of us. We used to muck about with the boats on the lake in Victoria Park in Hackney; we'd take them out to the island and sink them. To keep our clothes dry, we'd take them off and hang them in the trees, just going out in our underpants. Only this one time, when I went to get my clothes afterwards, some bastard had nicked them, and I had to walk all the way home in my Y-fronts. All saggy and wet, too.

We would hang out on the street and copy the older boys. I was a hanger-on with the Hoxton mob; I wanted to do what they were doing. One time we all got tooled up for a big fight with the Highbury lot. I grabbed a shovel, and they all laughed at me. 'What you going to do with that?' they said. Well, at the fight I laid into someone with the shovel and knocked him spark out. Someone from the gang called me 'Digger' after that, and I was pleased with my nickname. As a kid, in gang fights I'd wear a sling to look as vulnerable as possible – but I'd use it to hide my cut-throat razor.

We boys also hung out on the old building sites – so much of east London was still damaged because of the bombing during the war – and we'd think of ourselves as demolition men. We liked going into the old houses and knocking them down, which was our game. All the old houses were scheduled to be demolished, it was just taking a long time for the council or whoever to get round to doing it. The best were the prefabs. After people had moved out we'd knock all the walls out, just leaving the four corners standing. Then we'd hit the corners at the same time with our hammers and, wham!, the whole lot'd come down. LEB, as the London Electricity Board was called, used to turn off the power to the houses that were about to be knocked down, and they'd put up notices to let people know this had been done: LEB OFF they would say. Little Ted used to think it was a swear word. He'd tell everyone to leb off.

Ted had a bad mouth on him from a very young age. Once we went somewhere, the seaside or whatever, on a train – me, Alice, Little Ted, and Bubs (who was married to Frankie Shay, one of the chaps back then) and her daughter Frances. Little Ted, who was only just talking he was that small, was sitting by the window and one of the women said, 'Oh look, Ted, there's a gee-gee,' pointing at a horse in a field. We didn't go in for that baby talk. Ted piped up, 'That's a horse, you cunt.'

I taught Little Ted to fight like I'd been taught, making him stand up while I beat him black and blue. I taught him to play chess, and I read him books. I was given money to look after him, a tenner for the day, which was a huge amount of money for an adult to have, let alone a couple of kids, so we'd splash out. I'd take him to see the late-night movies. We saw Hitchcock's *The Birds* one night and came home with our jumpers wrapped round our heads to stop any birds attacking us. Well, Ted was only four at the time.

But actually he was fearless. My gang used to go on

missions together. There was this one place called Block End, a bombed-out area near Trafalgar Square – more ruins from the war – and we used to catch rats there. Big rats, too, like cats. Little Ted would corner them, size them up, then jump on them. Then we'd put them into big oil drums, put some wire mesh over the top, hold the mesh down with bricks, drop in a gallon of pink paraffin we'd buy from the machine, and watch them run around inside the drum, flames all over them.

The houses were usually covered with building stuff, and we'd use scaffolding poles to make cannons. We'd fill one end with cement to seal it, let it dry, then drill a hole (using Gary Roney's dad's drill) so we could put a fuse in. Then we'd empty loads of fireworks down the pole, wedge them in with cotton wool, then shove nails, broken glass and pebbles down. We'd plot it up carefully on the bomb site so that it just looked like a pole lying flat, then hide behind some bricks until our target came along. And the target was always the same: the police. When they were in range, which meant about twenty feet away, we'd light the fuse (which we'd taken out of one of the fireworks) and watch it blow. Then we'd scarper and hide out in another demolished house till it was safe to come out again.

Once in one of these houses we found a load of money stuffed up a chimney, round about forty grand, all in £5 notes. Johnny Bagshaw saw something hanging down from the chimney, this old sack; he pulled it out and there it was. We took it into school with us, but when the teachers saw us with all this money the police got called in and it all got confiscated. Johnny swiped some of it before they got to him, but no more than about £40. The money might have been no good anyway, and it might have been out of date. Rumour had it the money was from the Great Train Robbery, which had happened in 1963. The authorities were keen to catch all the robbers, so the serial numbers on the notes that had been stolen were looked out for – or so we'd all been told.

That wasn't the only money I got. I was ten years old when I did my first bit of office creeping. I just went into an office, up to the desk at the front and asked, 'You got any vacancies?' I always looked older than my age so maybe the man behind the desk thought I was fourteen or something. He looked at me, said, 'I'll go and check,' got up and walked off. So I jumped over the desk, grabbed the cash box and made off with it. I got £30. I was really proud of that one.

I bought my first pair of Levis when I was ten. I always had an eye for what was fashionable – I don't know where that came from – and one day I broke in somewhere, got myself some money and went out and bought some Levis from a shop called Smart Westerns. Forty-seven shillings and sixpence they cost me, and I was so proud of them. I always bought my own clothes after that.

I don't know where from, but I'd also got hold of a target pistol. A bloody big thing it was, over a foot and a half long, a Yugoslavian 177 that fired a little lead pellet. I used to shoot out the windows in the shed at the bottom of the garden. Then I'd shoot at the vicar over the wall. I hit his glasses once. They went flying off his face, spinning round in the air. I used to shoot at the police and their horses too, make them start and run off.

One time I was in Hoxton, standing on the corner of Falkirk Street and Hoxton Street, by this pole, holding court, and a policeman on a horse trotted by. I'm Jack the lad, giving it large in front of the other boys, so as soon as I see him I yell out, 'Get off and milk 'im!' The boys all laugh, only the copper does a Lone Ranger turn on a sixpence and comes galloping back up to us. He jumps off, ties his horse to the pole, grabs me and pulls me forward by the ear so that my face is right up against the horse's dick. It stinks of horse piss and God knows what and it's disgusting. He rubs my face in there a bit and goes, 'Milk him yourself, you flash cunt.' I'm wriggling away and yelling 'Get off me!' but it does no good. I expect he got a few claps on the back at the station for that one.

I've always been big. I took a size ten shoe and I'd have men's suits made for me at the age of ten, and I haven't grown much since I was eleven: I was five foot ten then,

I'm six foot now. I used to go into pubs when I was twelve, straight pubs where I wasn't known, and no one would say anything. I'd go in with Johnny Clarke and Bobby Parker, for instance – older boys from the Hoxton mob; four years older, in fact – and I'd get my pint of light and bitter, and *they'd* get asked if they were old enough. No one ever asked me my age. I suppose it was also because I was so serious. Serious Pete, I was known as. 'Don't be stupid,' I'd say to people. I hated frivolity, I didn't know how to do it. I didn't know what people laughed at.

It wasn't really a world to laugh about either. I was in a pub one time, in the Lion and Lamb, having a drink with someone when in walked this guy, a bad man, and the fella I was with said, 'Ah, I wanna see you,' got up, smashed a glass and, wallop!, cut right down the cheek of the man who'd walked in. You could see the damage right away. And the bloke who'd done it said, 'You wanna smile, do yer?' and smacked him right on the cut, opening it up from ear to lip. I could see the skin flop open and the teeth and the jawbone inside. Then the blood gushed out all over the place, splashing on to the floor. It was like something out of a horror film.

Home life wasn't much better. When I got bigger and stronger, I was the one who gave out the punches and clumps. I gave Fred one once. I had the hump over something that had happened in Crondall Street, and I got a hammer from Fred and smashed up a couple of cars that belonged to someone over the road I'd had an argument with. When I took the hammer back Fred started having a go at me so I boshed him. I was unhappy that I'd done it, but he was ever so proud of me. He was well impressed with how hard I could punch. That's all he could say about it. 'Fuckin' hell, boy, that was a good punch!' And then he was off, telling everyone how hard I could punch, how proud he was of that black eye.

By the time I left primary school, in 1968, I was pretty much unteachable I was so unruly. I was also still very much into fashion and into looking good, so for my first day at secondary school – Shoreditch Secondary Modern, in Falkirk Street, referred to by the police as a 'breeding ground for criminals' as loads of us came out of there – I got properly dressed up, even though I had no intention of staying there. I arrived at the school gates in a green-and-gold mohair two-tone suit, with a peppermint-green shirt, a striped tie, crocodile-skin loafers and a sheepskin coat with black fur. Remember, I was eleven years old. The only other boy with a black fur sheepskin coat, Twiggy, who was supposed to be the best fighter in the school, came up to me and said, 'You're not allowed to wear that, only I can wear a coat like that.' So I knocked him out.

I never went to school very much. I only went in to impress people with my money, to take some of the girls shopping down the market to buy them jumpers and things. I thought it was what I had to do. That's what the adult men I hung about with did. I was soon under notice from the ILEA regarding my attendance and behaviour. The notice was issued after I'd carried a bag of bricks and stuff into the playground at school and thrown them at the dining-room windows where the teachers were all eating their lunch, smashing every single one. I was expected to have a book signed by teachers at every lesson to prove my attendance, though how that was supposed to make me behave better I don't know.

I made it there for a few days, but not enough, and Alice got called in for a meeting with Dr Rushworth, the headmaster. I went along, but when he started dictating to me I jumped up, bent him over and used his cane on him. A similar thing happened with one of the teachers once when he tried to get strict with me. I was twelve years old, and I was in class sat next to my friend Eddie. The teacher had his back to us, writing on the blackboard. We spotted, there on his desk, some large blackboard compasses – the ones the length of an arm, with a spike the length of a man's finger – and I said to Eddie, 'I'm going to stick those in the teacher.' I was only messing around, but Eddie said, 'You ain't got the bottle,' so of course now I had to do it just to prove him wrong. I stood up, walking as quietly as I could to the front of the class, took the compasses off the table and jabbed them like a bayonet into the teacher's buttock. The teacher roared, turned, and tried to grab me, but I was already heading for the door. He started to chase after me, so I tore out of the room and down the hall towards the main exit. The doors out of the school were swing doors. I pushed through, then turned and kicked my foot on the door as the six-foot-four-inch teacher came through so that the door swung hard back into him, smashing him in the face. I got expelled for that, and I never went back to school.

I had a good time as a kid, I enjoyed myself. Although I can look back now and see things I don't like, I never thought then, 'Well, this is crap, ain't it?' It was what I knew. I didn't know that some kids didn't live in a house with a hole in the wall, or that when they got home they didn't get a slap, because I didn't care what they had; I didn't care about them. I was never motivated by envy. I never thought, 'Cor, I want what he's got,' because it was all much simpler for me. I saw something, and if I wanted whatever it was, it was mine. I took what I wanted, and put up with the rest.

Two

Stonewall Defence: On Remand

The other thing that happened before I was sent to approved school was that I discovered hard drugs. Already, as I said, I was used to going into pubs. From the age of eight I'd go in and grown men would call me over, get me a little drink, tuck a bit of money in my shirt and lean down and say, 'Tell Roy I looked after you, won't you?' I still had yet to discover why Roy, whom I knew only as my sister's husband, had such a hold on them; that was very far from my eight-year-old mind. But I remember only too well the day in 1967 when I had my first taste of cannabis. If nicking that Oxo cube was a sign of things to come, well, the day I bunked off school and met up with Colin Nelson was another.

I'd pretty much given up going to school regularly by the age of ten, so I'd get up and go and sit on the wall with all the guys from the factories that in those days were up and down Crondall Street. They'd give me a cup of tea and I'd have a fag (a Cadet), and then I'd hang around the cafés for the day. Most of the kids I knew would go and get their mark – that is, get themselves registered as attending school – then bunk off, but I just couldn't be bothered; even that seemed too much. We'd all meet up at the cafés mid-morning and hang out together.

Round where we lived was a bloke who started the National Front off in our area. Our little gang was sitting on the wall (where the Britannia Leisure Centre is now), hanging about, missing school and pissing about, when a rifle suddenly came out from the house behind us, followed by the man holding it. 'Clear off, you black bastard,' he said to our guitar-playing friend Dennis. We turned round and walked together over to him, fronted him and said that we'd rather be with a black man than a fucking grass – because he was. He never bothered Dennis, or us, again.

But it was the bigger boys who interested me; they were wilder, more dangerous, and I was into that. Like Colin Nelson. He was fourteen, a rough kid, and I was drawn to that. I liked him too, and me and him mated up. On Myrtle Street one morning he was sitting on the wall by the Russells' house and called me over. 'Got any fags on ya?' No, I didn't. 'Got any money?' Yes, I did. 'Go over to Harold's and get a threepenny [a single cigarette], will ya?'

Only too happy to please, off I went, got a cigarette and came back. He stuck it behind his ear, pulled a packet of Rizlas out and started sticking them together. I couldn't work out what he was doing. It was like a comedy sketch, the old one about Sir Walter Ralegh and the tobacco; I couldn't figure it out at all. I knew all about roll-ups but I'd never seen this. He took the cigarette, licked it down the middle, then ripped it along the wet line and dumped the tobacco into the sheet he'd made with the Rizlas. 'Hold yer hand out,' he said, so I held my hand out and he dropped the sheet into it. Then he dipped into his pocket and pulled out what looked to me like a ball of mud. He flicked his petrol Ronson and used the flame to char the mud, which he sprinkled into this giant roll-up he'd made which I was still holding for him. I watched all this closely without saying anything, but inside I was thinking, 'Cor, what's going on?'

He rolled it up, stuck a bit of cardboard in, lit it and pulled a long draw on it, holding it in.

'Ahhhh, yeah – nice bit of Afghani, mate.'

'What is it?' I asked.

'It's draw, ain't it,' he said.

Well, the only drawer I knew was what you put your socks in. I didn't have a clue. 'Do you want to have a go?'

Of course I did, so I had a go.

'No, you have to take it down.'

I had another go. And I felt this grin come over my face. I felt . . . different. Different in a way I wanted to feel again.

'Where'd you get this stuff from?' I asked Colin.

'From a black guy on Brick Lane,' he told me. 'Get yourself a dollar draw, a ten-bob draw.'

So off I went to look for a black man.

Of course, in those days if you weren't white, you were black. Pakistani, Bengali, African, we didn't know any different. All these Asian men up and down Brick Lane were trying to sell me Rothmans. Finally I found a big old black man standing on the corner of Old Montague Street and Black Lion Yard, and I asked him.

'What you want?' he said.

'A ten-bob draw,' I said.

He stared at me for a while, then reached into his mouth, took a lump of ganja out, and slit off a lump for me. It was all very exciting.

'Put it in your mouth,' he said.

Er . . . but I did, and it was all wet. Then I went home and smoked it.

Colin's dead now. He was found in a drug clinic, dead of an overdose.

I was hooked. I had loads of toys, good toys, worth a fortune now if I'd kept them – metal wind-up cars, stuff I was given all the time and never touched. The toys came from anyone in the family. We were never poor; I just had to point and I'd get. I wanted a bike, a racer, the best one, ten gears, top of the range. Whatever I had had to be better than anyone else's. I rode it for two days, then didn't want it any more. I had things, I was spoiled, and that afternoon I sold them all, immediately, to pay for drugs. At the age of ten.

It wasn't too long before I moved on from that to something harder – and I didn't have to go hunting around Brick Lane to find them either. Alice always gave me drugs, or money to buy drugs. To her, taking drugs meant you'd have a good time. When she took me to Hyde Park to see the Rolling Stones, the free concert in 1969, she handed over some LSD and a couple of Mandrax and said, 'Go and have a good time.' I wandered off and became fascinated by these two hippies making love under a tree; perhaps it was the drugs that made it weird, perhaps it was just the day. I had a walking stick and I was poking the bloke in his little bum as he went up and down on the girl underneath him, saying, 'Stop it!'

I was a *Clockwork Orange* man. I thought the lead character Alex was me. Not that I lived the film, but I was certain they'd filmed my life to make their movie – all except for the rape scene. I dressed the part too. I was the first skinhead in Hoxton, with cherry-red boots, Sta-Prest jeans immaculate with a crease, and every single Ben Sherman shirt going. Racks and racks of shirts I had: banana stripe, gingham, check, pin-stripe, plain – I had them all. I used to have a race with a boy we called Boof-Boof to see who could buy the most pairs of shoes in Topper's. I bought all my clothes from Cecil Gee and Take Six, and shoes from Topper's, unless I went up to Bond Street to get something special. I even had my suits hand-made for me at a place called Webster's. They only cost £30 back then. At the age of twelve!

We skinheads would go down to Southend regularly at the weekends. One day we were down there and I needed to go to the toilet, only the public one was shut, so I went down an alley, dropped my braces and my Levis and . . . ahhh, the release. Only, when I went to put my braces back on I heard a 'thud' on my banana yellow Ben Sherman. Oh no, I'd only gone and shat on my braces and pulled the turd on to my shirt. I had to go home with no shirt and no braces that night.

By that stage of my life I was already at approved school. The system for getting into an approved school was first to be sent to a place in Goldhawk Road in Shepherd's Bush called Stamford House, a classification centre for juvenile remand. From there I was sent to Essex Homes in Chelmsford. It was a Tuesday when I got to this great big place. They gave me a pot of tea and a plate of egg and chips, which I ate, then bread and jam, which I made up into sandwiches and stuffed into my pocket. Then I stood up, told them I was going to the toilet, and walked out the front door.

I was eventually caught, of course, and taken back, also on a Tuesday. I got caned for running away, then after my egg and chips and tea, and once I'd made my sandwiches and stuffed them up my jumper, I was off again. I was on the run for a while this time, in and out of home. The authorities knew I'd get nicked for something sooner or later so they didn't bother to search too hard for me. Sure enough, they were proved right.

'Fancy nicking a motor?' a boy called Stevie Comer asked me one night.

'Yeah, c'mon then, we can go to Southend in it,' I said.

So we nicked a Mini. Minis were easy to nick in those days: you just opened the bonnet, stuck a threepenny bit in the fuse box, pressed the starter button and away you went.

After I was caught with Stevie, the authorities knew better than just to ship me back to Essex Homes, so we were both taken back to Stamford House, still in our own clothes, and put into a room in Hastings House block. Another boy, Mank, was doing some cleaning in the room in his uniform – jeans, baseball shoes, stripy shirt. We saw a member of staff, a new woman who didn't know me, walking down the corridor towards us, so we put everything we'd brought with us away quickly, told Mank to sit on the other side of the table from us, and when she came in he said, as we'd coached him, 'My visitors are done now, can they go, please?'

And because we were in our home clothes she thought that was it, that we were saying thank you very much for our visit. So off we went, walking only till we got round the corner.

We started looking for a car to nick as that meant we could get away faster, but our escape had been noticed quickly and we heard whistles and shouting, and people were chasing after us. They caught up with us and surrounded us. There was snow on the ground so we couldn't move fast, and anyway, we were easy to follow. Stevie Comer went one way, me the other, but they headed for me first. Mr Johnson, a big black man who thought he could handle me, stepped forward and reached out as if to grab me, but I picked up a plank of wood and clocked him right round the earhole. Then they were all over me, punching me and kicking me, and I got taken back inside where I was immediately put into the closed unit. For the first time, living in a box. The cell was cool, I liked it. I was finally on the way to becoming one of the chaps. I'd arrived. Alcatraz, here I come!

Not long after that, towards the end of 1969, they worked out what to do with me. I was sent to a place called Hays Bridge. It had been called Court Lees, only that got shut down because of all the brutality that was going on there. But all they'd changed was the name; the staff, of course, were the same. When I arrived, I thought it looked all right. I couldn't have been more wrong.

The school was a big country manor, two wings connected by stone cloisters, with a dormitory in each wing where twenty-five to thirty boys slept. As it was already late I was taken straight up to the dormitory. It was quite intimidating when I first walked in. 'What's your name, mate?' and 'What you in for?' and 'Where're you from?' – the questions came at me from all sides. As I answered them, I became acutely aware of a giant sitting on a bed over the other side of the dorm staring at me. This giant turned out to be a fifteen-year-old kid called Smith, six feet seven inches tall and weighing in at about twenty-two stone. He was the school bully, the kid in charge.

'Lights out, boys,' a man's voice shouted, adding for good measure, 'and no fucking noise.'

'OK, Pop,' replied Smith, as if it was his responsibility. 'C'mon you cunts, you heard what Pop said, lights out, bed, and no fucking noise.' And with that Smith gave a skinny kid I'd learned was called Wellsy one hefty thump, sending him sprawling across the dorm.

It took me a while to get used to sleeping with so many strangers, so I tossed and turned that night for a long time. It felt like I'd just drifted off when suddenly I was wide awake; after the silence of my cell at Stamford House, any sound seemed loud. 'Hurry up, you skinny cunt,' said the voice, 'hurry up.' I looked across the dorm and saw Wellsy was giving Smith a blow-job.

The rest of the night was spent drifting in and out of sleep, the slightest noise bringing me to total alertness.

Morning call was a bit of a shock: 'Hands off cocks and on with socks, you little scumbags!' Mr Y, a member of staff, began his morning routine of going to each of the boys' beds and pulling all the blankets off. God help any boy who had his hand anywhere near his privates. Mr Y was a right proper bully. He carried this baton, a thick cane, and seemed to take great pleasure from whacking boys with it. He was also a bit of a pervert as well because he used any excuse to examine a boy's genital region.

'You the new boy, then,' he said at me – it was more a statement than a question.

'Yeah.'

No sooner had I answered than I got one almighty whack from Mr Y's stick.

'Let's try that again. You're the new boy?'

'Yeah.'

Whack, whack.

'You call me *sir*!' he shouted.

After breakfast some bloke came up to me and said, 'I'm Mr X. I teach maths and physical education. Follow me.' We walked out of the dining room, along the cloisters and out of the main building. 'I've been assigned to show you around,' Mr X continued. 'This is the school,' he said, pointing to a single-storey brick building. 'You'll do an hour a day there, then you work on the farm or gardens. If you're good at sport then I'll get you out of all that.' Back into the main building, along the cloisters and into the gym. 'We do football, rugby, cross-country, table tennis and boxing. Can you box?'

I nodded.

'Right, come on then,' said Mr X as he passed me a huge pair of boxing gloves, 'put 'em on.'

We stood facing each other, both wearing boxing gloves. Suddenly with no warning Mr X punched me full blast in the face with all his might. It sent me flying across the gym floor.

'Think you're hard, do you?' he said.

For a split second I wanted to curl up in a ball and cry, but a voice in my head – Fred's voice – told me, 'Never cry. Don't be a cry baby.' Dragging myself to my feet, I faced up to Mr X and said, 'C'mon then, you big cunt, I ain't scared of you.'

Head down and arms flaying like some sort of demented whirling dervish, I walked straight on to a right hook to the side of the head.

'Stay down,' came the order. 'You've proved your point.'

Of course, all the other boys heard about my set-to with Mr X and it made me a bit of a hero with them all. All except Smith, who saw me as a threat, someone he would need to bully and beat so as to maintain his position as top dog.

Luckily, all the football and boxing I'd done at home had made me quite an all-round sportsman. And I was particularly good at table tennis. I would play everyone and beat 'em. I got plenty of practice in the approved school and I won some medals from the Sussex league. I even entered the British Open, but got drawn against the number one in the first round at Brighton Dome and went out. I was gutted, but it helped me become Mr X's blue-eyed boy, much to the annoyance of Smithy. The other kids respected me because I wasn't afraid of anyone or anything; and, thanks to generous gifts from Roy and the rest of the family, to help matters along I always had money, tobacco and dope. Roy was now out of prison, and he would come down to Hays Bridge with a mate. They'd bring me my bag of bush, and my Driminyl tablets, a hundred fags, £20 – which was a lot – and I had everything I wanted, because of the power of money.

The farm was where I ended up most days, because I didn't want to go to any lessons. The first time I went up there, I got a job on the market gardens with Mr Z. 'Can you drive?' No, I said, because I couldn't. 'Well, you'd better learn,' he said, and chucked me the keys to the Land Rover. 'Hurry up then, you'd better practise. You've got to couple up those gangmowers and mow all the top fields.' So I had a practice, didn't do too badly, came back, tied up the mowers and did the job.

The shower block was a horrible place, white tiles

and a stone floor with rows of showers each side facing one another. It was where we went to smoke, it was where we went to fight, but worst of all it was where we went to shower. Mr Y was in charge of overseeing the boys taking their daily shower; in fact, he seemed to spend an awful lot of time in the shower block. At the end of the row of showers was a main stopcock or tap that controlled the water. 'Soap up' was Mr Y's command, then the water would suddenly be turned off. 'Make sure you wash your little cocks, you dirty little bastards,' he would say, then he would walk along the line and stop at his chosen victim. 'Hands by your side, boy,' he would say, then he would place his baton under the boy's testicles, gently lift them, and with his other hand he would take hold of the kid's penis and say, 'Call this clean? Give me the soap, I'll show you how you wash it.' Another of Mr Y's 'tricks' was to turn off the water while we were covered in soap and unable to see. 'C'mon, boys, wash those filthy little faces,' he'd say, and as we stood there naked, blind and scared he would give one of us a severe whack with the baton.

It wasn't just the staff that were a problem. Smithy started to bully me verbally, calling me a wanker and the like, especially when the staff were about and he was protected. One day I was having a kickabout on the field with a few of the boys when Smithy turned up.

'Oi you,' he said.

We all ignored him.

'Oi you!' he shouted

It went really quiet. The others knew it was time for me to feel the weight of Smithy. But I had prepared for this day from the moment I arrived. I'd planted various weapons around the grounds. Given the massive bulk he had to carry, speed wasn't one of the things with which Smithy had been blessed.

Looking straight at him, I said, 'You talking to me, you fat cunt?'

No one had ever spoken to Smithy like that before, or at least not to his face.

'I'll kill ya, I'll fucking kill ya!' he exploded.

Flicking the football up, I volleyed it as hard as I could at Smithy. It was more luck than judgement when the ball hit him right in his big fat gut. Letting out a yell of both pain and anger, Smithy came charging at me like a crazed elephant. The fat fucker had no chance, though, unless he got me in his grip – and the thought of him catching me filled me with horror.

I was off running, with fatty rumbling like a rhino behind me. As I headed towards the rear of the gym, I stopped to get a piece of wood I had put there in case of emergencies. Smithy came trundling up to me, red-faced and hardly able to breathe. I gave him one good clump with the wood and ran off again. A crowd of boys were following the proceedings with great relish, cheering me on. I had him; I had him beaten. My plan was perfect.

I trotted off down the path to the farm, putting a lot of distance between me and fatty. At the back of a barn I'd planted an iron bar and a sharp knife. It was time to put an end to all this bollocks.

Smithy was knackered as he came round the corner. He could barely walk, let alone fight, but to make sure I walked up to him and smashed the iron bar against his leg. A scream ripped through the quiet of the country-side, and Smithy fell to the floor crying like a big fat baby.

You'd think that would have been the end of it, really, but me being me I had to go that extra mile. I gave him a swift kick to the belly, knocking the wind straight out of him, then, leaning down, I grabbed his hair, pulled his head back and cut his face, yelling at him, 'Don't you ever fuck with me again, you fat cunt, cos next time I will kill you stone dead!' And I meant it.

I was the guv'nor in that gaff from that moment onwards, and I remained the guv'nor till the day I left some two years later. It was a horrible place, there was a lot of shit going on, and I knew I had to be at the top of the tree, because no shit rains down on you there.

By the time I finished, in 1971, I even had a little money-lending scheme going that involved not just the boys but also some of the staff – because I had the money to lend them. I didn't charge the staff interest, but the boys had to pay back what they borrowed plus 100 per cent; so, if you borrowed a fiver, you paid back a tenner. John Brookes was always into me for £20. Whenever we went to play basketball at Crawley, against the Crawley Eagles, the best team in the area, we'd get annihilated, but no one minded because on the way back we'd stop and I'd buy everyone – even John Brookes – fish 'n' chips. I knew how to be top dog. I never had discipline at home, so I thrived on it at approved school.

Three

Soho: Rattles and Needles

I bet you've got a calendar on the wall somewhere, maybe a diary by the telephone. I bet you know what you're doing next week; I bet you've got plans for the holidays, that kind of thing. Maybe you've got long-term plans: what job you want to do next, what kind of things you might learn to do over the next few years. Maybe you remember being young and making plans for your life.

I never did. We had nothing at home that told me what day it was, and because school meant nothing to me and nobody I knew worked a nine-to-five shift, five days a week, it didn't matter to me what day it was or even what month it was. I wanted to be with my friends, I wanted to have a drink or a smoke in my hand – that was what counted. I lived for the moment; that was all. All I knew was that I wanted to enjoy life, and in London in the early seventies, when I was young, there was no better place to enjoy life than Soho.

Soho was a proper place in those days, not like it is now, all cleaned up and everything. There were restaurants then, as now, and shops too, although there were more food shops then. But there were also dirty bookshops, newsagents selling stuff under the counter, policemen taking bribes, and discos everywhere, going on into the night. And thousands upon thousands of people, new ones coming in every night of the week. Some of them came to stay, but most of them were just passing through. Those were the ones I wanted because they'd be there to have a good time, and that usually meant drugs, which sometimes I sold them. Other times I'd rip them off.

There were people like me all over Soho, on every street corner and in every club, selling blues, bombers, downers, uppers, Purple Hearts, Dexys . . . whatever was your pleasure, you could buy it, and I could sell it to you. And if you wanted something else, something other than pills – drink, female company, even male company – then I knew who could supply that. Other fellas were playing the same old games: clipping punters, playing the three-card trick, hustling the people.

What was great about Soho then was the changing faces. White, black, brown, yellow – everyone went there, in their hundreds and thousands. Always fresh faces coming in, looking for a good time, and I was part of it, selling it to them. This tidal wave of girls and boys, all wanting to get pilled up with whatever I was selling, was exciting. This was the era of flares, of denim almost hanging off in sheets from people's shoulders the lapels of their jackets were so wide; of Bowie and make-up on blokes; of Led Zep and blokes with shirts open down to their waists; and girls, girls of every kind, everywhere. There was a geezer dressed up as a Red Indian, and another guy dressed as a cowboy, and they'd be dressed like that all day. There was another guy, Moses, older than anyone else, wearing his Crombie coat; he was still there years later, still smoking drugs. I loved it. I was only young – fourteen, fifteen – but it was like the world had come to see me and where I lived. I felt I was the King, that Soho was my kingdom and they were all my courtiers.

I'd begun partying and selling drugs to punters in pubs and bars and nightclubs in Soho when I was just twelve, even before I went to approved school. It was during that time that I discovered that Roy's name opened doors. Everyone knew I was part of Roy Nash's family, which allowed me to do what I did at that age; people even referred to me sometimes as 'young Nash'. The Nash family had been one of the big families in London in the fifties and early sixties, on a par with the Krays and the Richardsons. They were among the first to have nightclubs in Soho and in west London. Roy, who I thought was my brother-in-law, was like a father-figure to me, and I looked up to him.

It was Roy who helped get me started earning proper money. After one particularly good evening I arrived home at about nine o'clock in the morning and sat down to tell Roy what I'd been up to the night before. I asked him if he knew where I could get any more pills.

'What do you want with all them pills?' he said. 'They'll send you bonkers if you take too many.'

'Nah, I'm not takin' 'em all,' I told him, 'I'm sellin' 'em.'

Roy thought about this for a moment and then told me that it just so happened that he knew someone who might know someone, and he gave me a number to call. This 'someone' had four and a half *million* pills 'lying around' that I could sell. Up till then I'd mostly dealt speed, but having all these pills to sell opened all the doors of Soho for me.

Then I went to approved school, and went back to Soho when I was fourteen. I had a couple of years there before I went into borstal, and when I came out of there I went right back to it again. Soho was always a magnet for me because I knew what to do – I knew how to clip people. If you couldn't earn money in Soho then – I don't know about now – you might as well have given the game up.

Soho was mine to do with as I pleased, particularly the area to the north of Old Compton Street. I'd be in and out of the bars and clubs on Greek Street, waiting to see who wanted to buy from me. All the staff in those places knew me, and if anyone got a bit friendly with them and asked who had something for them that night they all pointed me out. I was living under the umbrella of the Nashes, though I didn't yet realize it, and that gave me the right to be in those places, selling those drugs.

Of course I took them all myself as well. I'd already been smoking weed – puff, I called it – for some years, and I'd started on some of the pills, like Dexys, before I was even selling 'em. I'd tried LSD – boy did I love that – and also blues and Purple Hearts, but now I also gave Mandrax and Tuinal a go. Valium was good, I liked that as well. And of course I was boozing at the same time. I was in Roy's clubs, so the whisky and Coke was always free, and the good-time girls who worked there looked after me. Whether that was because I was Roy's relative or not I don't know, and to be honest I didn't care. Their attention was enough.

I was horrible then, and sometimes I went out of my way to be horrible. One Sunday afternoon, the day before a bank holiday, me and Peter Murray, a friend from school, wanted to go to the Roundhouse in Chalk Farm to see a Welsh rock band called Man. This was the early seventies, and Paki-bashing, as we called it, was the thing of the day. We went to Old Street, and by the Leasham Mission (which isn't there any more) there was a doorway and there was this man standing there with an attaché case. He might have been Indian, he might have been Pakistani; I didn't know the difference back then.

But we went up to him and I said, 'Give us your wallet.' He didn't, so we gave him a right-hander and searched him to get his wallet. There was only a couple of quid in it so I said, 'Have a look, see what's in his case.' Pete took a look, and it turned out he was a scissors salesman. So we promptly stuck him in the legs and bum with every pair of scissors he had. He was on the ground with these scissors sticking out of him and we walked away leaving him like that. What a couple of bastards we were.

Tuinal was the drug we were into then, so with the little bit of money we got the two of us went off to the Roundhouse, but by the time we got there I was so out of my nut I couldn't walk. I crawled up to the door on my hands and knees, held up my money for them to take, and they refused to let me in. And I couldn't figure out why.

But LSD was my favourite drug. One night in Crondall Street – it must have been about four in the morning – when I was on LSD, me and the Wing had one little microdot of LSD left and we couldn't work out what to do with it. The way your mind works when you're tripping . . . I did, however, know that we had to go over the road to Fat Freddy's, that Fat Freddy would sort us out right away. I banged on his door, hammering away, and Fat Freddy answered.

'What's the matter? What's the matter?'

'We need to share this trip,' I said.

He looked at the pair of us, sighed, then put his hand

out and took the little microdot. He led us into the kitchen, put the dot down, then reached into a drawer, pulled out a giant carving knife, threw his arm back and whacked the dot, slicing it into two equal pieces. Now, I may not be right about this – it could just have been part of a hallucination – but I remember this giant knife and this mighty swipe he took. I used to like LSD because of the fun times I had on it. I don't think that scene, the knife and all that, would have been quite so funny if I'd been on something else.

There was one drug I didn't do. In all the clubs and bars uppers and downers worked because of the music that accompanied them, but heroin was something else. I'd walk through the underpass in Piccadilly Circus and there'd be these people laid out flat on the floor, and I'd think, 'Scummy druggies, I ain't never going to be like them.' They took no pride in their appearance at all, and if there was one thing I was into, it was how I looked. I had the sharpest suits and shirts; I wasn't going to let all that go for the sake of a drug.

China white it was known as in those days, because it was so pure. I'd heard what you did with it: you whacked some into the barrel of a syringe and stuck it into a vein (cooking up didn't happen until a bit later, when the impurities came into it). I didn't fancy putting something in a vein; I wasn't squeamish, but popping a pill or drawing on a roll-up of puff seemed far enough to me. Up until that point in my life I had never even seen heroin, let alone taken it, and I knew I didn't want to try it. I saw enough of the chaos it caused around me so I steered clear of it.

Until one night in Greek Street. I'd love to say that it was a busy night, that I was late getting to my patch, that the moon was out and the wolves were howling or any of that sort of bollocks, but I really can't remember. What I do remember is standing at the top end of the street, near Soho Square, and this dwarf coming up to me. Everyone who hung around there knew what I was up to, so when he asked if I had any blues, I wasn't surprised. I wanted to laugh really because he was wearing these funny high-heeled platform shoes and the dodgiest suit I had ever seen.

'Yeah, I've got some blues,' I told him.

'Wanna swap twenty blues for a five-quid bag of china white?'

Of course not! What do you think I am? Officer, arrest this man, he's selling dangerous drugs!

That's what I should have said, and gone my sweet and merry way safe in the knowledge that I had chosen not to fuck my life up and give myself over to an obsessive craze that wanted only one thing in return – *everything*. But I didn't; for some reason I was persuaded by this funny little guy. Maybe it was because I didn't want to lose face. I knew I could handle it, of course, because I knew I was stronger, way stronger, than any drug. Of course I was. I was Peter, I was Superman, I was invincible. This is just a little bag of flour, isn't it? So I swapped twenty blues for a £5 bag.

It weighed almost nothing in my hand, this wrap of china white. I didn't know what to do next, how to get this little bag of white powder into my arm, and I guess the dwarf must have seen some hesitation in me because instead of walking away he said, 'You know what to do with it, don't ya?' It was obvious from the expression on my face that I was totally clueless as to what to do with this bag of smack. 'You bang it up,' Shorty told me. Then, seeing that I still had no idea what he was talking about, he sighed and said, 'Follow me.'

First stop was Hall's all-night chemist in Shaftesbury Avenue. Shorty bought a two-millilitre barrel and an orange needle while I stood behind him and watched. We headed back out on to the street, and he said, 'C'mon, I'll sort you out down the Deuce.' The Deuce was a proper den of iniquity, a dive that called itself a nightclub but was really a place for the lonely people of London. Prostitutes, rent boys, junkies, pimps, crooks and homeless waifs and strays all visited the Deuce during the night.

We slipped down the stairs and into the Gents', and squeezed into the only cubicle – six-foot-something me and no-foot-nothing Shorty. It was light enough to see what was going on but I was concentrating so hard on watching what he was doing, learning from him, that I took no notice of how dirty the cubicle was. Shorty took the wrap of heroin off me and put it in a spoon that he'd produced from his pocket. He then placed that on top of the cistern lid, added half a syringe of water to the spoon, gave the mixture a stir with the tip of the needle, and sucked the ingredients back into the syringe. 'Roll your sleeve up and give me your arm,' he said. I did so. 'Pump it up a bit, give us a vein.' He indicated that I needed to flex my arm a bit to raise the vein in the crook of my elbow. I did so, then knelt down so the little man could reach.

So, in the stinking toilet of one of the most undesirable places in Soho, I did the one thing I had always said I wouldn't do: I held my left arm out and, displaying his battle-hardened skills, Shorty gave me my first fix.

I remember him flicking the syringe to get the air out – just like with Colin Nelson and my first joint, I didn't ask him what he was doing, I just watched closely – pushing the plunger so that a little drop came out, and then flicking it again. 'Lick this,' he said, and he gave me the spike to lick. That was the ritual that everyone did, then and now, even if someone else was pushing it into you. As he pushed the needle in I felt that little . . . like you're pushing a sewing needle into a tough bit of cloth and it pops through to the other side. It popped, and I watched as he withdrew the plunger and the blood came out of the vein. It swirled around in the milky liquid in the barrel, and then he pushed it all back into the vein, slowly and clinically.

Two minutes between going into and coming out of the toilets. Looking back, it's all in slow motion. I can still remember the moment when the contents of that barrel emptied into my vein. Why? Because I'd never known anything like that moment. It's near-on impossible to describe my feelings as the heroin began to surge through my blood. I could feel it racing through my bloodstream, hitting my heart and my toes and my ears and just everywhere, and everything, absolutely everything, felt different. Right away I liked it – no, I fucking loved it. It started a love affair that was to last the best part of thirty years, an all-consuming obsession that brought me to my knees.

Because I concentrated on everything that happened, I could do it myself the second time. If you concentrate and you look, you can get it. It's stupid and simple, this life. If it gets complicated, I know to pick the phone up and ask; everything's so simple when you do that. But I still made the mistake, didn't I?

I've a scar inside my left elbow because I didn't stop caning that vein. Once I'd started taking heroin, I didn't stop. Being a crook is bad enough, but add to that crook an addiction, well, that's when principles go right out of the window. I remember how I would frown at certain crimes – robbing old ladies, that kind of thing – and say things like 'scumbags' and 'I would never do that'. Robbing old people is called grunting; it's the next one down from being a nonce. Once you're an addict, though, everything becomes just a moment away from the crimes you'd despised before. Over the years I did the very things I said I would never do, all of them, and probably a great deal worse. Slowly but surely I sank lower and lower into the depths of degradation.

Using is like sex: at first it's the best thing ever, but it soon becomes a chore so you start adding to it, heightening the pleasure with other things. There's the phrase 'I take drugs', but it's bollocks really, because the drugs take you. They take you hostage and hold you to ransom. The prize? Your life. I always liked to say, in the beginning, that I enjoyed drugs, but by the end the drugs enjoyed me. That may be because I went further – took more – than the average Joe.

Stepping back on to the street that night, I knew I would take this drug again. And so I did. Soho remained the place I came to, but now I had a more urgent purpose to my dealing pills, because I used the money – not all of it; not yet anyway – to buy powder. But, despite it being my patch, and despite me thinking I had the protection of Roy's name, Soho was a very dangerous place to hang out, as I soon found out. I was living the life there too freely, and I came to the notice of one of Soho's predators.

Junior was a black man, quite well known in Soho, one of the 'night people'. He was also gay. Not that his homosexual tendencies made any difference to me: there were loads of poofs in Soho. You met all sorts of weird and wonderful people there, some not so wonderful as well. I was about fifteen when I met up with Junior and his cronies. At first I really thought they were OK, but once again I was so wrong.

Taking sleeping pills was the vogue in those days; stumbling about and falling over was our idea of fun. We must have looked ridiculous, I suppose, but that's what we did. I can't really tell any stories about being out of my head on downers because if the truth be told I can't really remember a lot. But one evening I ended up in a group going to someone's flat to continue the party. We left Soho at about six in the morning and made our way to the Tube. We were all a bit out of it, some more than others, and I remember ending up in Brixton somewhere. The next thing I knew I was in a flat with Junior and Peter something-or-other, some blonde-haired girl and four or five other blokes, and the downers were brought out. There was a jar of Nembutal and loads of Valium, which I was rather partial to. I got more and more out of it, to the point where I could no longer stand up, or speak without slurring.

What happened next will live with me until my dying day. Junior and one of the men waited until I was so far gone I couldn't resist, then picked me up and carried me into a bedroom where they stripped me and sodomized me. I was completely incapable of fighting back; all I could see were their smiling faces, them and the rest of the men who joined in the gang rape.

I don't know the names of the people, except for Junior. I always used to say to myself that if I ever saw him I'd kill him. And I did look for him, although fortunately I never found him. Junior's dead now: he got murdered on Brixton Hill, run through with a sword, not long after the event. Read into that what you will, but it was nothing to do with me.

I never spoke about this for twenty-five years, not to anyone. I was ashamed. A shitty thing to have happen to you. I couldn't go to the police as they didn't like me, and anyway I didn't want anyone laughing at me. Nowadays it would get a response, but then it wasn't really happening, at least not as far as most people were concerned. Also, if no one knew, I could pretend it had never happened. I look at boys of fifteen now and I think what I was like then and what I'd seen by that time. I never had a childhood. At a young age I was on the way to becoming an addict, and all I knew was violence and abuse. Maybe because I kept this rape secret it festered inside, and my isolation from other people just got worse.

After discovering heroin and being raped I became really wild, and the people around me – the old gang from Hoxton, as well as my family – encouraged that. I was more use to them when I was wild, because I'd dare to do more. Me and a friend used to take the Tube up to Hampstead and cruise about looking for girls. There were loads of posh girls who'd bunk off their schools for the day while Mummy and Daddy were out, so we'd hook up with them, go back to their houses, drink some booze and smoke some puff, have sex with them, then rob the place.

We all got into drugs, the old gang. Pudsy used to OD on barbiturates every Friday night, then go and sit in the hospital waiting room; they'd pump his stomach and send him home. So he'd get nicely stoned every Friday, safe in the knowledge that nothing bad was going to happen to him. He and I fell out when he kicked Roy's car, an Aston Martin. He'd asked me for some pills, but I wasn't just giving them away to him so I'd said no. He kicked Roy's car, I told him to stop it, he had one last kick, so I leant forward, grabbed him by the ears, drew him towards me and bit the tip of his nose off.

That was me, an odd contradiction. I'd discovered in approved school that I liked regularity, order and discipline in my life. I was Serious Pete still, using extreme violence (and the threat of it) to intimidate people. But I also liked to be completely out of my nut, really on one, when I took drugs. Then again, I also enjoyed mellowing out. There was a big squat at Charles Rowan House in Wilmington Square where we used to go to score; if you wanted heroin or LSD or puff, that's where you went. They'd build these giant bonfires in the centre of the blocks and sit around, smoking, all night. I used to go and sit there too; I liked that laid-back thing. I've never been to Goa or anywhere like that but I used to think that is what it must be like.

*   *   *

When I'd first come out of approved school Fred had taken me to one side and told me that I had to pay my way. So I started doing what I could, nicking stuff and selling on to fences. I was out with a friend, Ronnie, one night, 'screwing' – that's what we called burglary – and we broke into this little shop that dealt in old manuscripts. It took us quite some time as we were really careful. We didn't want to make a noise by smashing the window, so we carefully took the beading out, then scraped off the putty, inserted a screwdriver into the corner of the glass and gently levered it out. Once we were inside we didn't have to be quite so quiet, and when we came across the next obstacle, a heavy, solid, locked and bolted door with a small window with reinforced glass, I picked a rug up from the floor, folded it up to fit the window, got Ronnie to hold it in place and smashed it with a fire extinguisher.

The shop was like an Aladdin's cave, with books dating back to the sixteenth century, silver candlesticks, old maps, and a locked filing cabinet. We rifled through the open shelves first and stashed our swag by the door in some mail sacks we'd found, before turning our attention to the filing cabinet. I stuck a screwdriver in between the top drawer and the lock and with one hard pull downwards the cabinet popped open. I thought I was going to faint when I pulled open the bottom drawer. It was full of money. Fifty-four thousand pounds in cash we got away with, along with the silver and the books. I couldn't believe it, and nor could the family, who were well pleased with me for the night's work.

I went out the next morning and bought myself some clothes and a nice watch from Bond Street, then went to the Queen's Head and bought the most expensive bottle of champagne in the place. We were two fools who thought no one would notice us splashing our cash about. We planned to sell the stuff and then go abroad for a bit.

Johnny Mac, a small, dark-haired man with the features of a rodent, was the one to sell to if you had anything a bit special to get rid of on the hurry-up. Mackeson's stout was his favourite tipple, so we called him Johnny Mac. We met him at Ronnie's mum's house – she was holding the stuff we'd swiped – and there was a great deal of umming and ahhing. 'This stuff's a bit hot, boys,' he told us, and we noticed it was taking him a while to get to a figure, 'because most of it's listed. That'll make it harder to sell.' He stared out of his beady eyes for a while, then said, 'Eleven grand.' Well, we were a bit sick really because we'd done our homework and knew the value of the stuff we had, but we had no choice. So we agreed to meet him in Victoria Park on Saturday morning; Johnny would be there with the buyer and we would do the trade.

Sitting on a park bench with a hundred thousand pounds' worth of stolen property is quite scary, especially when your buyer is late. A bad feeling crept in. 'Where the fuck is he?' said Ronnie. I didn't know, so we decided to leave. I hadn't noticed anyone lurking about, but as soon as we'd stood up two cars and a van came hurtling towards us and screeched to a halt, and men appeared from everywhere, surrounding us.

'You're nicked!' one of the policemen shouted.

The next thing I knew I was face down on the floor with my hands cuffed behind my back. The bag with the books and silver remained propped against the bench we had been sitting on. Without even a glimpse into the bag a policeman said, 'Where did you get these books?'

Ronnie and I had been set up by Johnny Mac. I mean, how on earth did the policeman know that there were books in the bag without even looking? Turned out Johnny Mac had recently come out of jail and the police leant on him; to make sure he didn't go back right away, he sold us out.

So I found myself back on remand at Stamford House. By this stage I was well versed in the art of manipulation, and when we had a court date coming up I said that I wanted to go to a barber's. 'If I'm going to court I want a haircut to look my best, it's my right, blah blah blah.' So they took me up to Shepherd's Bush, and as we were walking along I said to the geezer with me, 'See you later!' As he went 'What?' I hopped on to a bus that was going by, waved goodbye to him, and was off. Of course I was caught again fairly quickly, and although we pleaded not guilty to the burglary when we went to court (and, to the judge's annoyance, were found not guilty, because they couldn't prove that we'd actually stolen the stuff), we were found guilty of dishonestly handling stolen property and got sent to borstal. Although I was too young to be named, I was called 'a professional thief' in the papers, which I was so proud of. It made my day when I read that.

I was sent to Wormwood Scrubs and put on B Wing; you went there to be taken off to borstal. It had been an ambition of mine to get in there since I was twelve years old. I'd been shown it on a visit to Hammersmith Hospital from Stamford House. 'See that place?' the warden accompanying me to the hospital said as we walked past the Scrubs. 'That's where you're going to end up one day.' If only he'd known that what he was saying to me wasn't a threat but a promise. I couldn't wait to get in there. Prison meant I'd arrived – that's how warped my thinking was. Prison meant I'd joined the chaps in their exclusive club.

The night I arrived in the Scrubs I had a visit, but not from outside, from a screw over in the main prison block. Freddie Foreman, who later became known as the Managing Director of British Crime, was over on D Wing at the time, and he was a good friend of Roy's. When he heard that I was inside for the first time he wanted to make my time easier for me. Freddie was a man with clout, and that's why he was able to get a screw to carry a parcel across to me. The first I knew of it was when my door opened and this screw was staring at me, as if trying to work out why he was doing this, as if somehow what I looked like might explain what was going on. But it wasn't clear at all to him, and he shrugged his shoulders and said, 'Freddie Foreman sent this over to you.' He handed over this pillowcase and went away, shutting the door behind him. I looked inside and there was tobacco and sweets and everything I needed.

I smiled. Thanks, Freddie.

There was also a bookie in the Scrubs called Billy Gentry, also from Hoxton. Billy sorted me out with a job in the probation unit. The same screw who'd brought me the stuff on the first night stuck his head round the door, told me that's where I'd be working, then added, 'Don't worry, it's all been sorted out.' So now I could pick up my tobacco and use the phone. The only problem in there was the stink: the probation officer, Mrs Pelly, we called Smelly Pelly because of the perfume she slopped all over herself.

The boys going through the system were being sent off to Portland or Rochester or Dover, and then all of a sudden a screw said, 'We're allocating you today. Do you want to go to Huntercombe?' And I thought, 'Yes, that's the posh geezers' borstal, out by Henley. I'll have a bit of that one.' Straight away I got a job in the kitchen. I sorted out Sid Swan, the kitchen screw: he would bring me in my bits and pieces; I'd sit in the kitchen and eat steak.

Borstal was not too bad, nothing like the approved school. There was a bit of marching here and there and a lot of physical exercise, but I enjoyed that. It was all about instilling a bit of discipline into you. I was happy with that, I kept my head down, and a year later I was back out on the street, back on the job again, a super-fit disciplined criminal.

When I got out of borstal, I ended up being sent back to Stamford House for some misdemeanour, only they wouldn't have me there, and they couldn't keep me in the police cells, so they had to send me to a children's home in Hackney. Trowbridge House, that's where they put me, and I loved it. The nightwatch lady made me hot chocolate and a bacon sandwich and put me in a nice soft bed in the hospital ward. There was an open window and I could have jumped out and disappeared, but I thought, 'Soft bed, cup of cocoa, I'm all right.' I'd been in borstal, I'd been in the Scrubs, and now I was in a children's home, so I stayed there. When I got up that first morning I found out I was a novelty, a serious guy among some girls – and there were nice girls there – so for a while I didn't know what to do. It appealed to me to stay, but after a while I'd had enough, and walked out.

I remember Trowbridge House because that was the last time I ever felt like a child.

Four

Larging It

When you stop being a child, you become an adolescent, and that's when confusion sets in. You're not sure where you're heading, you don't know what you want from life. Things happen around you that sometimes freak you out a bit, and the illicit treats of adult life come a little sharper into view.

You could say I had a head start on most of this, that my teenage years had come and gone by the time I was twelve. I'd certainly grown up quick, but coming back from borstal and being at home again in Hoxton – well, on my return I found that things were different. Not the place, and not me either, not really. It was what was going on around me that was different. From then on, something unspoken started to happen around me; I started to be treated in a different way from how I had been before. There was respect. I don't mean people doffed their caps to me in the street or stood up to salute me as I walked into the pub. What I mean is, I was no longer just someone on the outside of what was going on, on the periphery; things happened around me instead.

Take the time I got wronged by Lenny Bonkers. Lenny was a lot of things, but one night I needed him to fence something for me, a diamond ring that I'd stolen. I didn't mean it to be him – someone else would have done the job just as well – but I showed it to Lenny and he said, 'Yeah, nice one. Let me have it and I'll see what I can get for you.' And that's precisely what he did get for me – nothing. He sold it and fucked me over for my money. I went into the pub and saw him there; he just looked at me and turned away. Now I was still just a kid, and he was a big man, so there was nothing I could do about it. It made me mad, so I stormed out of the pub. I couldn't do a thing about it.

Or so I thought, because as I said, this was when things started to get a bit different for me. I was standing there fuming and Bill the Bum (he looked like an egg on legs) came out to talk to me. 'What's going on, Peter?' he asked. I told him. 'Wait,' he growled, then headed back into the pub. A few moments later the door shot open and out flew Lenny, closely followed by Bill, Carrots (so-called because of his red hair) and Fat Arthur (a half-Indian cockney, a genuine and happy bloke). They laid into him and gave him a right hiding before telling him never, ever to do that to me again.

Now this surprised me, of course. It's one thing helping your pals out, but what was going on?

It was another incident that made things clearer for me. I was round at Billy Clarke's house, whose son Binsey was in our gang. Charlie Dodd was there; he must have been about forty and he'd just come out of the nick. I had a bit of cash on me from the night before, from selling pills, so I pulled out a few notes and gave them to him, told him to get himself sorted now that he was out. This old boy looked at me and at the money in his hand, then smiled up at Billy Clarke. 'See this boy here,' he said to Billy, 'he's going to be the guv'nor one day.' And then they both looked at me expectantly.

So that was it – I was not just going to grow up, I was going to grow up to be The Man. That was why people were doing me favours. When I was younger, whenever I went into the pub the men fell over themselves to buy me a drink, but then it was always 'Tell Roy I looked after you,' that kind of thing. Now it wasn't for Roy's sake, it was for mine. I'd been brought up to think I was something special, but now it appeared that other people thought so too. Here, in Islington and Hoxton and all the gaffs in between, I was going to be something special. I quite liked this idea.

Charlie Dodd went straight back to doing what he'd done before, working with Hawaiian Dave doing a few jewellers'. I used to go out with them. Once we were inside they'd sling me in the window to clean it out while they put everyone on the floor and did the shop. I didn't care that I was on show to whoever was walking past. I thought it was all a laugh.

So what had I learned, to be treated like this? What had I picked up in borstal that marked me out as a leader of men? Because I'd not learned anything at school that was going to help. I'd come out from Huntercombe fit and healthy, and discovered that I was going to be promoted to the rank of 'one of the chaps', but that was it. After that, I didn't have a clue. I knew that if anyone took the piss I had to cut them or stab them, but that was about the extent of my interpersonal skills. I didn't have a clue who I was, so it just seemed easiest for me to fit in with everyone else's plans. If they wanted me to be something I wasn't, well, best not to show that, best instead to get on with being The Leader. I knew how to handle myself in a fight, I'd learned enough on the streets of Hoxton and the terraces at Arsenal as a young boy, and approved school and borstal had taught me more. I was on my way to being a gangster.

We'd swan about in big coats, in all kinds of weather, because we were gangsters, weren't we, so we not only had to act like one, we had to dress like one too. A couple of the chaps even carried swords hung under their armpits, hidden by the coats. I watched 'em use them once on someone they'd dragged up to the top floor of a block. They tied a noose round his neck and told him to jump. He didn't really see things their way and thought he wouldn't, so by way of encouragement they took out their swords and stuck them into him, proper jabs they were. He had no choice, and he jumped. Only they'd had their fun with him, so they pulled him back up, told him he'd been taught a lesson and sent him on his way.

When we had gang fights, guns were involved and everything. It was like military planning. We'd have snatch squads. We'd run in and crack baseball bats on their legs and arms but we'd avoid their heads. That way they'd do the same for us. I became immune to the savagery. I lived and breathed it. It was what we all did. Violence was all around, and I dished it out too, because I was supposed to be going up a gear. Everyone was expecting big things of me.

Johnny Buck, for instance, a big old boy from Bethnal Green who was always robbing people. One time I was standing about outside the Nag's Head selling blues when Johnny came over, pushed me against the wall and took the whole bag off me. He was always doing things like that – he was a bully. Then he went inside, and Roy was drinking in there, so I followed him in and with Roy collected a few chaps together. It all kicked off and I got my blues back. I was one of them; they were going to look after me. These were the people I was with. Their ways were my ways, and the things I saw – well, I wanted to do that too.

The chaps had big bellies, and they sat around in the pub on a Sunday afternoon, cigar in hand, talking about the 'little woman' back home getting their dinner ready. So I did, too, even though I was no more than sixteen. They'd think nothing of brushing someone aside to get what they wanted – it's how they got those big bellies in the first place – so neither did I.

I started to look at how they lived, their code. The drinking I could understand, but some of the rest of it got to me. That Johnny Buck again. We were all in the Nag's Head. I was at one side of the bar drinking, Johnny was at the other end, drinking with a guy called Eddie Hoskins. Now, Johnny had pissed someone off because as we were standing there the door opened, a gun was pointed through the crack, it went *bang bang bang*, and Johnny was shot. He wasn't dead, though. He got carted off to hospital and came out right as rain.

And then he took a right liberty with a drug dealer, a Greek guy selling trips. Out from the pub went Johnny. 'Right, I'm off home,' he said, and off he went with his big lolloping walk. He was just passing the steps of the children's hospital when all of a sudden someone got out of a car with a shotgun and went *bam*! We were over fifty yards away but we could see it all clearly: the gun exploded, and Johnny Buck's back opened up in a haze of blood, like someone had come out of his shirt and thrown a tin of red paint in the air. Johnny crashed down on to the steps, but somehow he survived that as well.

Fuck me if he didn't then go and top himself. Crazy.

Another one who got shot was Big Jimmy. We were in the King's Head having a drink one night, and Big Jimmy was thought to be having an affair with the wife of Robin, the guv'nor of the pub. I'm not sure who believed this, but obviously somebody did because a geezer walked in, balaclava on his head, carrying a sawn-off shotgun, and fired it off. But he had dried rice in it, which cuts right into whatever it hits but doesn't kill you. He let go with both barrels at Big Jimmy's legs, and the rice went right through Big Jimmy's strides, shredding them on the way to his legs. Obviously somebody wanted to get a message to Big Jimmy, not to kill him. So there was Jimmy standing there, and we were all a bit shocked because of the noise of the gun, loud in that small space, and the fact that his trousers had been blown almost right off and there was blood pouring down his legs. Jimmy went 'Ooooh,' then barely paused before pushing his glass out and saying, 'Give us a pint of lager.' Oh, how we laughed.

Jimmy did bird. Before he went in he was a thug and everything that goes with that; while he was inside he did a creative writing course, and since he came out he has written things for radio and really turned his life around. Gentleman Jim he's called now, a good man. Always got time for you.

Shootings, guns, they were all around us, although I never handled one myself. The whole of Hoxton was full of crooks, and sometimes they were good to us and sometimes they weren't. I remember sitting outside Andrew and Eve's café down Hoxton one Christmas Eve and someone said, 'Is that Fred over there?' And Freddy Davies came over with two carrier bags full of money, two leather shopping bags full to the brim with fivers and tenners. 'Come here, boys,' he said, and we wandered over while he dug his hands deep into the bags and pulled out big handfuls of money which he just pushed at us. 'I've had a good 'un today,' he said, 'so have some yourselves.'

But then there was Tommy the Talker, a notorious old-time fence who ripped us right off. We'd get diamonds and things and take them to Tommy's. He always had a coal fire going, nicely stoked up, all year round, even in summer. But we never thought about why, not till his daughter told me about it. We'd take the stuff round to him, spread it out over the table, he'd get his glass out and 'All right, boys, I'll give you a fiver for that, a tenner for that, and that's rubbish.' He'd throw the rubbish on to the fire, like he was doing you a favour, getting rid of the evidence. And when we were done he'd pay up and we'd leave, after which he'd carefully rake the coals and take out the diamonds he'd thrown in there, because of course the stones don't melt, only we didn't know that, and of course it was the really good ones he threw into the fire. I was quite old when I found out what his little game was. I had an affair with his daughter, I was talking about her dad, I said something about him always having this fire, summer and winter, and she said, 'You know why?' I thought it was pretty good really. I didn't feel too bitter about it.

Fell off a bus, Tommy did, and died as a result of his injuries.

So although now I can say I properly understand, there were things going on around me then that I just didn't get, and things I just didn't like. I went along with them, but I knew it wasn't what I wanted to be. The expectations to behave in a certain way – to turn up at certain pubs and have a drink there on a Saturday night, to talk to the right people – it was too much like *having* to do something and not much like *wanting* to do something, so it started to piss me off.

The one thing I did want very much was to get out of my tree as often as possible. The drinking was easy: we all did that; it was expected of you. Smoking puff wasn't too bad either – no one thought much about it. But one thing separated me from everyone else, and that was my growing addiction to heroin. Because my friends and family were totally against intravenous drug use of any kind, and derogatory towards anyone even suspected of involvement in heroin use (although it was of course OK to sell it), my addiction was for many years one of the best-kept secrets in London; and because I was still going out drinking with the chaps, standing at the bar and sinking pints with the best of them, I really thought that sort of made my addiction to heroin OK in a way.

On the face of it I was the person it seemed everyone I knew wanted me to be: I was a crook, an up-and-coming villain, destined to become a big shot, a major player; I had respect, and increasing numbers of older criminals would often take me along on their jobs. The other me skulked around the dark and dingy areas of Soho, hiding in the shadows in case I was spotted associating with the 'scumbags', which is what my family called anyone who wasn't dressed in Cecil Gee or Dior clothes. There I was, drinking and committing crimes with people who were well respected in the crime world, all the time planning when I could leave them and go off to the squat in Wilmington Square where I could score.

Truth be told, I never felt I belonged in either camp. I never really felt part of any group. I went to football matches and surrounded myself with thousands of people, I spent lots of time in Soho where life never stops, I went to pubs and clubs solely to be with people, but in all these places, no matter how many people were there, I was lonely.

Taking drugs became a way of life for me. I lived to use and I used to live. I look back now at a life of madness, sadness and badness, and there came a point when it had to stop. Taking drugs was good, the feeling was good, it took me away from the present and eased my sense of isolation, the unhappiness I sometimes felt in my lonely little world. I created my own little world to live in, and although I knew it was shitty I didn't care, because it was mine, and no one else knew about it or could do anything about it. In that world I could do what I wanted. I could take drugs, get drunk, break into houses, factories, shops; I could rip people off, and I could hurt people before they hurt me. To me, that's what people did: they hurt you all the fucking time. Maybe they never physically hurt you, or maybe they never realized that what they were doing was causing pain, but that's how it felt; so I shut myself away from them all, tucking my emotions up. I didn't know what emotions were, really; and because I couldn't allow myself to have any I couldn't allow anyone around me to have them either. People just seemed to drift in and out of my life, leaving me alone in my world.

Living this dual life – being treated as The Man by some when I was in the pub drinking, then being strung out on drugs the rest of the night – really started to fuck me up. I didn't know what I wanted, but inevitably the two worlds collided.

I'd done some business with a man called Charlie

Swift, and he'd knocked me up for my money. I was on downers, and it got into my head that I needed to do something about it. I decided I'd get my revenge. I knew he lived in a block of flats so I went there looking for him. He wasn't in, so I waited on the first floor till I saw him coming in through the main door below, then jumped in the lift as he called for it, so that I would be there and ready when the lift reached the bottom. The doors opened, Charlie went to get in, and I stepped forward and stabbed him.

In court, I had to say I was on drugs and didn't know what I was doing. Neither Charlie or I mentioned anything about our past. Well, you wouldn't, would you? 'Oh yes, officer, I recall the reason I stabbed him, now that you ask. It was because he'd kept some money back from a robbery I'd done and he was going to sell the gear without paying me back.' So no one knew why I'd done it. He was sixty, I was sixteen; everyone thought I was in the wrong as I said nothing about the money. It wasn't their business. I got three years.

I was sent to Onley, near Rugby, which is where I started to go mad and bad. I was on the segregation block, where I read a book called *The Dice Man*. Now if you don't know the book I won't spoil it for you, but what it meant for me was that every morning I based my decisions on what to do that day, just like the hero of the book did, by rolling dice. I'd then have to do what the dice had chosen from the options I'd given it, and the madder and badder these decisions, the better. One time I hit a guy called Chalky White over the head with an iron; another time I slept under the bed, not on it; once I went down to breakfast naked.

It was all bravado. I had my head shaved, and I grew a little pointy beard – all the better to look mad, bad and dangerous to know. But prison wasn't a bad place for me to be. I had plenty of puff, and other bits and pieces, and just as in school, where I'd found out that having money meant people would do things for you, I always had my firm around me. I'd look after them, but they had to do what I told 'em. I was sixteen when I got my first three years. By the time I was seventeen I'd created such a fuss. I wouldn't do drill or any marching, all that nonsense. I'd go to the gym, but that was for me, that was my time; I wasn't going to do anything for anyone else. I was in the punishment block almost all the time.

I wanted people to be afraid of me, and for them to do what I wanted. There was a Welshman who had a Seiko watch and I liked the look of it, so I asked him for it. He said no. I got two guys, Fingers and Slim, to ambush him and take his watch off him, but that wasn't enough, so I had them hold his head so I could kick him. I ran up and booted him so hard in the face that his jaw broke. Once I sewed up someone else's mouth. Mailbag needle and cotton, through the lips. I'm not even sure he'd done what I thought he'd done – you know, grassed on me; it was just a rumour. Again I had him held down, my little gang around me.

I had to prove myself, all the time. I had to be someone; I wanted to be someone. I thought I was a gangster anyway, so I might as well be one of those real violent feared people. Charlie Dodd had said I was going to be the guv'nor one day, so I had to be the ultimate guv'nor; I had to let people know that they should fear me. If they had to fight me, they had better be prepared to kill me, because if they didn't then I was going to kill them. I wasn't an animal, but the screws called me one so I started to act like one. Nor was I mad, but they told me I was so I acted as mad as they wanted me to be. Me being me, that had to be the maddest, baddest animal they had ever seen. And of course it was always the system's fault, never mine. How could I have thought otherwise?

I couldn't let on who I was, underneath it all. I couldn't ask for trust, or help, or love, because it frightened me. It was too much to risk being rejected. And anyway, I didn't know what trust or love was. I didn't know what either of them looked or smelled like, and I was brought up to believe only in the things I could hold in my own hands. I knew nothing about the things that could have made a difference in my life, but I knew everything – or I thought I did – about the things that would do their best to destroy it. Heroin, alcohol, crime – each of them came close to killing me over the years, several times, but something swung my way each time and I survived. Once or twice people told me they loved me, but I never believed them; it was a lie designed to get me off my guard so they could hurt me. Keep away from me, I don't need friends, and I definitely don't want all that love stuff. Nothing worse than someone saying 'I love you'.

Why did I think like that?

I even kept friends at arm's length, or worse. About the time *Star Wars* first came out, when I was twenty, I went to do a job someone told me I'd make about a grand, a grand and a half from. I came away with over £8,000, and as it was my mate Terry Pridgeon's twenty-first birthday I splashed out on a VW Beetle for him. A few days later we were out and about in it, Terry was driving, and something was said out of turn – you know, turn left, not right; I said left, you dumb fucker; that kind of thing. The car was stopped, I had a fight with him, and I bit lumps out of his face. I had to go down to Charley Wright's (as the Queen's Head was known) to smooth things over with Terry's brothers to ensure they weren't going to come after me. Nothing came of it, we shook hands, and it was all over. But I couldn't stay in the pub with them there so I walked over to the Nag's Head, wanting a drink before the lock-in.

Terry's girlfriend Joanne was in there. She really started insulting me, going at me, smashed a glass and stabbed it in my hand. I went fucking berserk and clumped her, and anyone else who was around me. At the time the owner of the pub was John L. Gardner, the British champion boxer, and he hid behind the bar while I smashed the optics and threw stools around. I even hit Alice with a glass ashtray – I didn't know I'd done it, but I did. On the way out, Nicky Gerrard, who was known to be a hitman, stopped me; he was a nasty piece of work, fucking mental. I'd just hit everyone and smashed up the pub, and there he was in the doorway, blocking my way.

'See you,' he said, 'you're fuckin' mad, you are.'

'And you fuckin' ain't, are you?' I replied.

I couldn't believe this person who went all round London sticking it in people's nuts. The audacity of the man – how dare he call me mad. He's dead now anyway. He came out of his daughter's birthday, they knelt him down in the street, then blew his head off. He'd gone one step too far.

Stories like his, and my experiences in prison, changed me. When I came out, I was different. I'd had a taste of prison, and it didn't frighten me. I knew what it was like in there, but the people I knew who were doing the things I was expected to be doing, they were getting eighteen, twenty, twenty-five years. That's a life gone. I wanted to enjoy mine, not spend it inside four little walls. I wanted clothes, sex, drink, nights out, money, music, the occasional punch-up, drugs, and I knew that if I carried on as I was I'd be missing out on all of that. I didn't want to be involved in all this gangster stuff after all. Deep inside, you see, I wasn't as nasty as I pretended to be. I don't know where that hidden feeling came from, as my family hadn't brought me up to be nice. Then again, when there was a fight, or whatever it was, I had to win, I had to be the best, and they didn't instil that in me either.

Once I realized how serious all this stuff was, how long these guys were being sent away for, and how much effort it took them to get to where they wanted to be, I decided that I didn't want to be a gangster. I was happy being a thief, a vagabond, a scallywag, but I never wanted to be thought of as a Bad Man. Was I confused? Probably.

I also realized that I was going to need someone's help to turn me away from the gangster trail. And that's where One-Thumb Norman came in.

Five

The Apprentice

Perhaps because of who I was, or rather who I was being groomed to be, I was taken in hand by two men who treated me as if I were their apprentice: One-Thumb Norman, who taught me burglary, and the Old Boy, who taught me con tricks.

When I came out of prison the first time, and I was about eighteen, Norman was at the house when I walked in. He offered to take me out with him that night; he decided he was going to do me a favour and teach me his trade. If you'd met him then, you'd have thought Norman was gay. For a start, he was Leslie Holt's friend. Leslie, the King of the Cat Burglars, was gay, and he and Norman had started off together. Norman was a very handsome man with a shock of dark hair, quite effeminate in his movements and his actions, always immaculately dressed, nice, kind and polite. That man had manners; he had this *je ne sais quoi* about him. What Norman liked, though, was amphetamines, nice cars, money – and women. He was the greatest womanizer I've ever met in my life. He had a way with women I could only aspire to. Even in his fifties he had a harem living with him, all sorts of girls.

He was called One-Thumb because rumour had it that he'd had a run-in with the Kray twins. It wasn't polite to ask him what happened, but this is what everyone thought had gone on. One of the Kray twins' men caught him carrying on with his wife, and they caught up with Norman walking along Bridport Place one night. Ronnie and Reggie pulled up in their car, stopped him, pulled out this big pair of boltcutters and told him they were going to cut his dick off, stop him using it. Well, of course Norman didn't really want to go along with this so a big struggle ensued. The three of them were wrestling on the street. One of the twins managed to get the boltcutters fixed on to what he thought, in the dark and in the rush, was Norman's dick, but Norman had shoved his hand into his trousers, so when they closed the cutters – *crunch* – it was his thumb that fell on to the pavement. No one ever dared to ask Norman about his thumb, so this story of the boltcutters remains folklore. Once it healed up, Norman bought a selection of silk cravats – they all had to be silk, because he was debonair – and he'd wear one over the absent thumb. The silk hid, to him, the ugliness of the stump.

Norman loved his cars, always flashy, showy ones. The first car he had that we used to drive about in was a Zodiac; then he had a Humber Super Snipe, then a Jensen Interceptor. I wasn't alone in thinking Norman was cool: my mate Stevie Lee, who died recently, thought the world of Norman. Norman was his absolute hero; Stevie modelled himself on him. Except for the silk cravat, of course. And the missing thumb.

That first night Norman took me out we headed up north, the other side of the North Circular Road, to a place he said he'd heard was worth going into. Norman stepped out of the car, looked over the wall, then said to me, 'Come on.' Over into the garden we went, and we waited for the security lights to go off. Then in one of the windows a woman appeared. She started undressing, right by the window, with the curtains open. 'Right, there's nothing going on here for a while,' Norman said to me. 'You go back to the car. I'll wait.' So I went back to the car, but, curious to see what he was up to, I didn't get in. I just waited a moment or two, then slipped back over the wall and sneaked back into the bushes. And there was the woman, still stripping by the window, and there was Norman, playing with himself in the bushes. That made me laugh. Norman was a bit of an old pervert, albeit a harmless one. I went back to the car and didn't let on what I'd seen.

The first time we ever did anything that earned us some serious money came as a result of Norman picking up a bit of information while socializing: there were thousands of pounds in this particular room in a house down in Hampstead somewhere. He picked me up to go with him, and we drove over to the house and parked outside.

'What we doing here, Norman? Whose is this gaff?'

He told me, and I knew the name. It was some old-time gangster, very well known, and he kept a mistress in this house. It was the stuff he'd given her we were going to steal.

'You've got to be fuckin' kiddin' me!' I said after hearing the name. 'There's no fuckin' way I'm going in there! He'll do us! He'll skin us alive! He'll feed us our own arses!'

But Norman told me it was going to be OK, and he hadn't put me wrong so far, so I went along with it in the end. And it was OK: we got in, took the stuff we wanted, got out, and got rid of it. I spent the next few days looking over my shoulder nervously, but nothing came of it so I stopped worrying.

Norman knew his job very well, and once we'd been out that first time I was happy to go out with him again and again. He'd drop round and ask if I wanted to do 'a bit of work', and we'd be off. He'd have had someone tip him off that a house was worth going into, so we never wasted our time breaking in and having nothing to show for it.

I learned loads from that man. Norman taught me about witnesses, people walking by on the street you could ignore because they wouldn't notice if you acted casually; about people's weaknesses, how people will get complacent when they get home and they're indoors. People think they're in control inside, but they're not – they're complacent. They don't lock doors; they leave their back doors open, or just pull them to; or they'll have a cat-flap for us to put our hand through to catch the key as we pushed it out through the lock – chances are there'd be a mat anyway and we could catch it when it dropped. Believe me, there's no great skill in burglary, unless you're a bell-man, someone who can take out an alarm system. That's when skill comes in. But there's no glamour, no Raffles turn-out. It's all about tip-toeing, the open door or window, being very quiet, and not having any fear.

We'd head up from Islington. Coming from Hoxton, I thought all these places we'd go to – Golders Green and Finchley, places like that – were posh. I'd be dead impressed when Norman told me what we'd find inside, as they were pretty affluent areas. It's a Jewish community, and the first time we went up there I asked Norman, 'Why are we going up on a Saturday?' That's when I learned that Jews went to synagogue on Saturdays. I also learned that they like silver, so that's what we went for. I learned that Indians liked gold, so if we went into a house owned by Indians then that's what we went for.

When we'd done enough of the houses in those areas we'd head out of town. Norman would hear something, and we'd get in his car and go away for the day. Me and Norman would go everywhere. West, sometimes, or down south. How would we know where to go? It was all about keeping your eyes open. We were going through Westcliff-on-Sea one time, driving along, when all of a sudden Norman pulled up and said, 'I've seen one.'

'What do you mean?'

'I've seen one. It's all dark. There's a milk bottle with milk in it on the doorstep. That's ours. Come on, let's go and earn some money.'

Nowadays people think about those sorts of things – you know, not pulling the curtains, leaving a light on, cancelling the milk. But even then there were things we could do to find out if anyone was around. We'd park up somewhere and saunter up to a door, perhaps have a bit of paper in our hands so it looked as if we were calling about something. When we got to the front door we'd open the letter-box and look down. If there was post on the floor, chances were no one was in; if there was a lot of post on the floor, there was definitely no one in. You can cancel your milk, but not your post.

At this house in Westcliff we got a right result: a

full-length chinchilla fur coat, some diamond and sapphire rings, a three-foot-long gold chain and some crystal vases. It was a good haul; we got three grand for those crystal vases. After that I started learning about fur, because I didn't know what a chinchilla was. Norman had to tell me what it was and why it was worth so much (basically because it's rare; mostly the good furs are rare furs). Once I knew what I was up to, I went into the fur trade, literally: we targeted all the fur factories and coat shops, stole what we could and sold it on.

If we'd done well, like that day in Westcliff, we went home. Sometimes things didn't go smoothly, though. Another time we went all the way up to Stratford-upon-Avon but only managed to get about £300 each, so we thought we might as well have another one on the way home. And if that weren't enough, we did another one after that.

We were professional. We went out and looked for it. We didn't just go out and go in, slam bang crash. We'd knock a place up, and if no one was in we'd go back later, maybe at night. We had a routine; we were good at what we did. If we knew nothing about what was inside a house but we liked the look of it from the outside – we could see no one was in, it looked posh enough to have something worth nicking, that kind of thing – then one of us, probably me, would knock on the door. If there was no answer then we'd both go and look through the window, to see what they had. If there was something nice we'd want to investigate further, so I'd go round the back and have a look. If we could see some nice paintings, maybe a bit of silver, the chances were that upstairs there'd be some jewellery, maybe some cash, perhaps even a safe. And if it was on display, which people tend to do with silver, it was our bit of silver. Mine.

While we drove around we were always looking, remembering things, writing stuff down – we had a little book to note down things like addresses. We'd creep up to gaffs and look through the window to see what was in there. That was the only way to know whether it was worth breaking in somewhere, unless we'd been given information, but there was never enough of that about.

Once we did a complete block of flats. Eight flats, starting at the bottom and working our way to the top. When we got into the block we made sure no one was in by ringing all the bells. When we knew it was empty, we used a fire extinguisher we found on one of the landings to bang open each of the doors, and then we went through the whole block like a dose of salts.

After this 'apprenticeship' I didn't work with Norman for more than a year, although our long-lasting relationship went on for much longer than that: if there was a scam going on we'd ring each other up and get each other involved. I evolved, moved on to bigger and better things. But the real reason was that Norman did what he did to enjoy life, whereas I did what I did because I Had Needs. Norman could do things leisurely, but I had an addiction; no matter how well disguised they were, my needs were greater than Norman's. Norman'd phone me up: 'I've got some work.' 'Sweet,' I'd say. But if I called him and Norman said, 'I've got nothing on,' well then, I was off – I've got something to do. 'Norman, got any work?' 'No.' 'All right, talk to you later, I'm off out.' I had to be. It was my weakness, although of course I didn't realize that at the time. I'd always been brought up to believe that I mustn't have weaknesses, because then my defences might come down and I'd be vulnerable. No, I just thought it was fun, a release. The reason I stole from people was to have money to spend as I wanted.

One time I was in jail somewhere – can't remember where – and Frankie Fraser was inside with me. I offered him a bit of puff, some tobacco, and he said, 'Nah, I don't do any of that, I don't have weaknesses.'

'What do you mean?' I said.

'I mean I don't have weaknesses. Nothing can hold me.'

And I remember thinking that wasn't a bad way to be. But of course I did nothing about it.

Years later I was walking across a park and I saw Norman, only it had all gone. He was a down-and-out. He was filthy, he'd pissed himself, and he didn't know who I was – that's how far gone he was. It was sad and all that, but it didn't hit home that it could happen to me. It just didn't hit home.

I've known the Old Boy all my life. He'd done ten and a half years for attempted murder, and when he came out I was told to look after him, which meant I had to try to stop him doing anything stupid. Mostly this wasn't too hard as he was silly drunk all the time, but someone had tried to help him out by getting him set up as a dealer. They'd given him huge amounts of speed to sell, to get him back on his feet, but he was so drunk all the time that he kept giving it away. He'd offer a 'sample' to someone who looked as if he'd buy from him, only what he'd dish out was huge so the punter never bothered to buy it from him.

It was the Old Boy who taught me about people's greed, that this is their downfall. Look for the greedy people, he'd say, look for their weaknesses. Greedy people are the targets for every con man; if there wasn't greed there would be no con. No matter who they are or where they are from, most people want something for nothing. The idea of making a fast buck appeals. And that's how we worked: we'd tempt people with offers of cigarettes, or TVs, or videos, things like that, and they'd all want to get something for less than it was worth, so it was easy to sucker them in. 'Working the corner', we called it. It's an old Hoxton trade. People from Hoxton were always supposed to be good at cons. Don't ask me why, it's just what we did.

I really excelled in the world of the confidence trickster; it was something I found especially enjoyable. I particularly liked role-playing, becoming all these different people. It was the best time I had and the easiest money to get when I worked on cons with the Old Boy. It was easy because the suckers did most of the work for us.

There were those who wanted to believe that they could get something cheaper if they knew the right people – us, usually – that if they slipped us two grand in cash they'd get ten grand's worth of fags. Then there were the people who enjoyed getting involved in something a bit dodgy, people who got a thrill from stepping outside the norm. Taking a risk is something the majority of folk never do, so when presented with such a chance the adrenalin tends to cloud their judgement. So, if we showed them a large cardboard box with hundreds of packets of fags inside, a big weighty box, they'd jump at the chance to give us money for it. Only the box came from the back of another shop – we'd collect them, telling the shopkeeper we needed them to move house. We'd then put a brick in the bottom to load the box down, fill it with paper, and place three cartons of fags at the top. Stacked right, it looked like they were in a box of twenty cartons, and we'd only allow a quick peep before we closed the box up.

The best deals, though, took place in what we called Heartbreak Alley, down Great Sutton Street, Berry Street and then Sutton Lane, right opposite a pub called the Slaughtered Lamb. It would take time to set up a deal, so we had to be sure they had the money and that whatever we were going to pretend to sell them was expensive, so that the deal we offered them was too good to miss out on. There were two things we did that made the con work. The first was that they held on to the money right up until the end; we'd say no if they tried to pass us the money too early. The other was that I travelled in the car with them, so that they always felt they knew who I was, and that they were in control.

The con itself was simple: we'd offer them something, usually TVs, and say that we had someone in a warehouse who could hand over the gear, and they could sell it quick and make money. Only he wouldn't deal with anyone else, only me, so they couldn't take delivery at their place or collect it themselves, I'd have to go with them, and then they'd have to hand me the cash so I could go and pick up the stuff.

We'd get the guys in a car, I'd be in there with them, holding a newspaper, they'd have the money, and by now they'd trust me and be nervous enough to want me to hold the cash for them. 'No,' I'd say, 'keep it. Don't give it to me. Hold it there.' We'd drive down the road, and I'd point out the CCTV cameras that were outside the offices there. 'Park here,' I'd say. 'We're between the cameras here, they can't see us.' Then I'd tell them, 'Right, I'll get out here, go knock on the back door of the warehouse. The guy will be expecting me. I'll go in, make sure everything's sweet, then come out and get the money, hand it over to him, and then we'll stick the TVs in the back together.' And I'd get out and make a show of walking down this alleyway, turning to my right, and knocking on this door at the end. Only there wasn't a door, there wasn't even a building, it just looked like there was from where they were sitting in the car. If they'd followed me they'd have seen that the alley was a dog-leg, and that what looked like a dead-end to them was just the point where the alley turned and carried on up to the next road. So it was very important they stayed in the car as I stood there, pressing an imaginary bell.

After a moment or two I'd smile, say hello to the empty air in front of me, turn to the car and give them the thumbs up, then walk round the corner as if I was walking into a building. Then I'd just stand there, passing the time, having a roll-up, reading my paper for a bit, before coming back into view, pretending I was leaving the warehouse, saying 'See ya in a minute', that kind of thing. Then I'd go back to the car, stick my head through the side window and say, 'Quick, the money now, in my paper, before the camera sees us,' which I did to get their adrenalin going and to make sure they were looking at the cameras and all that and not at me.

So they'd put the money in my opened paper and I'd fold it up and go back and pretend to ring the moody bell, then leg it round the corner and run as fast as I could to find the Old Boy in a car out on Clerkenwell Road.

We called it Heartbreak Alley because we broke so many hearts there. Must have had half a million out of that place. Once we came to check it out and someone had put a gate across. We soon sorted that out so we could still make our quick getaway.

For a con to be worth doing it had to be repeatable, and it had to be worth real money. No point in doing something complicated that we couldn't do again, and no point in doing something that didn't earn us a proper wedge. For instance, I used to love doing the snide jewellery. I'd get brass rings and sell them as gold ones. I knew someone who could put a fake hallmark on them so they'd look real and I'd sell them by the tray. I was trying to sell them once to a punter in the architectural salvage place in Dalston; he was keen, checked the hallmark and all that, but just when it looked as if the deal was sweet he opened up a bottle, dripped some acid on the ring and melted it in two. I was invited to leave promptly. But I still tried to get him to pay for the ring he'd melted.

Or we'd get a good ring – say it was worth £30,000, and I'd nicked it from somewhere – and we'd go to sell it to a punter. We'd get some snide ones made up to look just like it – maybe we'd get a ring that looked OK, and we'd get a bit of glass put in it, say, to make it look like the real thing – and then we'd show the valuable ring to a punter, get them to get it valued at a jeweller's of their choosing, and then get them to make us an offer. They'd always want to buy it because it was a valuable fine-quality ring. We'd refuse their first offer, take the ring back and wait for the next offer. We'd keep the good ring hidden in one hand, and once we'd agreed on a price, give them the snide one we'd had made up and take their money. 'Switching the groin', it's called. Once, Fat Arthur and Carrots were doing this and Fat Arthur got confused and handed back the good ring by mistake. Carrots was furious. The Old Boy and Carrots were taught by Albert. Albert was loaded. He had a huge house in Hampstead. He was probably the one who sold London Bridge to the Americans. He was like that.

I also had snide bracelets, the chunky gold ones. I'd get a bit of brass and a fake hallmark from my contact in the jewellery trade, and I'd go out with one on. I'd lean across the counter in the kebab shop and waggle it about a bit. Someone would offer me fifty quid, I'd say no, get lost, this cost me loads more than that, they'd come back with a bit more, we'd haggle, I'd say yes, and I'd walk out with sixty or seventy quid for something that only cost me three pounds. And a free kebab.

I never got any comeback from the people I sold stuff

to, or conned. Maybe they didn't want it known that they'd been greedy and stung by the likes of me. There was only one time when I had problems, and that was when Carrots and I made £6,000 on some dodgy rings. This was in 1978, and six grand was a decent amount to make. I went off to celebrate and was in the Trafalgar having a drink when some blokes with guns came in wanting their money back. I was sitting facing the front doors and I saw them come in and thought there was going to be trouble, so I told the girl I was with that it was about to kick off and that I'd just slip out the back. But they'd thought about that and had sent someone round that way, and I had a gun pressed to my head. Of course I'd spent my share of the money, so I had to ring Alice to help me out. They had the phone box surrounded, guns all over; there was even a bloke in there with me. I had to laugh. They thought I was mental. 'What's wrong with you, mate? We've got guns and you're laughing?' I told them, 'You snooze, you lose,' which was my motto back then. Alice turned up with the cash and I paid them off, only I wouldn't tell them where to find Carrots, so they waved the guns about a bit more while I was warned to stay away from them. Then, as they drove off it was all 'See you later' and that, like we were friends or something.

Other bits of work I did involved the Post Office. It was easy then to go to Somerset House and get a birth certificate in someone's name, if you knew what to ask;

and when you had that you could open a Post Office savings account with it. The idea was to get the chap behind the counter to stamp the book really hard when he entered the details of the deposit you made to open the account, because if he did it hard enough and left enough of an imprint in the savings book I could 'lift' the stamp off using the foil from inside Wrigley's spearmint gum, then use that to stamp the book with fictitious deposits. When you'd loaded enough into the account book you'd go to another Post Office and withdraw the whole amount.

Another good little money-earner was the cheque guarantee card, when they came in. When they first started to be used they only covered thirty quid, but we found out that we could buy the adhesive strips in W H Smith to put on the back of cards and write our own signatures on. W H Smith withdrew them from sale, so we learned to use Milton baby-cleaning liquid to 'clean' the ink of the signature off, then write our own. With a cheque card and book you could write your own money. We'd take it in turns to go out and cash cheque after cheque after cheque.

Those times weren't all just about money, though; they were also about football. Football was, and still is, one of the great loves of my life. Away games were, for me, a proper buzz. I loved going to places such as Wolverhampton, Southampton, Coventry, and all grounds in between. Only not for the game. The match was of secondary importance, if I'm honest. It was the crowd, the gang of travelling fans, the hooligans that I loved being among.

As with everything else in my life, my plan was simple: manipulate the crowd into doing what I wanted, take control, and lead them. Every army needs a general to lead it into battle, so why shouldn't that general be me? After I got out of the schoolboys' enclosure, it took little or no time at all for me to establish myself as a fearless warrior on the terraces. I had no regard for any form of authority and often provoked confrontations with rival supporters and the police at a match. I climbed the North Bank hierarchy at the old Arsenal stadium in Highbury with ease, stabbing and slashing my way to the top. It seemed as natural as kicking a ball.

Football hooliganism and vandalism seem to go hand in hand. I noticed that at away games the hardcore hooligan element often targeted shopping centres to run amok in and wreck. I hatched a plan. Saturday came, and a couple of hundred Arsenal supporters boarded the train at Liverpool Street station bound for Norwich. The usual songs, chants and banter took place as always, and everything was normal. As the train passed through Ipswich I put my plan into action. 'Fuckin' yellow wankers!' I shouted. 'We're gonna smash your poxy carrot-crunching city to pieces!' And with that I began to smash the windows of the train. By the time we arrived in Norwich we were a trainload of lunatics baying for the blood of any Norwich City fan that could be found.

As we got off the train I made my way to the front of the crowd and shouted, 'C'mon, let's smash the town up!' I led everyone towards the shopping centre, and when we got there I steered them into a department store and began throwing anything I could lay my hands on up in the air. The delighted crowd followed my example. My plan worked perfectly. There was total mayhem in the store, shoppers and workers running scared, hiding wherever they could find safety, so it was easy for me to bash open the tills and help myself to the money inside.

What with the thieving, the con tricks and the burglaries, I was making a good living. I was certainly taking in more than I was spending on the booze and the drugs. And everyone seemed to want me to steal. Once – it must have been the mid-seventies – I was nicked for stealing a carriage clock, and the duty solicitor was called in to see me, but instead of asking about me and what my defence was, he simply said, 'This carriage clock, it's a nice one – any chance you could get me any more like this?'

'Yes,' I said. 'Yes.'

And, of course, every chance, when you lead a life like that, of landing in the slammer as a result.

Six

The Warehouse

Prison was known as many things, but to us, the inmates, it was the Warehouse – because it was a meat warehouse, and we were the meat, hanging about in cold storage. At least, that's what it felt like to us. Perhaps in the old days it was a place the criminal classes feared more – sometimes I think the old days had it right, because at least the inmates got taught some kind of trade – but to my generation at least it was just a place you had to go to sometimes. It was neither a good nor a bad thing as far as I was concerned; I'd go in, do my time, sometimes it'd be OK, sometimes not, and then I'd leave and just pick up my life where I'd left off. Prison made no difference to me, in that I learned nothing there to stop me taking drugs or breaking into places. It was just what I got lumbered with if I'd been dumb enough to get caught and unlucky enough to get sentenced.

I'm always being asked what prison's like, what it feels like in there, and what the different prisons are like. I've been to many prisons over the years. At some point or other I was in every prison in London except Belmarsh, and as far afield as Oxford, Norwich, Camp Hill and Parkhurst on the Isle of Wight, Portsmouth, Birmingham, Dorchester, Winchester, Albany, Coldingley (near Bisley), Downview, Lewes, Stocken at Oakham, Lincoln, Blundeston, Wayland, Leicester, Bristol, Cardiff, HMP Weare (a prison ship off Portland), The Verne (near Portland), The Mount (at the end of the District Line), Channings Wood, Newton Abbot, Guy's Marsh and the open prison at Hollesley Bay – to name but a few. Some I spent a fair bit of time in, others I was there for just a day: if I didn't like the look of a place, or someone I knew when I got there told me I wasn't going to like it in inside, then I'd just make sure I wasn't wanted in there, and I'd get shipped off somewhere else. So I could tell you lots about the places I've been to – how one prison had fresh air because it was on a hill by the coast, but another got all foggy because it was in a dip by the coast; how the food was OK in one and the drugs were easy to come by in another. But the truth is that all prisons, even the really horrible ones like Dartmoor, are just prisons – four walls and a bed. Nothing can take that feeling away, no matter how much bravado you can muster when the door shuts behind you. There's you, your cell, and that's it. Even a plush hotel's no different, really: a carpet may be nicer than a bare floor, the bathroom cleaner, and you can walk out when you want to, but it's still four walls and a bed and you're still alone (usually) once you're on the inside.

So in that respect, one prison is very much like another. What makes them different is the people inside, your fellow prisoners and the screws who lock you in. Dartmoor is horrible because it's at the end of the earth, and so are the people who are in there. You've got to be the worst of the worst to end up in Dartmoor, and that goes for the screws as well. Some awful things have happened in that place.

Most of the time I was in prison awful things happened around me, because I thought then that the only way to stop being frightened of other people was to make them frightened of me. If they were too scared to do something horrible to me, then I was safe. This is how I coped with prison. In fact I coped with it so well that prison became a way of life for me. It would be fair to say that I became a professional prisoner. In prison, at least when I was younger and I still thought drugs were something I had control of, I was well known. I could command respect, everyone knew who I was and a lot of people feared me. I actually used to like being in prison. If I wanted drugs while I was inside I'd just take them off the dealers, and then challenge them to a fight if they wanted to take 'em back.

Taking all those drugs, drinking all that booze – over the years I just lost track of time. Dates never meant much to me anyway, like I said, and when the only way you can tell the difference between a Friday and a Monday is that there are fewer people in the pub on a Monday, there's not much hope, is there? So when one day in prison was very much like the one that came before, and the one that came after, I can only say that when I think about my time in jail it all seems to boil down to one long sentence: *Peter Woolf, I hereby sentence you to eighteen years inside with occasional home visits; your time spent in jail will be to you a drug-induced haze of boredom punctuated with moments of great violence and aggression.* That's what it seems like, and that's what I ended up with. Doing life on the HP, I used to say.

People also ask me, 'What do you do in prison? How do you pass the time?' Well, I could say you'd get up, and if it was in the bad old days and you were in one of the older prisons you'd have to slop out, then you'd wash and get some breakfast . . . but that's not what prison's about. At least, it wasn't for me. Day after day could pass with nothing to show for it, just some pointless conversation with someone you'd never see again once you got out – but that wasn't the point, either. Most of my time in prison was spent on drugs. That's what I did all day, that and go to the gym. That's how the days passed. That's how I lost eighteen years of my life. I only knew which day of the week it was because of what I was served for dinner. I'd wake up, slop out, get let out for breakfast, and get put back in my cell to eat it. Then I'd be let out for an hour's exercise, perhaps, back in for dinner, and then tea – the last meal of the day – at three p.m. I'd stay in my cell from then till the morning, to start again. It's hard now to appreciate how much of my life I wasted in jail, days of watching nothing and doing nothing while nothing happened around me. I lost days, weeks, months, years to this.

Markers in other people's lives – where you were when Elvis died, that kind of thing – I know only by which jail I was in at the time. In the case of Elvis's death, in August 1977, I was in Wormwood Scrubs. That might have been the time when we used to get a free daily show from one of the nurses in the block opposite. The Scrubs is built right by Hammersmith Hospital and the nurses' accommodation used to face on to one of the wings. We used to make a right ruckus when we saw one of them, except for Rosie, as we christened her. She'd come to her window, and we'd all make sure we were looking out of ours, and she'd do a full strip in front of us all, then close her curtains. I guess she was finishing her shift and just wanted some peace and quiet. Well she certainly got that because it was as quiet as anything on our wing after she was done.

Some prisons are nicer than others. Coldingley, for instance, is nice: good facilities, good food, good surroundings, everything's cool. The Scrubs, however, is horrible. There are twenty-five hundred people in there, in atrocious conditions. Before going in the Scrubs I'd had a short stay in Wandsworth, which was a prison I'd been desperate to get into ever since I knew anything about the life I was in. To me, it was a symbol of having made it. I wanted to go there more than anywhere else, so I begged the screw to let me in when I was being taken across London to jail somewhere else. 'Go on,' I said, 'it ain't gonna hurt you to put me in there, is it?' So they did. I was only seventeen, and technically a minor, and therefore I didn't belong. I was what was called a 'lodger'. But to me, being in Wandsworth, where so many of the people I mixed with back at home had been or still were, was like a badge of honour. In fact it wasn't great, really: if you didn't have a job, in the shops somewhere, then you were in your cell almost the whole time, twenty-three hours a day.

Being stuck in a cell meant that we couldn't pass things between us, so we had to come up with other ways of doing so, and the usual way was by swinging a line from one cell window to another. In Wandsworth once we used carrier pigeons. We caught the pigeons by tempting them down to our cell windows with some bread, then tied a package to them with mailbag twine before throwing them from one window across to the other wing. As the pigeon would automatically land on the highest point, in this case my mate Lee's cell, Lee would grab the twine dangling down from the pigeon and then pull over to him the package we'd attached. This didn't always work, of course, and sometimes the pigeon would fly off.

I made it back to Wandsworth in the mid-eighties, when Walkmans had been allowed into prisons. I spent my days lying on my bunk, taking drugs, listening to a Tom Petty tape. It was the only one I had for eighteen months, but I didn't mind. I'd sit in that cell all day and it was fine, 'Freefalling' and all that. I used to prefer staying in Wandsworth because I could just sit there, take drugs and wait for release day, and that was fine. I didn't have to do any work or anything, and there was only one alternative to work – your cell. I still had my exercise time, so I could do press-ups or whatever. The big event of the day was when I was in the exercise yard, where I could maybe swap a bit of heroin for a bit of puff, or a bit of puff for some heroin. One bath a week, one shower and clean clothes once a week. Sometimes I didn't even bother to do that.

Now, when I said I wasn't changed by prison, that wasn't quite right. There was one that changed me, I suppose, and that was Lewes. And I changed in Lewes because of Charlie Richardson.

Charlie was inside because of what was known in the

papers as the Torture Trial. I once asked him if he'd done any of the things they'd said he'd done – electrocuting people, pulling out their teeth with pliers, cutting their toes off with boltcutters – and he said no, it was the other mad bastards. But then I suppose he would say that. I could ask him things like that because we got on well. The first time I met him he said to me, 'Make us a cup of tea,' and I said, 'Piss off, make it yourself,' and he liked that; he thought it was funny. He asked me to take the cell next to him, and because the jail was old and we were down one end of the wing, at the end of a blind corner, we had privacy. No one was allowed to come to our end of the landing without our say-so. We had a table outside the cell, and Charlie and me would sit there and talk about what he'd read.

Charlie was the most well-read man I'd met up to that point. He used to like reading the paper in the morning – he took the *Guardian* – and when he'd done with it he'd pass it to me. I was supposed to read it through too, as he wanted to talk about what was inside. So I would read the paper and then run down to the prison library to read up on what they were talking about, so that I could hold my own in a conversation with Charlie. Where was this place in Africa? I'd never heard of it. What was this business selling? How'd they make money from that? Just sitting at a table with Charlie Richardson kept me on my toes; I was expected to know so much. I loved it, though, and I learned a lot that time. One time Charlie passed me a book about sugar, and how bad it was for you. 'Read this,' he said, so I did, and I never touched sugar again, from that day to this.

Still carried on taking the heroin, mind.

I got into the habit of reading when I was in jail, which eventually became one of the things that saved me. The majority of my education has come from reading books while being locked up in a cell. There wasn't a lot else to do, really. I only read properly when I was in prison because keeping my heroin addiction going on the outside was a full-time occupation, and anyway, it was hard to read when I was full of narcotics and alcohol. So my reading was either feast (in jail) or famine (on the outside).

After a few hundred crappy paperbacks I decided to go for books that made me think. I really developed a taste for reading, and I would devour books at a rate of knots never seen before. My friends and family thought I was a bit weird because I used to talk about authors like Kafka, Steinbeck, Orwell and Dickens. They really had no idea what was going on in my head. My thinking really changed when I read Desmond Morris's *Manwatching*, which made me realize that we are all pretty much the same underneath it all. It doesn't matter what sort of spoon you're born with.

Alongside the reading, the gym, as I said, was the other thing I really got into in prison. I'd enjoyed the boxing I'd learned at approved school and liked getting fit. Over the years I became just as addicted to exercising as I was to booze and drugs.

Now Lewes was, in the seventies, the place where it was decided they'd experiment with the prison population, mixing everyone up together, which wasn't common then. The Home Office, in their wisdom, decided to put all those who were never going to get out, the worst of the worst – the dregs of the prison system – with all the others, on one wing (I had always been a Category B or C prisoner – at the end, to my surprise, a Category D prisoner – because I'd never done anything serious enough to warrant being Category A). Of course this policy had its drawbacks, as some of the prisoners were a little less popular than others. Well, if you've got all types of offenders on the same wing, that means sex offenders, murderers, rapists and child molesters mingling with run-of-the-mill robbers and thieves like me. Then chuck a serious gangster like Charlie Richardson in for good measure and you've got the makings of some serious problems.

We were allowed certain privileges that weren't standard in other jails. We could spend our own money, even send the warders to the shop once a week to do our shopping. And they turned a blind eye to drug taking. To be honest, they openly encouraged us to smoke dope; there was even a screw who would bring bottles of booze in, as long as you paid him. It was like a lunatic asylum, with the loonies running the show. Drugs became a way of life in prison very easily. Once, a screw came into my cell and I was sitting there with tin foil (from a Kit-Kat bar: always popular in prison, they are, for the foil to smoke heroin off) in my hand and a tube hanging out of my mouth, chasing the dragon, and the screw said, 'What the fuckin' hell are you smoking there?'

'Well it ain't fuckin' Old Holborn, is it?' I replied. 'Now fuck off.'

'All right, I was only asking,' he said.

Homosexual activities were rife – don't ever let anyone tell you different about prison. Certain prisoners were affectionately known as Mr and Mrs X, or Mrs Y. On our landing there was a man called 'Mary' – Bill in reality – who was the wing prostitute. I suppose if you're in for life you change your tune about what you will and won't do, but for some it was just what they'd always done anyway.

The screw who would bring us booze would sometimes bring in a bit of dope along with the bottles of vodka, and to pay him off we'd invite him along to one of our parties. He'd come and get stoned with us. We'd be in Patsy Mac's cell, with loads of drugs and booze, 'Mary' would be on the table doing a 'go-go girl' routine, Pink Floyd would be blaring out of the speakers, and we'd all be totally smashed. One night I put on the screw's uniform and he sat there wearing nothing but his boxer shorts and T-shirt, sniffing lines of cocaine and smoking dope through a home-made hubbly-bubbly pipe. It's a miracle that he had any kind of control over us at all; it was only down to the fact that we quite liked him.

So, who was in my little gang then? Obviously Charlie had nothing to do with the drugs and the parties; that wasn't his thing at all. There was me and Patsy Mac, and Tony Hall, a lovely man, the only man in all Her Majesty's prisons who had permission from the chief psychologist to carry a tennis ball around with him at all times, on account of what he did to his girl-friend. The tennis ball was there to give him something to squeeze on to make sure he didn't do it to anyone else, to keep his mind on the here and now. Then there was Billy Corella, who was doing twenty-five years.

I came in from the gym one day and my whole room was gone. There was nothing left in it but the bed; everything else had been taken. I was sitting there in shock when Tony Hall came in, a bag in his hand. 'Here's some of your stuff,' he said. 'Billy fancied it. He's gone loopy. Leave him alone, will you? I know you're pissed off, but I'll deal with it. Just don't mention it to him, it'll make him worse.' Well, I was steaming, but I didn't do anything. Billy had lost the plot; it had got too much for him. Tony sorted it out, and eventually I got all my stuff back – the carpet, the stereo, all of it. A little while later Billy came up to me.

'Sorry I done that, Peter. Dunno what came over me.'

In Lewes, I used to slip the nonces half a packet of tobacco, and I smoked puff with them sometimes. I didn't feel sorry for them, and I didn't think they should be let out, but I thought they deserved to be treated like the rest of us, even though I'd never have said so to any of my gang as the nonces were regarded as the lowest of the low. It wasn't a good idea to have your own opinions about the prison population. For instance, there was one fella called Jimmy I thought was all right, but I was told otherwise, and our friendly screw showed me his file. At the age of sixteen he'd killed his grandmother, and they'd found his semen in every orifice of her body; he'd even cut off her fingers to get her rings. And then there was The Frog. He'd bitten a baby to death so we used to throw things at him, the heavier the better. In the workshop it'd be bolts and stuff. Even the screw in charge of the workshop would join in.

Our little gang got along OK together, getting by anyway. I'd read every morning, exercise all afternoon and party all evening. Until the day we heard that the Poison Dwarf was coming to Lewes, which put a black cloud over the whole jail. The Poison Dwarf was the worst, an evil bastard, a prison poof who'd tried to rape Patsy Mac in another jail. Whatever the weather, he just wore these little swimming trunks, because he was very proud of his body. He was very fit and very strong and he looked as much like Mr Universe as I've ever seen someone look. Patsy was in bits when he found out this bloke was coming here.

The first night he was in his cell I fronted it out with the Dwarf. When I walked in he was sitting there with Tony Hall. I introduced myself, offered him a bag of puff, and then said that Patsy Mac was in here with us and there weren't going to be any trouble, now were there? I didn't want to fight him – to be honest, I wasn't sure I'd win if I did – but I think he knew that if he wanted to get at Patsy he'd have to go through me first and I had enough friends to make his life horrible if he did anything to me. After a pause, the Dwarf told me slowly that no, there wasn't going to be any trouble. Which was a surprise and a relief, because our gang had talked about it beforehand and we'd decided that if he didn't agree there was only one thing left to do, which was to kill him.

We all learned very early on that Poison Dwarf had a temper, and that it wasn't a good idea to be on the wrong end of it, so most of the time we made sure that we didn't upset him. Like the time I walked in on him with 'Lionel', an inmate who at his trial had had Lionel Blair as a witness, so Lionel he became to all of us. Lionel was decked out in suspenders, stockings, bra, the lot, and the Dwarf was giving him one, furiously. I backed out of the cell as quietly as I could.

We did give in to temptation eventually, of course. One day we stuck everything of the Dwarf's to the top of his locker with superglue. Poison Dwarf decided to be hospitable and offer us all a cup of tea, and we sat there, faces frozen, trying not to laugh, as he reached over to get his china mug off the top of his locker. The mug stayed put. The Dwarf looked a bit puzzled and pulled harder. Nothing happened. He put two hands on it and really yanked hard, and we were biting the insides of our mouths, trying not to howl. By now the Dwarf's muscles had muscles bulging out of them. He pulled so hard that he snapped the mug clean off the top of the locker, leaving the base stuck there. Silence. Poison Dwarf, who'd turned purple with the effort, now turned red with rage and pulled out the biggest blade I've ever seen. 'Whoever the fucker is who done this,' he said, 'I'm going to find out, and then I'm going to kill someone.' He meant it, so we sympathized with him, cleared out of his cell as fast as we could, and went back to our cells, our hearts beating like drums. Then we had to talk him down without ever letting on it was us.

We'd play dice every evening, and bet on the outcome. Usually the bet was for small amounts but sometimes it'd be stupid amounts. One time we had this kid in the cells with us, Sam from up north, who was inside for stabbing someone who'd bullied him. He was doing OK until one night when Poison Dwarf put his dice down and glared across the table at Sam. 'I've got a better idea,' he said. 'Just me and you, Sam. You win, you take the money.' He gestured at the small pot in the middle of the table. 'You lose, you're coming back to my cell.'

Aargh, we all thought, how are we going to stop this? Because the Dwarf had this awful look in his eyes. He was like some tiger with its prey in its sights; you could almost see the saliva drooling out of his mouth. Somehow again we managed to get him off that idea, but Sam was as white as a sheet. He knew how close he'd come to it that night.

Sometimes I had visitors. I'd send out a VO, a visiting order, so someone could come in and drop stuff off for me. You'd have thought it would be hard to get drugs in prison, but no, it isn't. I knew people who were making two to three grand a week selling drugs inside Pentonville at one time. With a room provided and meals paid for, it was a pretty easy life for them. It wasn't as if you even risked losing the money either, because although all that honour-among-thieves stuff is just bollocks (if you snoozed, you lost, remember), before drugs became the overriding factor in prison, putting more people behind bars and driving more desperation into those inside, it wasn't too hard to hold on to your own stuff, if you were careful. Tobacco would be nicked sometimes, but to be known as a cell thief was scandalous. Still, it became acceptable as the stakes got higher.

One time Alice came up to see me on a visit with a bit of puff and some LSD, and she said, 'I've got you some stuff here called scag, do you want to try it?'

Well, of course I was game for almost anything, but at the same time I liked to know what I was doing. I was always curious. 'What the fuckin' hell's scag?'

'It's all right,' she said, 'it makes you feel nice.'

I took the package back to my cell and opened it up. I'd seen brown heroin before, but I didn't call it scag. It was henry to me; it wasn't scag, or brown, it was henry, or a bit of horse. A different vocabulary; just like when I first started using, withdrawing wasn't called clucking, it was hanging out. Still, once I looked at what Alice had brought me it was like all my Christmases had come at once: she'd bought me a quarter ounce of the fucking stuff. A quarter ounce is seven grams; out of one gram you can get eight ten-pound bags, or even, if they are little bags and you're short-changing your customers, ten ten-pound bags.

In those days inmates weren't allowed to use the phones. We had to write to anyone outside, which meant you had to use codes, so that if your letters were read no one could tell what you were on about. Or so we thought, anyway. I might write something like 'You looked nice in those black jeans, can you get me a pair?' which meant I wanted some nice black hash. This time I wrote to Alice after her visit, 'That brown jumper you got me was fantastic, get me loads of them!'

Of course it wasn't all taking drugs and drinking and reading books and going to the gym when I was in prison. Sometimes I found it downright nasty, but then I suppose that had something to do with the company I was keeping. Take Freezer Fred. Now he really was a strange one, the ugliest man I had ever seen. He'd murdered his boyfriend by stabbing him in the heart, and kept the body in a chest freezer. Every now and then he took the body out of the freezer and warmed it up in a hot bath in order to have sex with it. Nice guy, though, and handy to have about. Then there was the time when we were all round the TV watching the horse-racing on a Saturday afternoon and in a cell nearby one man pulled out a rolling-pin and smashed in the head of his cell mate, cold as you like. Didn't even seem to have a reason for it.

I was offered money to kill someone in prison once. I was in Pentonville at the time and was working as the prison barber. I'd got the job after cutting the wing principal officer's hair. I'd lied about being trained as a barber, of course, but had managed somehow to pull it off. Well, nobody complained anyway, but why on earth not I've no idea, it must have been dreadful. The PO was quite senior too, so it could have gone badly wrong for me. Anyway, there was a supergrass in the prison waiting to be transferred somewhere else, and because he'd have his hair cut like anyone else and because I'd be holding a sharp pair of scissors up to his face I was offered £50 to kill him, to cut his throat while doing his hair. But I'd got to know him in the jail and I quite liked him, so I wouldn't do it.

I went back into Lewes a few years later, by which time they'd stopped their experiment, mixing everybody up. It was 1982, and the Falklands War had started. I'd been sent to Lewes because I'd not returned from a home leave out of Camp Hill, on the Isle of Wight, and I brought about a hundred LSD tablets in with me. I sold a few, gave a few away – making friends in the process – and took the rest. One night we were all watching TV and news of some attack by the Argentines on the British forces came in. We all started cheering for the Argies because most of the screws were ex-servicemen and had squaddie friends out there. They hated that, us cheering.

Camp Hill was, for me, pure violence. I worked there as a blacksmith, so I had to spend my working hours standing by the side of the forge banging metal. I didn't take it that seriously, but you had to do something while you were there, and at least doing this kept me fit and warm. One day I was on my way to the forge when someone came rushing up to me, said, 'Here, get rid of this for us, will you?' and shoved something into my hand. I slipped it under my jacket then went into the smithy, where I took a look at what he'd handed me. It was a home-made knife and it was sticky with blood. I never asked whose, I just did as I was told, and melted it down in the forge.

My thumb was nearly severed while I was in Camp Hill. I was on my landing and this geezer was coming towards me, out of his pram, and although I was trying to be nice to him he wasn't having it. He was coming down the landing one way, I was going the other. I stepped out of his way and said, 'Excuse me, mate,' but he stood there and said, 'You, don't talk to me. In fact, don't even breathe near me.' All right, I thought, and stood back to let him pass.

I waited till he came back again, and when he came up to me I said, 'Oh, by the way . . .' As he went 'What?' I shoved the cup I was holding in my hand into the side of his face. It cracked, tore open his cheek, and blood spurted all over. Of course all hell broke loose after that and I was dragged away by the screws. What I didn't know until I was in the segregation unit was that I had a large shard of the cup stuck in the base of my thumb. I pulled it out and blood shot all over the place. I had to go to St Mary's hospital to have the wound stitched. They gave me something for the pain, some morphine, but suddenly the pain got a lot worse – oooh, the pain! – and they had to pump me full of more morphine. Lovely. Three days. I would have stayed longer but the food was better in prison.

But I used to like Camp Hill because you could go to the gym, and you were let out in the evenings for association time – a game of cards or a game of table tennis, something like that. Or to someone else's cell to take drugs. It was quite a social thing for me, then, to take drugs. I hadn't yet started to hide myself away.

I did OK as a blacksmith at Camp Hill so I was put up for a welding course, which meant a transfer to Parkhurst, also on the Isle of Wight. But I didn't like that work so I stopped. In other prisons, after this, I didn't get to learn another trade, so that was a waste of an opportunity, on both sides.

I continued to use, of course, throughout the eighties. Drugs were always easy to come by in prison – more so now than ever before, I shouldn't wonder. One day during the summer of love, the era of rave music and Acid House in 1987, a couple of mates came to see me just before I was due to come out. They were talking about a rave they'd been to, going on about 'being on one', 'banging tunes', all this kind of chat that I didn't understand. They gave me some heroin and three ounces of puff – which I had to wedge, as usual, up my arse to hide on the way back to the cells – and a couple of pills that they called Es. 'Take these tonight, mate, and make sure you've got some music on. Nice one. You'll never want to take that heroin shit again.' I didn't have a clue what they were going on about but I never say no to a drug, so once again I said, 'I'll give it a go.'

I went back to my cell and gave one of the tablets to my mate Martin John Robinson – Nosnibor to us (his surname backwards). We waited till lock-up, then I called out, 'You taken yours yet?' And Nosnibor said, 'Yeah.' So I took mine, then put my headphones on and slipped a Simon and Garfunkel tape into the Walkman. Twelve hours later it was time to open my cell door and I hadn't stopped wanking all night. I saw Nosnibor staggering out of his cell. He looked across at me, and I could see he'd been doing the same thing.

'What the fuck was that stuff?' he said. 'I'm not having that again.'

I was in Brixton prison in the early nineties, at the same time as Lenny McLean. Lenny became properly famous after he died, really, because of his appearance in the film *Lock, Stock and Two Smoking Barrels*. The book *The Guv'nor* came out and suddenly everyone knew who Lenny was. To me, Lenny was a friend of the family. I'd known him since I could first tell that what looked like a mountain standing in the front room was in fact a man, and a friendly one at that.

Lenny was huge, a big, big man who was well known by all of us as a prize-fighter. He was inside for murder, on remand awaiting trial. I hadn't been in for a while – a fact I hadn't realized until a solicitor pointed it out. I'd got nicked flogging some computers I'd stolen from some office block in Clerkenwell – dishonest handling, that kind of thing – and my brief said, 'Here, look at this.' He showed me my record. 'You've not been inside for the last seven years. Maybe the judge will think that's to your credit – you know, trying to stay on the straight and narrow.' This was unusually optimistic for a solicitor. They usually think pessimistically, because anything better when it comes to verdicts and sentencing makes them look like great chaps. I replied, 'Maybe the judge will give me credit for that, or maybe he'll think I just haven't got caught.'

Now, who do you suppose was right in their prediction?

So I was inside again, alongside Lenny, who had a nice little job working behind the hot plate. He'd stand there, arms folded, glowering at everyone who went past. Well, no one was going to nick an extra sausage with Lenny looking at them like that, were they? If Lenny boy, all twenty-two stone of him, said 'Jump,' all he'd get back would be 'How high?' And that's the screws, never mind the inmates.

I came down one day and there was Lenny boy, guarding the sausages.

'All right, mate?' I said.

'All right?' he replied. 'All right? It'd be all right if I was on a beach in Marbella with a blonde on each arm. No, I fuckin' ain't all right.'

The wing went deadly quiet, which very rarely happens in prison, and everyone turned to look. I could tell what they were all thinking: Lenny's got the hump; let's watch Lenny turn him inside out. People were hanging over the rails to see what was going on.

I just stood there, in the silence, and put my finger to my chin, as if I were deep in thought. Then I leaned over, pointed at Lenny and said, 'Don't fuckin' talk to me like that. You forget who you're fuckin' talking to. I remember you when you was the window cleaner. Don't forget that.'

Now everyone was waiting for the two of us to launch into each other. And round from behind the hot plate Lenny rumbled – and we're talking about a man who thought he'd lost a bit of weight to reach his twenty-two stone. Everyone was getting ready to watch me get pummelled, but as he came up to me Lenny stuck his right hand out to clasp mine, and with his left hand he clapped me on the shoulder (which felt like it was going to collapse under the weight).

'Sorry, boy,' he said, 'I forgot who I was talking to then. I got out of bed on the wrong side.'

I looked him in the eye and said, 'All right this time, but don't let it happen again.' And with that I helped myself to breakfast and went back up to my cell to eat it.

From that point on I was looked at differently in Brixton – the man who'd stood up to Lenny McLean. What nobody else knew is that we weren't playing it for laughs, it wasn't some kind of game. Lenny thought that if he made me cross I'd tell Roy, and Lenny was terrified of the Nash brothers. For that one moment he'd forgotten that he wasn't allowed to talk to me like that. He had to show me respect. What Lenny didn't know, though, is that by then my relationship with Roy was dwindling away, so I was no threat to Lenny at all.

Lenny didn't handle prison very well. I used to sit in his cell and read stuff to him – he wasn't too good at that – but I couldn't handle his whinging. He would moan a lot about being inside. One evening he sent a screw up; I was on the second floor landing, Lenny was downstairs. The screw said, 'Lenny wants you to come down and have a talk with him. He wants you to move in with him, into his cell.' I said, 'Tell him no.' And Lenny never mentioned it to me. He was too proud to ask me to my face in case I did what I'd done, which was to say no.

I remained a keep-fit fanatic even though I was still taking a bit of gear. I used to get Lenny out for press-up competitions in the exercise yard and he could never beat me. I'd train in the morning, take an hour-long nap at lunch, then train all the rest of the day. I'd get out in the yard, strip off – I had stars-and-stripes boxer shorts – and run round that yard all the time I was out there, just going round and round. I got too fit for the screws. They wanted me to stop, and barred me from training in the exercise yard, but I still did press-ups in my cell and squat after squat after squat. It was a cross-addiction thing for me, that's all it really was. I wanted to beef right up. I wanted no-neck muscles to go with my shaven head and my goatee, my keep-away-from-me look. Don't come near me, I'm baaad.

Prison, in the end, got to me, and I did go stark raving bonkers. I was perfectly happy marching about with a book, and I'd stand on the landing and shout out, 'Listen to this!' And all the inmates would have to listen, or I'd want to know why. It wasn't as if I was reading out something that they wanted to hear either. No cheap thrills from me, oh no. It'd be Voltaire's *The Philosophy of History*, or something like that, and I didn't want to hear anyone tell me that they didn't want to listen because then, for that moment, Voltaire was The Man. They had to listen, because I needed to be listened to, and I was quite fortunate to have a captive audience.

I was reading Voltaire, of course, because Charlie Richardson's need to have someone discuss ideas with him had taken root in me. I read everything I could get my hands on in prison libraries, and I soon found that I didn't like reading the novels most of the other prisoners read while we were all locked up. Whether I'd read enough to see how the patterns were constructed, or I just understood it, I don't know, but whenever I started a book I could quickly see what was going to happen, and then I'd get bored and put it down. This got to the point where I could see by page six the direction the story was going in, so reading the book became pointless. I started to read more non-fiction, and that's how I picked up the language of psychiatrists and criminologists that I used to like to use in court and elsewhere to baffle those people who thought I was stupid. And while at first I liked to listen to the radio for the music – I can remember when Capital Radio started, listening to Nicky Horne, and Radio One's Alan Freeman on a Saturday afternoon – I also started to listen to the plays on Radio Four. I can still remember hearing Peter Shaffer's *Equus* and being really wowed by it. It was an amazing piece of theatre, and it inspired me to try my hand at drama in prison.

By this time I was at Channings Wood in Devon. There was a little acting group there, and I took it over. I didn't want to act but, surprise surprise, I liked directing, telling everyone where to go and all that. I can't remember what the play was, and to be honest I only went to begin with because the drama teacher would let me look at her tits behind the screen. But I got caught up in it. And I wrote a play with someone. It was called *The Phone Card*, and we won an award, a Koestler Award, which is something given to people in prison who write. I was taught by a great man – Neil Galbraith was his name. We won £60, and I donated my winnings to charity, to a local children's hospice. I'd never won anything in my life before.

We had other ways of passing the time, and some prisons I associate with certain things. For instance, Coldingley, near Bisley in Surrey, in particular I remember for the card games. We'd always play for cash, so there was often a large amount of money on the table. One time I remember playing a game when there was over £2,000 in the pot. We'd play poker, and kalooki.

Sadly, although I was good at table tennis and chess, I wasn't that good at cards and I never won.

We inmates would bet all the time, just to make things seem exciting. In another prison, to win a game of snooker meant you'd make £50 – not bad money. Once, in Lewes, the bank robber Johnny Johnston was playing football and won a penalty. I yelled, 'Fifty quid says you miss it!'

'You're on,' he said – and promptly missed it.

Sometimes when I tell these stories about life in prison it sounds as if it was all a great laugh, that there was a camaraderie among the inmates and that we all stuck together because we were all in it together. Don't believe that, it's wrong. It may sound that way, the way I'm telling it, but the truth is that you had your mates and you stuck with them so as to keep safe. When I first started to be sent to prison regularly I had my little gang around me because I was top dog, and they all knew it; sticking with me would get them something on the outside when we all got out. The lesson I learned at school, that money could persuade people to do things for you, was one I put to good use in prison.

But after a while I had fewer and fewer mates in prison, and that's because I had one special companion who took up more time than any of the rest of them, and that was heroin. I just wanted to sit in my cell and smoke drugs. I wanted nothing to do with any of them out there; unless they could give me more drugs, I didn't want to know. Up till the time the heroin started taking over, I'd always been a rebel. I saw myself as a martyr, as someone fighting back, although against *what* I couldn't have told you. But when it seemed easier to stay put in my cell and chase the dragon, I used to think of myself as less of a rebel without a cause and more a rebel without a clue.

It was in Pentonville that I started changing, around 1994. I stopped sending out the VOs, the visiting orders, because I didn't want the hassle of getting up out of my cell and going to speak to someone who'd come up to see me. I couldn't see the sense of it. That's how bad it was starting to get for me. The drugs had started to isolate me from people, which was the worst thing that could have happened to me at that time. I'd always been lonely. I felt that no one understood who I was. My family thought I was one of them when I felt different from them, and the drugs intensified that, making me feel different from everyone in prison. I really hated the loneliness. I felt isolated in the world I had created, the world I could find no escape from; yet no matter how lonely I was I still took refuge in isolation. It's the vicious circle that drug addiction creates. You hate your reality, so you escape it, only that makes your reality worse, so you have to take more to escape that. The life I was leading was slowly driving me mad.

I would sometimes find myself stuck in solitary

confinement. I can't say I didn't deserve this, because I probably did; but sometimes I demanded it, because it got me out of the general population. If I owed money for drugs to someone, for instance, I could get myself shipped out into solitary in another jail and get away from the debt. So I used solitary for myself sometimes. However, I don't think that's the point. The point is, was it doing me any good or simply harming me? There were times when I preferred to be on my own – usually when I had some drugs I didn't want to share – but there's no doubt in my mind that long-term segregation had a detrimental effect on my mind.

When I was in Lincoln prison, where I'd got myself a cushy little job as landing cleaner, I met someone who was as keen on heroin as me. We were approached by a chap from Nottingham to start selling heroin on a commission basis. Of course, we didn't sell as much as we took so we wound up getting ourselves a massive debt. The two of us flipped a coin to see who should take the blame, and inevitably I lost. We hatched a plan: I'd get myself into the segregation block and then get slung out to another prison, which would allow my new friend to act all innocent and say that I was the one who'd taken the money and that he knew nothing about it, blah blah blah.

I tried all my usual tricks to get myself put into solitary – smashing up offices, refusing to go into my cell, and the like – but nothing worked. In the end I walked up to a screw and told him that I owed a couple of grand for drugs and couldn't pay; I went on to say that this meant big trouble not just for me but also for the screws, because I would kill any man who tried to give me a hard time. That did it. I was in the seg straight away.

But no attempt was made to move me out of Lincoln; instead they seemed happy to let me rot in solitary. I had to escalate things. First I stopped washing, then I stopped going out of the cell, forcing them to bring my food to me. Nothing seemed to move them along, so I stopped speaking altogether. I refused to communicate with them at all. This went on for ages, months in fact. I said nothing to anyone, and eventually people gave up and stopped speaking to me too.

One day the door opened and a screw said, 'All right, get yourself ready, you're being transferred.'

I was shipped out on the bus and taken to Onley where I was lodged in a great big holding cell with up to thirty or forty other men while we were all being processed. It was a bit like being in Victoria coach station – lots of people saying hello to one another as they passed in and out. And of course someone I knew came in. He walked up to me and said hi. I was huddled in the corner, completely freaked out by all this noise and all these people and all this talking. I had not seen so many people for ages, let alone interacted with them. I opened my mouth to say something to him but I couldn't speak. I'd almost forgotten how. That really scared me, and after that I stopped using solitary as a means of escape quite so readily. I still went into solitary when I'd broken rules, but that wasn't my own choice.

The best means of escape for me remained drugs. One time the doctor of a particular prison was either very sympathetic or completely misguided because I was prescribed eight DF118 tablets, four blue 10ml Valium pills and two Mogadon sleeping pills *every day*. This was about four times what I would have expected to get, and better still, when I picked up my supply they gave me a whole week's worth in one go, all in a paper bag, like the ones you get sweets in. I could have killed myself with that lot; instead, I took loads and swapped some that very day for some gear. The next day I went back and told them that the bag had been lifted from my jacket when I was out on exercise, and I got a repeat bag, just like that. The doctor clearly just wanted an easy life and thought that having a load of catatonic inmates was the answer. When I had spoken to the doc on my initial entry into the segregation unit I had said that I needed to be kept 'drugged up', to which he readily agreed. In effect, then, the doctor was maintaining my habit. This particular prison was known as 'the Smartie factory' because pills were so readily available.

Of course, I got in trouble again. I knocked out a Yardie calling himself 'The Axeman' and then had a fight with three screws, so I was back in the seg. I had my solitude, a radio, books, my personal exercise yard and – the icing on the cake – drugs supplied by the system. It should have been a Utopia for me, but this particular period of solitary really started to do me a bit of damage.

There is that old chestnut about 'talking to yourself', but that's pretty normal when you're in solitary confinement. I used to do it all the time. After all, who else is there for you to talk to? But on this occasion, drugged up as I was, I started to fantasize that I was not just talking to someone else, I was talking to loads of people. They were all me, but they all had different personalities, so I began to create different voices for them. For some I adopted a Manchester-style accent, for others an American voice, then a French one, a Pakistani one, and so on. I found the northern accent particularly hard to snap out of and would jabber away for hours to myself about anything and everything I could think of, questioning myself, answering myself back, telling myself about little things I'd said and done earlier in case I hadn't noticed them. I was well and truly gone.

I did get out, in the end, and once I came off all those pills I started to shape up again, but it was a time that frightened me. It still does, really, when I think about it. I regard it as one of my close calls. A few more days or weeks of being on my own and I'd never have woken up out of whatever trance I was in. I'd still be inside somewhere dribbling, sat in a chair, watching life go by. I realized then that I really didn't like solitary, so I kicked up if it ever looked as if I were going back there again.

When I was sent to HMP Wayland, in Norfolk, I didn't like it there so I started a fire to get myself moved on. I was sent on to Norwich jail, and when I arrived there was a great big deputation of screws ready to welcome me, ready for this Bad Man – the prison governor too. Only when I stepped out of the van, he came up to me and indicated the kind of welcoming committee I could expect. And he told me it didn't have to be this way. 'Excuse the pun,' he explained, 'only you come here under a cloud of smoke.' I don't think even any of the screws laughed at that one. 'Now, I'm supposed to send you to solitary, but it's Christmas and I don't want to do that. Instead I want to put you on the wing so you can associate with the other prisoners. But I want your word that you won't cause any trouble if I do that, at least until after Christmas. Will you shake hands on that?' Well, I thought he was decent to have explained all that to me, to have given me the choice, so I shook his hand and stayed out of trouble for a few weeks.

I was often getting shipped from one prison to another. One time it was to an actual ship, HMP Weare, off Portland. I had a screw there who'd fetch me an ounce of tobacco and a phone card and slip them under my door whenever I wanted. The land-based prison at Portland, HMP The Verne, was a weird place though. The Verne was right by the coast in a hollow, where the fog came in so thick you couldn't see anything. Stretched right across the exercise yard were posts for us inmates to use to feel our way along so that we'd know where we were walking. When I arrived there I was taken up to C Wing where I was given my own key and told to find my own cell. It was all very casual, and I suppose it was designed to make prisoners behave better – you know, treat them like adults and they'll behave like adults. I made my way up to the landing. Inmates were lying about on the stairs smoking puff, and they asked where I was from. 'Oh, there's a Londoner up there,' they said when I told them. When I got to my landing I discovered that the 'Londoner' was a Turkish geezer called Dennis who I knew, Fat Dennis from Green Lanes. There was another fella from London in The Verne who was a top chess player and a first-class table-tennis player. Howard was his name. He was a bit effeminate but he was the only one who could beat me at chess in jail. We must have played well over five hundred times before I finally beat him. And once I'd beaten him, that was it, I'd no interest in ever playing him again. It took me a year to beat him, and once he'd admitted that I was better than him I never played him again. I was a terrible show-off and would play four games simultaneously in prison.

Other places had a totally different attitude to the men in their charge. When I was transferred to Guy's Marsh in Dorset I arrived just in time for food, so I was standing in the dinner queue when a screw from the Isle of Wight recognized me (oh, the hazards of being inside so often). He said, 'Hello mate, you ain't going to like it here.' Then I recognized another inmate, Dave from Portsmouth, and he said the same thing: 'You won't like it here.' I asked, 'Why's that?' and he replied, 'It's like a kids' home. You can only go to the gym when they let you, and that's no more than three times a week for any of us.' Now I wasn't having that. I liked to go to the gym as often as I could; it helped me let off steam, apart from anything else.

'What are you doing about it?' I asked him.

'Well, I'm out of here tomorrow morning,' he said. 'I'm going to Dartmoor.'

'Right, I'm coming with you. I ain't staying here.'

So that night this screw I knew from before, he was the head of security and he came up to find me and asked, 'You ain't going to perform, are you?' He knew what I was like and he didn't want me to bust up his prison.

'No,' I replied, 'I just want to go to Dartmoor.'

'All right, you can go in the morning, I'll sort it out for you.'

What he didn't do, though, was tell the other officers, so when I went out on association that evening I was called down to sit and give my details for my induction. I said to him, 'Don't worry about it,' only the screw on duty thought I was taking the piss so he came right up close to me and said, 'What do you mean?'

'I'm not staying,' I told him.

'Oh, yes, you are,' he said. 'You'll only go when we say you go.'

It looked for a moment as if things were going to get a little heated. He was getting stroppy and we were both starting up with the you-listen-to-me, no-you-listen-to-me stuff. But just then the security gates opened and the guard said, 'Woolfie, it's all sorted out, you're off in the morning.'

'See what I mean?' I said to the screw.

Now, as I've said, Dartmoor has a special place in the system; it's where you get sent to when you've reached the end, when there's nowhere else for you to go. I've seen some awful things there. And it wasn't just the place of last resort for inmates, it was also the place of last resort for screws. The first time I was taken there I couldn't believe it – grim, colourless, and miles away from absolutely anything that I recognized as living. It was so forbidding-looking, and it had this terrifying motto above the main entrance: 'Abandon Hope All Those Who Enter Here'.

I loved it, of course. Being there was like a kind of testament to my being a horrible person, a seal of approval on all the terrible things I'd done. Of course I had no idea, absolutely no idea, how bad that place could be. Two screws were suspended for 'demanding sexual favours'. Once, the screws allegedly beat a boy from Bristol so badly that he died; it was said that they kept his body warm on the hot plate so as to make it too difficult to determine exactly when he died. Of course, this could just be some kind of urban myth, the kind of thing the authorities are happy to let lie because it convinces inmates the place is brutal. Who knows?

When I got to Dartmoor I was met by a screw, but instead of giving me a hard time he was out there shaking my hand, clapping me on the back and making sure I got a cushy job. Why? Because of what happened back in Pentonville some years earlier.

I was in my cell, and I'd got my Rizlas, cigarettes, foil and heroin, but I hadn't got a light. I was banged up for the night and I couldn't even get a line across from someone else's cell so that they could send something through for me. The geezer in the next cell, Richard, was a posh chap, and I banged on the wall and shouted for him to pass some matches under the door, saying that I'd get the night guard to pick them up and give them to me. So I rang the emergency bell to summon the guard, and blow me if the voice on the other side of the door wasn't Mr Bickle, the principal officer. Right flash officer, he was. I needed to do my best to be polite.

'Awfully sorry to bother you, Mr Bickle. Some people are addicted to drugs, some to alcohol; for me, it's nicotine. I can't get to sleep without a fag, and I need a light. Could you do me a favour and pass the matches that are on the floor by the cell door next to mine?'

He spoke back through the little opening in the door that all the cells had: 'I don't do cons favours.'

I remained diplomatic. 'Oh, please, Mr Bickle.'

Nothing doing. 'I don't do cons favours,' he repeated, and *slam*, he banged the hatch shut.

I rang the bell again. He returned to my door.

'Mr Bickle, please, come on.' But he still said no, so I was left with no choice. I shouted through the door, 'Well, you're one right nice cunt you are, aren't you?'

The next morning I got what's called a telegram, a charge sheet, against discipline. I was handed down three days' remission and three days' loss of pay.

That night, same time, I rang the bell. The night guard came this time.

'Is PO Bickle on tonight?' I asked him.

'Yes, he is. Why?'

'Well, as you may or may not know, we had a little altercation last night and I want to see him about it.'

So off he popped, and *bang*, Mr Bickle was almost immediately outside my door again, slamming the hatch back, standing there, legs astride.

'Yes? You have something you want to say to me?'

'Yeah, Mr Bickle. Last night, about them matches. I asked you to do me a favour?'

'Yes, that's right.'

'Well, unfortunately it got a bit heated and I called you a right nice cunt, didn't I?'

'Yes, you did.'

'Well, you ain't a right nice cunt. You're one horrible cunt. Now fuck off and get away from my door.'

Well, of course, he went ballistic, didn't he?

The screw who came to see me when I turned up at Dartmoor was Mr Bickle's son-in-law. Far from wanting to clump me for tormenting his father-in-law, he was pleased to see me; I got the impression that he must have hated the man. I was straight up on to his landing, and was made the cleaner. All I had to do was push the broom and mop about, leaving me free to go to the gym, and then pop into the landing officer's office. Len was his name. He'd call down to the tea boy – 'Toasted cheese and milky coffee, please, twice' – and we'd sit there and tuck in. It was marvellous.

As time wore on, being let out of jail made little difference to me. I might not have been stuck in my four-walls-and-a-bed but I was in a prison in my own head as I stumbled around London. I'd read a lot of books about animals when I was inside and I knew about breeds of dogs, all sorts of things; I'd also read a lot of psychiatry books that talked about 'the inner beast' and all that sort of rubbish. So what was I? Was I something that would have to stay caged up for the rest of my life? I was a mad person unleashed upon the world whenever I left prison. Could I be trusted to safely run free?

Seven

Party Animal

On the occasions when I was out of jail, I chased three things: drugs, women and booze. I committed crimes because that's what I did. That got me money to buy drugs, and I had women because that passed the time when I wasn't taking drugs. For long periods, though, I was a successful drug addict – successful in that I could have the life I wanted without losing anything. And the key to it all was money. I was a good thief. I broke into places and stole stuff, and the money I got from that got me everything I wanted – whether it was a room in the Savoy or oysters and champagne at a smart City restaurant – as well as all the drugs I needed.

Going into the Savoy was a spur-of-the-moment idea. One day my mate Terry Bridges said, 'Wouldn't it be funny to stay there, with all them posh people?' so I said, 'C'mon then, let's go.'

We walked in, not carrying any luggage or anything, and the girl behind the desk said, 'Can I help you?'

I nodded. 'Yes. I'd like a room for the night.'

'Sorry?' she replied.

To prevent this one being dragged out too long, I slammed a load of cash down on the counter – a huge wad of notes, it was.

She smiled up at me. 'How long will you be staying, sir?'

I went back there one other time to impress a bird. We were in our room and I suddenly fancied some cold water. I rang down for a bucket of iced water, and when the girl brought it up I offered her a tip. 'Help yourself,' I told her, because all over the bed was cash, strewn about. She picked up a ten-pound note and tucked it away quickly in case I changed my mind.

Going into places that were smart didn't bother me. I'd go into restaurants and order food, even eat with a spoon if I wanted (I'd never learned to use a knife and fork properly), just because I could. I nicked stuff from an embassy once. I went in, ducked down to avoid being seen by the woman on duty, and leaned against a mirror as I did so – which swung open, revealing a concealed corridor. I crept in, went round and took loads of stuff. Some lovely gold ornaments I got.

Other times I liked to go into places other people might have thought were risky, like a police station. With my friend Gary Roney, I used to break into the police station car park in Old Street. We'd wait till the officers had left their cars and gone into the station, then we'd nip round and nick the wallets out of their jackets which they'd left hanging up in the back of their cars.

For a while, one of my bail conditions was that I had to sign on in the police station in City Road. I would regularly take glass vials of stink bombs – the kind that smell like rotten eggs – into the station, hiding them in my mouth as I walked in, then crack them under my foot as I was standing by the desk signing the book. Only one time I was jogging up the stairs, hit one step a bit too hard, and a vial cracked in my mouth. I spat it out fast and got rid of the glass, but it was too late to do anything about the stuff inside. My mouth stank; oh, it was disgusting. 'All right, sergeant?' You could see him recoil from the stink. My breath reeked for days.

Another time I was in Hoxton market and there was a police car parked up. I went and knocked on the window. They looked up at me, and I opened my palm and showed them five blues in my hand. They scrambled to get out of the car, but I downed them all in one so they had no evidence to arrest me. It was all part of the game – tit for tat.

The violence was part of it too, and in the days before CCTV cameras and taped evidence and all that, you expected them to beat you up; it was just what happened. The police lifted Gary and me one time and drove us all the way out to Epping Forest in the back of their van. I expect they were fed up with us both by then. We got more than a few clumps on the way as well. When we got there – and this was in the middle of the night, so it was pitch black – they took our shoes off us, chucked us both out of the van, and told us to walk the ten miles or so home.

There were all sorts of games I liked to play to steal from people. A disguise is always a good one because then people see what you want them to see. Often the simplest disguise is the best, and not just because you can put your bits and pieces down and walk away quickly should you have to. When I was twenty, maybe twenty-one, I had some clothes stashed at my sister Carol's (as I then thought she was) that I'd put on, like working overalls, and a bucket and a mop, and I'd set off to see what I could nick. One morning I slipped into this undercover gear and set off down the road, and a little old lady came out of her door and said, 'Are you a window cleaner, dear? Can you do my windows?' Well, I could hardly say no, could I, with all the gear on me, so I said yes and asked to look at the place to give her a price. All the while I was thinking, 'There'll be something in here; she'll have hidden something away,' so I hummed and hawed while I took a look. 'I want 'em done inside and out, mind,' she said, and I said, 'Sure.' I got on with the job, still looking around as I did so, to see what I might be able to get, but she was a nice lady. She gave me tea and biscuits, chatting away all the time, so I did her windows and left without nicking anything – and without taking a penny for the job, either.

Other times I'd just have other disguises, and use different voices, and props like a backpack, a raincoat or an umbrella. I'd be an American, a northener, even a cripple. I'd wear a beret, or a scarf. If I was being a tourist, I'd carry a map I could open up and pretend to consult when I wanted to look at something close up.

I was so successful back in the old days that I only had to 'work' once a month. I found it easy to come by money and even easier to get rid of it. As a result, money lost its value for me. A £4,000 vase I nicked from Bond Street I sold for £300. If I got ten grand, I'd just spend it till I got down to a hundred. Then I knew I had to go out and start again. I'd go to nice night-clubs, like the Candlelight Club in Mayfair, a private members club, and drink in there; it was a good place until the East End mob came in and ruined it. I wanted to be different from them. I tried to act appropriately for the situation. I used to go to the Speakeasy, in Margaret Street I think. It was the place all the stars used to go, so I adapted – I acted like a star. I wanted to be accepted. Everything was about acceptance in life. At least, it was for me.

One night I was in the Speakeasy when I saw Phil

Lynott, the bass player with Thin Lizzy, over in the corner. I really liked Thin Lizzy; I'd seen them at the Roundhouse. I'd had a nice earner that day, so I called a waitress over and said to her, 'Take that man over there a bottle of champagne.' So she did. He raised his glass to me in thanks, and I thought, 'Yeah, this is what it's all about.' He even sent one back to me. In fact we spent some time sending bottles of champagne back and forth to each other. Then he walked past me, and said as he did so, 'Here, come with me.' I said, 'Yes, sir,' and we went into the toilets where he pulled out a bag of charlie and we did some lines together.

After that he took me to a party in Cheyne Walk, and this for me is the dog's bollocks: I walked in, Phil introduced me – 'This is my friend Peter' – and these smart, rich, glamorous people looked *at* me, not *through* me, for a change. I went to a few parties there with him. When we arrived there'd be piles of blow – not lines, but bowls of the stuff. He never asked what I did, he'd simply say to people 'This is my friend Peter' and we'd get stuck into the booze and the drugs. But it didn't matter that he didn't know who I was, because we were just people who took drugs together, that was all. Phil Lynott wasn't a friend, he was just someone I took drugs with, although on a grander scale than I was used to.

It wasn't all glamorous West End nightclubs and Chelsea parties for me, though. There was a club round the bottom end of Old Street, near where the road goes off up to Hackney, and I'd heard this record – 'Mr Big Stuff' – and I liked to think it was about me. So I paid the DJ there a tenner to play it whenever I walked in the place; whatever record was playing came off, and on came 'Mr Big Stuff'. That was me. I was living a movie. I did it all the time.

I'd try any little scam for money. I was in someone's place once and I met this guy who worked the bar on that boat on the river Thames, *Tatteshall Castle*. I came up with a scheme: I'd go in, order a drink and give him a pound note (that's how long ago this was), and he'd give me change as if I'd handed him a tenner. I liked this idea, but at the end of the evening he wanted something for himself, so I told him to piss off. I was greedy. I didn't see why I had to share any of it with him.

One summer Little Ted and I were on holiday down in Clacton and we fancied some oysters. Only we couldn't find any down there, we were told they'd sold out, so we drove about for a bit and eventually joined this yacht club. We had to join in order to use the restaurant, but as soon as we'd marched in and sat down the waitress came over and told us that there were no oysters that day. So up we got and off we went again, only this time we drove in Ted's little Fiat Uno – Ted never passed his test; he paid someone else to do it for him – all the way back into London, up to Smithfield, where we went into Rutland & Stubbs in our shorts and flip-flops. Yes, at last, they've got oysters. We ordered plates and pints of Guinness, and the oysters were great.

'Fancy some champagne?' said Ted.

'Why not?' said I.

So we ordered a bottle, Cristal of course. Ted told the barman to pour it into his Guinness, to make a Black Velvet. Well, the French barman was horrified – this expensive champagne, mixed with Guinness? But he didn't understand. We could do, did do, anything we wanted. We had no rules, and all the money we needed, so we did as we pleased. If I wanted to sit in a smart place and ask for a spoon to eat with, why shouldn't I? I didn't care. This was my playground.

It did all seem like a game sometimes. We learned how easy it was to appear invisible in an office; no one notices you if you're wielding a screwdriver or carrying a tool box. Me and a mate of mine, Winkle, got hold of some British Telecom uniforms and a few tools along with a field phone and, posing as BT workers, started going round the City. We'd turn up at office blocks and tell the bird on reception, 'Morning, we're here to do some fault-finding.' Usually we'd get the nod-through, but if there was ever any bother I'd say, 'Can I see your boss then?' Once the boss came over to see us, we'd start up on the patter – basically the same, just a bit jazzed up. 'There's been a lot of trouble with the lines in this area, so what we are here to do is trace any faults on your line, and at the same time upgrade your existing service.' We'd bullshit away. 'You'll get high-powered fax lines, new handsets and in some cases a brand-new fax machine.'

With this load of rubbish out of the way, we'd be in. We'd mooch about, up and down corridors, looking for anything of value. If anyone was working in the office we wanted something from, we'd just go in and start working – that is, pulling phone wires out of the wall and heaping things up in a pile so as to create the maximum amount of inconvenience for them. If they didn't take the hint, eventually we'd say, 'Listen, sorry for any grief, but maybe it would be quicker if you went and got a coffee and we can get this done with minimum disturbance.' Nine out of ten times they would oblige us. Job done.

I'd nick and sell anything. I'd sell fire extinguishers I'd taken from an office. I'd just go through a building, nick them, and go and get a fiver for each one. I might do that all day; get a taxi waiting outside and go in and get them. In the days before security cameras and tagged clothes, I'd go into any department store, big or small, find a rail of nice fur coats or nice dresses or suits, pick up the lot and walk out, straight into a taxi I kept waiting outside for me. No one would try to stop me. If anyone did, I'd tell them to piss off out of it. I started doing this with a mate, Jimmy G. We used to take holdalls in. We'd go up to the cashmere rack, take the whole lot off and cram it all into the bags, treading them down to get them to fit in. Then we'd drag the bags out of the store. We'd have a motor outside, or a waiting cab, the door would be open, in we'd get and away we'd go. The cabbies knew what I was up to, but they didn't care, as long as they were properly paid. I had regular ones I used for work, and I gave them my daily rate of £100 a day. If I made less, they got a third of what I'd earned, but if I got £1,000 they'd get the daily rate.

Or I'd wander round Smithfield – St John Street, say. There would always be roadworks there. I'd wait for my chance when the workmen were on a break or they weren't looking and I'd steal one of their yellow jackets, go into an office and tell whoever was behind the desk to turn their water off. Inevitably they wouldn't know where the stopcock was, so I'd say, 'Oh, I'll go and do it for you,' and I was in. I'd go round the office nicking purses, wallets, etc. I can even remember the first time I pulled this one off. It was in an optician's, though I can't remember how much I got.

In Smithfield Square one Friday I had a great result. Outside one building was a load of workmen's tools and things, so I picked up some that were lying about and wandered into the building.

A bloke came out from one of the offices and said, 'Are you nearly finished?'

I didn't even blink. 'No, mate, sorry,' I said, waving

my hands about me. 'I've hardly started. I'm gonna be here all weekend just to get it done for Monday.'

He looked frazzled, cursed a bit, then said to me, 'Look, I can't wait here any longer. You'll have to lock up yourself and let yourself in tomorrow as well. I can get you the keys but I can't leave you these ones. Come back to my place and I'll give you a set.'

Sweet.

'Fair enough,' I replied.

We climbed into a taxi, drove back to his home, and he hopped out and fetched me a set of office keys, which he gave me along with the taxi fare back to Smithfield. I went back to the building and over the weekend cleared it out, every last stick.

It's easy to get people to believe you. You just have to believe enough of what you're telling them not to get found out, and be ready to give it up and clear off or run out on them if you have to. Most of the time you feel exhilarated when you pull it off, but occasionally there is a feeling of regret. There's one chap in particular I stole from I still feel bad about.

I'd headed off one morning to Hampstead. I'd got myself a one-day travelcard but I'd had to borrow the money (£2.40) from Carol – that's how broke I was. I'd made myself some sandwiches, and I went to that big pub, Jack Straw's Castle. I'd go up there to nick stuff from the cars parked nearby, cameras mostly. I'd 'ping' the windscreen with a spark plug that I'd wear on a bootlace round my neck, banging it once on the window, then reach in and grab what I wanted and be on my way. But that day things hadn't gone as well as I'd expected – not many cars about, perhaps, or not so many with stuff lying about inside that I could sell – so I took a breather by going into the reception of the youth hostel, where I sat down on an L-shaped sofa with a pot of tea next to a geezer who was asleep and a girl from New Zealand.

I turn the TV on to watch the racing and the bloke wakes up. Turns out he's from Texas and I know – just a fact I picked up somewhere – that it's twenty-four hours for him to get to London from there, what with all the travelling and the time change. I let him know this and of course he thinks I'm a fellow traveller. I let him think I'm staying there, that I travel a lot as I've a rich daddy, and that I'm on an allowance. 'Let's have a good time in London,' I suggest. 'I'll get some girls for us.' So I go over to a phone and pretend to make some calls, giving him the thumbs up and all that, and then we go out for lunch. 'It's on me,' I say, though I've only about sixpence left.

I've seen his wallet. It's bulging. Plus he's stored his bags in the left-luggage space, and I can see some new cameras. (I learned about cameras when I was in jail, reading up on the best models and all that, so I knew his gear was worth something. In fact, I knew my stuff in whatever place I happened to find myself – which were the decent guitars, what was a real fur coat and what was a fake, not to bother with Amstrad computers, that kind of thing.)

We find a nice restaurant and we eat lunch. I make sure there's loads of booze, and I'm ordering all the best stuff, all the time wondering how I'm going to get out of this one. I can't pay the bill, and anyway I want to get back to the youth hostel and pick up his bags. The meal goes on for a while, we're both enjoying ourselves, and it's a warm summer's day, so by the time we've finished eating I fancy an ice pop.

And then an idea comes to me. I ask him if he got his ice pop when he arrived.

'What?' he says.

'It's a British tradition,' I tell him. 'You arrive at the airport and you're given an ice pop. You didn't get one? Shocking. I'll get one for you right now. Stay there.'

I march out of the restaurant, jump in a cab, and get back to the hostel. I go into the left-luggage office, grab his bags – nobody ever stops you if you look like you should be doing whatever it is you're doing – and jump back in the cab. 'Essex Road, please,' I say. I know I can shift the cameras there.

I start going through his bags. There's about £500 in cash, plus loads of new clothes from Bloomingdale's. These were the days before that shop had been heard of over here, so again I knew I could flog them easily. And then the cameras: two Nikons, loads of lenses,

Hasselblads, and a huge fourteen-inch telescopic lens. I peer inside this lens, and what do you know, it's stuffed full of dollars, a bloody great big thick roll of dollars.

'Hold on,' I say to the cabbie, 'change of plan.' I tell him to take me home instead, where I go through every inch of the Texan's stuff in case there's any more hidden cash. I keep the clothes – Nike stuff, again not known over here yet, even Nike socks – and go out and change the dollars. I get about £5,000 for them.

As I said, I still feel really bad about that one. It makes me feel really ashamed. If that Texan bloke is reading this, Christ, I owe you one, I know, but what can I say? Nothing will make me feel better about doing what I did to him. Even saying sorry isn't enough.

And it's no good telling people to be more careful, to watch out for people like me on the street. If you want to believe someone, you will, no matter how crooked they are. All I can do is tell you to watch out for certain things. And it's never what you think it'll be, like crowbars and whatnot; you can get nicked just for carrying those sorts of things around. What you need to keep an eye out for is someone carrying something like a newspaper.

A newspaper is a multi-purpose tool. Watch out for people walking around, looking about and carrying a large newspaper folded up on their arm, as it's very useful to hide their hands behind as they reach into someone's pocket or bag. It's good for opening up and reading too, trying to look like they're doing something when what they're really doing is looking at a place, waiting to see whether it's worth robbing, and if so, when. It's good for passing the time with while they're just waiting. Folded up, it's also good for holding things in, like cash, when they're handed it on the street. No brown-paper packet is as invisible as a newspaper. Fold it up tight and roll it and it can be used to slam someone in the side of the head. Rolled up tight and held under a coat, it can look like a gun, if the person holding it acts and sounds convincing. A newspaper can be useful in so many ways.

I once used it as a form of camouflage. I was walking along in a nice part of London and I saw a couple come out of their house and shut the door. Something about it intrigued me; maybe I caught a quick glimpse of the interior, maybe it was the way they said goodbye to each other that let me know the place would be empty for a while. So I sat there, reading my newspaper, for all the world looking like someone who was meant to be there. No one came back. I carried on reading for two, maybe three hours, then got up and walked away. The next day I went back, same time, and the same couple came out and left to go to work again. This time I hung about till five o'clock, to see what time they came back. One more day of watching, to check; yes, they went at eight and came back at five. When I was sure of the timings, I went in right after they left and emptied the place out.

Now, nicking stuff is all very well, but you have to be able to sell it. You have to know who to go to. If I had stolen some rugs, say, or perhaps some nice antique guns, then it was off down Hatton Garden to see the Fat Man. If I'd been into the Bloomsbury Book Auctions and stolen some fine old books, then it was Mick the Book I sold 'em to. I also sold him some miniatures I stole from Smithfield. But I never really liked him, he was snide. It worked both ways, of course: if you knew someone who bought stolen gear off you, stands to reason that you could take your money back off them too.

There was someone I met who lived up Highbury way; we used to sell him TVs and all that. He was the one who bought that £4,000 Bond Street vase off me for £300. I suppose as it was a listed item he knew he couldn't sell it on to anyone else; perhaps he just fancied having a nice piece around the house. God knows he could have done better domestically. His wife was awful, a bit of a dirty whore in truth. She used to love it when we turned up. She'd have her housecoat on and make sure that we saw she had nothing on underneath, and then she'd put her hands all over us, everywhere, while we did our business with her husband. One time, the Old Boy and I were scratching around for something to do, some way of making a decent score, and he asked me if I had a clue. I thought about it and I said, 'Yeah, probably.' Well, we got our man down to Heartbreak Alley, telling him he was going to get a load of cheap TVs from this bloke in a warehouse – the usual – and took about £2,500 off him. He was pissed off with us, and I heard he went about saying that if he ever saw me again he was going to shoot me with a flare gun. I wasn't really scared, but then again a flare gun shoots phosphorus flares. Can you imagine that? The burning would go on and on. I never saw him again, thankfully.

Extreme brutality was still the order of the day, and I heard about all sorts of terrible things people did to each other with baseball bats, meat skewers, swords, you name it. Some people were horrible, although I can count on the fingers of one hand the number of times I did something brutal.

The brutality I'm personally guilty of is revenge. In 1979, Alice – I still thought of her as my sister then – got nicked for possession of heroin with intent to supply. I was in prison at the time. She was of course guilty. She'd had bags of the stuff at home and I used to help myself to little bits every now and again. But at her trial the conviction came about because three men testified against her: Trevor Pareham (the man I had used to pretend to be my chauffeur), Johnny Gray and Scottish Neil. Trevor was nicked for defrauding clearing banks of £31,000, which he said he had to do as he owed Alice for £32,000 worth of heroin, and Neil said he'd been buying heroin off Alice for three years. I can't remember what Johnny Gray said, but he also stood up in court and helped put Alice behind bars.

I had to wait eighteen months until I was out of jail. I went round to Neil's house, he opened the door and threw his arms open wide to say hello, but before he could I stuck a knife in his chest. Then I went round to Johnny Gray's and broke his legs with a baseball bat. Trevor I caught some weeks later in his BMW outside a pub. I'd been walking in Rosemary Park and he was outside these two pubs, the Ones and Twos, at the top of Shepperton Road, with Bobby Leonard and Dirty Deb in the car with him. I leaned through and took the car keys out so he couldn't drive off. First thing I did was have a go at Bobby Leonard (he's dead now, died of cancer). I said to him, 'How dare you associate with Trevor. He's a bad man, you're fuckin' wrong.' I was smoking a cigar – though I never usually smoked cigars – and I stuck it in Trevor's eye, pushed it about, dragged him out and smashed the car door on his head, really doing a *Goodfellas* job on him. I felt I was entitled to, after what they did to Alice. I know I should feel really bad about doing these things, but I felt then and I still feel now that these men had betrayed Alice, and as a result got whatever was coming to them. You could say they felt the same way as there was no comeback from the police over what happened to them.

And then there was Alan Archer; he's also dead now, an overdose. He owed Alice five grand, but because she was inside I just knew that this little debt wasn't going to be paid. He obviously thought he could get away with it if Alice was locked up. He lived down the Crescent, where Alice lived, so I went round there, knocked on his door and asked for the money, pointing out that Alice could really use that money right now where she was, although of course I only intended to spend it on myself.

'Oh no, it's been sorted,' he said.

'It ain't been sorted,' I replied. 'Now, I want five grand off you.'

'Well, you're not getting it,' he said. 'It's been sorted. Alice is going to get it when she comes out, and that's the end of it.'

'I'll be back,' I warned him, 'and I want five grand, or else you're in big trouble.'

I went out, got a Wildcat Crossbow, went back to the Crescent and knocked on his door again. He opened it, and I asked again if he had the five grand. He said no, so I shot him in the leg with the crossbow. The bolt embedded itself in his thigh bone, and the shot was so powerful it dislocated his hip. Then I took hold of his wife, put her on the floor, reloaded the crossbow and threatened to kill her if he didn't produce the money. He didn't produce all of it, but he produced quite a lot of it.

Sometimes my brutality took a different form. I knew a guy who lived above a fax shop in Old Street who'd got hold of some fine heroin, some white Thai, which couldn't be smoked as it was so pure, and as he was one of those who can't inject themselves – there's always someone like that around, squeamish for some reason – I was only too happy to help him. When I got round there he took the heroin out of his bum, where he'd been hiding it in a little bag. I got all the gear ready and I injected him; in fact we both had a little hit. It was powerful stuff, and it was nice. I wanted it, and, as I used to say then, if I wanted something it was already mine; it just happened to be in someone else's hand at the time. I asked him if he wanted another hit before I went, and he said, 'Yeah.' So I gave him the biggest hit he'd ever had. He went out cold on the floor, I got his pants off and took the bag out of his arse. I left the flat without knowing if he came round from his trip or not. It really was a case of dog-eat-dog in the drug world.

I was on the receiving end of some of this, too. Mad Danny once tried to run me over in his brown Mini. He's in Broadmoor now. I'd taken his girl, Jeanie, out to do some book-and-card – cashing cheques with a fake card that we'd signed. Only she lost it in the first shop she went into: they challenged her, she got scared and walked out, and I called her an idiot, and worse. Danny tried to run me over as revenge. He used to work at the print for one of the daily papers, and tried to get me to go in with him. Four hundred quid a week it was, pretty good money then, but it meant working for a living, and that wasn't for me. That Jeanie girl drank herself to death.

I can't hide my violent past – I don't want to. I've got to own up to everything I've done. I don't know why I was that violent, except that I didn't want people to know what lay behind it. I used to fear being found out as a nice person, so I had to hide that by doing extreme things.

I always knew I was going to win any fight, except for the last fight I ever had, that time I broke into the house in Canonbury Square; that was the only time I wasn't sure of myself. So if anyone interrupted me while I was robbing somewhere, whether it was a photographic studio, a recording studio or a clothes warehouse, and whoever they were, whether a guard, a cleaner, the owner, whoever, I'd just walk out, and offer them a right-hander if they tried anything.

I sometimes thought about a different life, a life in which I couldn't be bothered by anything or anyone. When Sony Walkmans first came out, I had a little day-dream that I would be a roadsweeper. I'd get a Walkman and walk the streets all day, pushing my broom about, listening to educational tapes, cleaning the streets. Nothing and no one would trouble me.

But the drugs – always, always the drugs – inter-vened. I tried to give them up, I really did. Even when I was young I tried. Just not very hard. One time – I can only have been about twenty-one – I checked myself into detox, on the City Road, just down from the Angel Tube, not far from the City Club, owned by George Nash, where George Bell got shot – well, right next door in fact. The club was known as the Blood and Buckets. You might not think this was the best place for me to try to quit drugs, but in truth what I really wanted was a rest. I had no desire to stop, I just needed a rest. After two days I checked out, although first I got myself some drugs, using a carving knife to 'persuade' this Irish guy to open the pharmacy, and then to let me out. Sometimes rehab was pretty much like prison and you were locked in at night, which was the case in this place.

Some of the crimes I committed were so petty as to be almost ridiculous. Most people would think that the longest sentence a criminal earned would come from the most serious crime he committed, but in my case that didn't happen: one of the longest I got, three years, was for bunking off a fare on a train. It was 1978 and I was with the Hock, who looked like one of the vultures in *The Jungle Book*. Like me, he was from Hoxton, and he was called the Hock because he was so skinny, like a hock of bacon. We'd both been to a football match, Arsenal versus Crystal Palace, and as we came back through Bethnal Green Tube station this little ticket inspector asked for our tickets. 'Fuck off,' we both said. He reached out to grab us and the Hock shoved him away, reaching for a small bag of change before we legged it – we'll have that too, thank you very much. It amounted to £2.17. We were chased (I dislocated my shoulder falling down some stairs), nicked for it, and given three years, mostly for the robbery. When I went to jail there was someone in there moaning about his sentence, how it was so unfair and all that. I told him that I'd got three years for bunking off a train fare and taking £2.17. That soon shut him up.

I went back to some places again and again. If I'd got a result somewhere, then I'd make sure I went back there; knowing something about it made it an easy take for me. Twice I did a jeweller's down Bartholomew Lane. The second time I used a piece of timber to jam the door shut, then broke the windows with a scaffolding pole. The man inside couldn't get out and some builders were shouting, 'Oi, what do you think you're doing?' I just yelled back, 'Mind your own business.'

When I got pulled in for that job, I was thirty-four and in prison with about six weeks to go on my current sentence. The police had to come and collect me to drive me up to London to charge me, so they had to obtain a 'production order' to take me out for the day, up to Snow Hill near the Old Bailey. All the way up I was handcuffed to the policeman beside me, and nobody was speaking, me least of all, as I didn't know what I was being taken up there for and I didn't want to say the wrong thing. In London all was made clear, so on the way back the policemen escorting me were a little more relaxed. I was no longer cuffed, and they even stopped at a services and bought me some lunch.

So there we were, travelling south on the M3 in an unmarked police car. At one point the officer in the passenger seat turned round for a chat.

'You were hard work tracking down,' he said to me. 'All those aliases and being adopted and everything.'

Rule number one: never, ever show anything to the police. That's what I'd been taught. My stomach had flipped over – Adopted? What the fuck? He must have the wrong fella, surely? – but outside I was all calm and seen-it-all-before.

'Oh yeah?' was all I said.

'Yeah. Here, you might as well have these as we won't need 'em any more.'

He handed me an envelope containing a birth certificate and adoption papers, and turned back to chat to the driver.

I stared at the papers in my hand. There was Alice's name – my mother, Alice. I'd held the man I thought was my father, Fred, as he died, and I'd had to go through Lizzie's death too, and now I learned that they were my grandparents, not my mum and dad. At that moment I was very angry with Alice because I realized that one day I was going to have to cope with my mother's death all over again. Funny, the irrational thoughts that come to you in moments like that. I seethed with rage all the way back to jail.

I don't suppose I said anything to Alice about this when I came out, but I did go and tell her that I knew. And I went straight back out thieving, taking stuff from offices and from people's homes. I didn't feel bad about it because it was all just work to me. I'd nick stuff and go on to the next one when I was done, I'd spend it, and when it was gone I'd go out and get more. Drugs, clubs and betting shops took all my money. But not women. I wasn't very good with women. I wasn't horrible to them, I just couldn't form any kind of relationship with them. Even when they wanted one.

The first woman I spent any time with, the first relationship I ever had, was Jane Harrison, who went missing long after I'd finished with her. No one knows what happened to her. I'd just been let out of jail – this was 1978, or thereabouts – and I was celebrating with a drink in the Three Brewers. I was being one of the chaps, everyone was round me, I was showing off a little, and this attractive young lady stuck her head through the crowd and said, 'Are you going to buy me a drink or not?' I hadn't heard a squeak out of her before then, but I gave her a ten-pound note and told her to buy her mates a drink and keep the change. We went on to the City Club and I didn't see her for a couple of weeks, but then I bumped into her again, and that was it. It wasn't long before I moved into her place, in Cherbury Court.

Aged four: me and my Guinness.

With my nan, my mum and my dad (or so I thought).

Hopping with Fred.

Me as a baby outside a pub during hopping

On a scooter waiting outside the pub in Cliff Street.

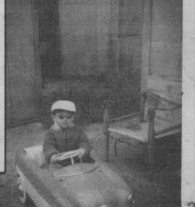

My getaway car outside the prefab in Newton Grove.

Newton Grove. Johnny Smith and me with my bow and arrow.

Pissed on whisky and Tizer.

My new guitar. The day I got it I smashed it over Fred's head when he was hitting Nan (Lizzie). I jumped up on the table and, copying one of my favourite cartoons, walloped him. It broke.

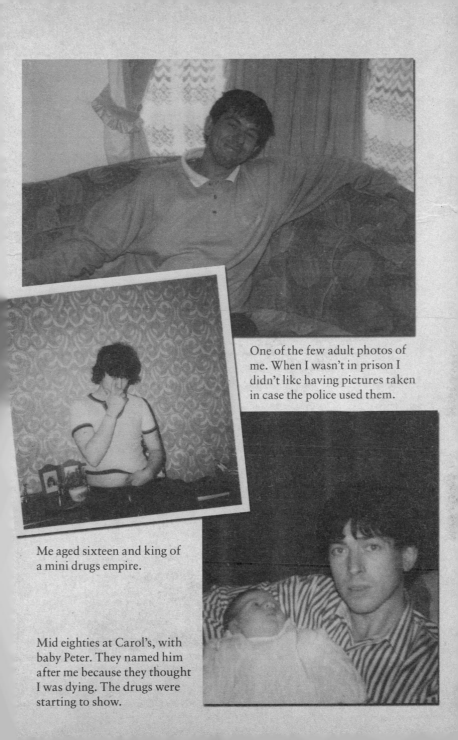

One of the few adult photos of me. When I wasn't in prison I didn't like having pictures taken in case the police used them.

Me aged sixteen and king of a mini drugs empire.

Mid eighties at Carol's, with baby Peter. They named him after me because they thought I was dying. The drugs were starting to show.

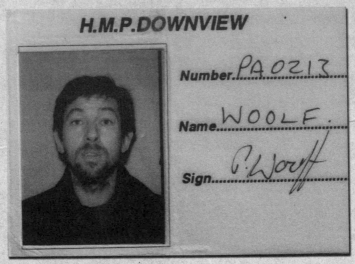

My prison card. This was shown when you signed for your weekly earnings, and spent money in the prison shop.

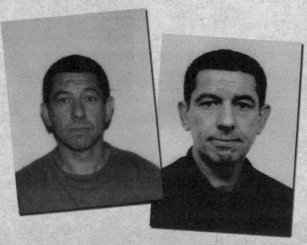

Prison pictures. I had these taken to send to women penpals.

With Will at a Restorative Justice conference in Bristol.

ouise and me on our wedding day.
ow I'm smiling.

With Princess Anne at the RJ
conference in Bristol.

No longer dodging the camera – this photograph was taken for the police magazine *The Sharp End*.

I didn't know anything about relationships (thinking about it now). I knew I liked Jane, but I didn't know how to have a relationship with her. All I knew was that she was gorgeous and everyone was envious of me. She was like a prize, a trophy. I just wanted to have as much sex as possible, and that was really and truly what it was all about for me. I don't know if I loved her; I still don't know. I just wanted to do what I wanted to do. I've always been a caring person, I've always believed I was a kind person, but in the world I was in it didn't pay to be kind and caring. It just wasn't the done thing.

I was with Jane for a couple of years, but our relationship was all about me. I just wanted to do more crimes, take heroin, and drink; she said she wanted me to get a job. I told her she was off her head, but in one moment of weakness her uncle Jimmy got me a job down Covent Garden, working on a site, smashing out the innards of a building. After an hour or so I thought, 'I ain't having this, this is ridiculous,' so I said to Jane, 'Either take me as I am or don't take me at all.' There was a bit of a kerfuffle, I said, 'See you later, then, I'm off,' and that was it.

I just didn't do relationships. If I wanted to stay round someone's house, I stayed there. I might turn up on a woman's doorstep and they might say, 'I've got someone here,' and I'd just tell them to tell whoever it was to go: 'I'm staying here, and that's the end of it.' I had run-ins with a couple of people. The footballer

Peter Storey was one. I turned up at this woman's house and he was there. He was there for the same reason as me: to get his leg over. 'Hello, what you doing here?' I said. 'What are you doing here?' he said. 'Never mind that,' I said, 'time for you to go, cos I'm tired and I want to go to bed.' He looked at the girl, and I said again, 'I think you'd better go.' If he hadn't, I'd have taken him outside and I'd have given it to him.

Another girl I spent time with came about when Alice was inside doing her four years for supplying heroin. I was out, and she wrote to me and asked me to come up and visit this girl, who came from Norwich. Her name was Julia. I went up to Holloway and saw her; I'm the gent, taking flowers and all that. Anyway, I gave her some puff, sent her a few tenners after that, but then forgot all about her. Then she wrote and said she was coming out. I went to meet her, but she had come out the day before. I shoved the flowers I was carrying into a bin and drank the bottle of champagne I'd brought along to welcome her back out. And forgot about her again.

Some time later – quite a long time later – Alice came out of jail. I was at Bianca House in Crondall Street and there was a letter for me. I never got any letters, so I held this one at arm's length to read it. It felt important, so I treated it accordingly. And it was from Julia. She wrote that she'd put on weight, and this was why she hadn't wanted me to see her when she got out – all that sort of nonsense. But she was in London, and she gave a number, so I picked up the phone and spoke to her.

We met, and my memory had obviously been playing tricks on me, because she's gorgeous. We went for a walk along Regent's Canal, holding hands, but nothing further happened. I wasn't bothered because what I really wanted to do was go off and get drugs. Which I did. Bye bye, Julia. Again.

Then one time when I'm with Jane, I fancy something a bit different, and I ring Julia's number, which I'd kept. A woman answers and tells me Julia's gone away. However, she knows who I am, and Julia's left a number for me in case I called. It's out of London, I think it's Norwich, but she says, 'I'm in Surrey, d'you want to come and stay?'

'All right, then,' I say.

'Just throw a few things in a bag and get the train down to Weybridge.'

So I go and meet her. She picks me up in a car at the station, and tells me she's a housekeeper. I'm thinking it's a B&B, but no. We drive on to St George's Hill where we pull into this house I recognize, because of course I've been down there, out nicking. Millionaires' Paradise, it is. The house is now owned by a Saudi prince who uses it for when he wants to go to watch the horse-racing, so that's six weeks in a year, at most. The rest of the time it's hers: sauna, squash court, tennis court, a pool, inside and out, a staircase you expect to see Fred and Ginger come dancing down, you name it – even credit card numbers up by the phone in the kitchen so you can call for food.

Well, I love this. I'm happy there, and I use it as my base for a while, until it's time to get some money. And I'm being horrible now: I tell her she's got to go get the money, I don't care how, sell her body if she has to. She says, 'Why don't we nick here?' And of course the place is loaded so that's a great idea.

I go round and see my friend David Wright, who's got a removal business. He comes over and we clean out the place. There's antique guns, Fabergé eggs, a £24,000 chinchilla fur coat, silver, all sorts, and we sell the lot. I reckon the value's a million to a million and a half, although of course we don't get that.

Six months later I get arrested for it. I come out of Jane's mum's on Balls Pond Road – her mum was on holiday at the time and we were living there – heading out to get my breakfast. I've got on espadrilles, shorts and an orange string-vest. I get my paper, twenty Embassy, milk and some bread and I'm heading back when, *whoomph*, cars come in from everywhere. There's blokes jumping out with guns (because we'd nicked guns, you see), and I'm pushed to the floor with a gun to my temple and another one to my cheek. Guys leaning on every part of me.

'You're nicked.'

No, really, you think?

I'm bundled off to Upper Street in a car and shoved into a cell. I've still got my plastic carrier bag with me. Time passes, no one's coming, so I bang on the door and the desk sergeant comes over.

'Give us a clue, what's this all about then?' I ask.

'I dunno,' he says. 'You're wanted by the Walton-on-Thames Regional Crime Squad, and they're on their way to collect you.'

Well, I think that's OK because I've never been there so they must've made a mistake. I'll be on my way shortly.

So I'm driven down there in an unmarked car with escort and put straight into an interview room, without booking me in, a uniformed officer either side of me. With my plastic bag still. No one tells me why I'm here.

In walks a detective inspector – Bowles, I think was his name – in a smart Savile Row suit, which immediately lets me know it's serious. He's got two flunkeys with him carrying huge piles of files. And he's as nice as pie. Asks if I want anything, offers me a cigarette, arranges for breakfast to be brought in to me. And then he says, 'Do you know someone called Julia blah-de-blah?'

I immediately relax. This'll be fine. That's why there were serious guys about with guns and smart suits – she's been murdered. Well, that's nothing to do with me. They're just eliminating me. I'm not in trouble after all. What a result!

'Yes,' I reply, because I'm sure they know I've visited her in prison. My name would have been written down somewhere.

The DI leans forward. 'And do you know David Gerald Wright?'

The penny drops. Ah, hmm . . .

'Before we go any further and start involving solicitors and no comments and everything, read these,' the DI says, and he shoves two huge files across the table. Two detailed statements, one from her and one from him, naming me as the man who did the robbery, forcing them at gunpoint to help me. She says I was a Bad Man, and a bully, and I threatened her. But here's the strange bit: the amount listed as stolen was only about four to five grand's worth.

I go to trial, pleading innocence. First trial I say that I loved Julia dearly, she was the love of my life, and I came home and found her giving my best mate David Wright a blow-job. I was devastated, and I beat them up (the truth is that David could really fight and he'd have killed me if we'd fought). The jury can't reach a verdict so I get a retrial. I want it to be away from Surrey, but it's put in Guildford Crown Court. When the jury's being sworn in you have the right to challenge some of the members, so when I see a scruffy-looking old geezer I nod my head to my brief to allow him. Only the next day, the first day of the trial proper, the scruffy geezer turns up all suited and clean-shaven, hair slicked back, and I'm prepared to bet that he is a retired police officer. Just my luck.

The trial goes ahead and I go through the same defence. Afterwards, the two prison officers with me – because by now I'm in Coldingley doing time for something else I've done – say, 'You're going to get out of this one, son,' as the jury's been out for a while. David's been charged with me, though they've done a deal with him, and Julia's been given immunity. I'm alone in the box, waiting for the jury to come back out and say 'Not guilty.'

Then word comes back from the jury room that they have a question for the judge. In they all file, and the foreman hands over a note which is read out. One of the jurymen – and once again I'm prepared to bet it's the formerly scruffy one – has noticed that there were two men listed on the indictment but only one standing in the dock. What happened to the other one? The judge turns to the jury with a big smile on his face and says, 'I can answer that one, ladies and gentlemen of the jury, it's a simple question to answer. The other man's already pleaded guilty.'

So that's the end of that. *Boom*, I'm found guilty too.

I'm on the wing in Norwich jail and I find other people I know, so it's good. I like it there. I'm going to the gym one day and I hear someone call out, 'So-and-so, visit.' Now this name is an unusual one, and it's the same as Julia's surname. So I ask along the wing to see him, but his mates think it's trouble so they take it the wrong way. I can see why: I look like a right mad lunatic with my bald head, and I'm always in the gym pumping iron. Anyway, we do meet and I ask him who's this Julia.

'Ah, my ex, that rat,' he says.

I tell him the story.

'I heard about this, but I heard it in a different way,' he says.

'Oh yeah? Have you got her address?'

Indeed he has.

I write her a letter. Two years have gone by now, so I write, 'I forgive you for what you done, I know there was no alternative, why don't you come and visit?' I put up a VO – I had loads – and she comes along. She's brought a bit of heroin up, and I say, 'Right, this is what I want from you. I want you up here every day with a gram of heroin.' She agrees, and comes up five days on the trot.

On the last day, she says, 'I think I've paid my debt back to you now.'

'Oh, all right, sweetheart,' I say, and lean over the table to kiss her. Only I pull my right arm back and knock her spark out.

All hell breaks loose. I'm standing up, screws all over me.

I don't hit women as a rule, but there are times, and this was one of them.

David's dead now. I think it was an overdose.

Someone kept setting light to his flat, but it wasn't me. Julia's living in Norwich now, too, not far from me. I'd like the opportunity to say sorry to her, but I can't blame her if she wants to stay away from me.

So there was the Bad Man, always there at the front, and lurking behind him, unseen, unrecognized even by me, was someone else, a different Peter, the one who wanted to see the world, not the one who took drugs and stole and treated people badly. I knew there was something else, something different out there, but I didn't know how to reach it. Every now and again I'd catch glimpses and I'd feel a yearning to be part of it, to fit in with something – one thing I did know was that I didn't really fit in with my world – but it never happened. Whether or not that was because there was something in me that prevented it, something that blocked the change, I don't know.

One time I nearly gave in to the yearning to change was early on when punk rock happened, and everything seemed altered when I came out of prison. In the short period I'd been locked up this whole new language, new music, new way of dressing, new way of behaving towards one another had come into being. To me it was as if the whole world had changed. One thing about punk rock I got wrong when I first heard about it when I was inside was that I thought it was a fashion, nothing more, and that punks only dressed like that when they went to see bands at the Marquee. An old mate from Hoxton days, Jimmy Dix – whose beard was so big that one day he scratched it and a roast potato fell out – took me down the King's Road and they were all sitting outside the fire station. I couldn't believe it. There was a bird dressed in a green dustbin-liner, or what looked like one, and I went, 'Fuckin' hell, look at that!' And she spat at me.

I liked the music, the Pistols and all that. I wanted to have pins in me too, in my hooter. But I couldn't, because I had to look the part of a gangster. I didn't want it, I didn't want to do what was expected of me, I really hated all the stuff that was being put on my shoulders, I didn't want the responsibility of being me, I hated being me, I didn't like me, but I had to do it.

It was quite crap, really. But I had an answer to my problems. At least, I thought I did.

I had drugs.

Eight

Decline to Fall

There comes a time, if you're an addict, when the scales tip over the wrong way. You are no longer in charge of the drugs, they're in charge of you. Instead of drugs being a feature of my day – the way I relaxed, the thing I chose to do – almost overnight they became the be-all and end-all of my life. My days revolved around the acquiring, taking and – unfortunately for me – coming down from drugs. Specifically, heroin.

Right from the age of fourteen, it was always heroin. Heroin, heroin, alcohol, heroin. Heroin, heroin, alcohol, cocaine, crack, heroin. Heroin, heroin, heroin. It overtook me, like a plague of locusts swarming over a field. It was everything. Even all the songs I loved, Lou Reed and that, they were all about heroin. The obsession, to take and get more heroin, drives you on. It's described in one of the treatment programmes as 'the Doing and the Getting of More'. It's all about More. I love that quaint phrase, 'What's your drug of choice?' I would roar back, 'More! Whatever you've got! MORE! That's my drug of choice – more of whatever you can give me!'

It's odd, really, how I could have known that I was addicted yet carried on regardless. I lived in this weird fucking world where my head would be out there, my body would be over there, and my heart would be somewhere else. I'd be ripped in pieces half the time – a weird fucking life when I look back on it. This was the addiction. All the time, I felt I had not a split personality but a shattered personality. I had twenty different personalities, if not more.

The maddest thing, what destroys you in the end, is that heroin takes all the rest of life out of you. One time I booked a holiday – me, who never went on holiday – to go to Sardinia, with my friend Terry Amis. I paid for it and everything, but I didn't get my passport so I couldn't go. It was just too much trouble. Couldn't be bothered with waiting in the Post Office. I never bothered to get a passport because I was too busy getting heroin.

I'm proud of myself now – not proud that I can look back on it, just glad I'm not like that any more. These days I won't even touch most painkillers, so if that's the most you've ever done in your life – by way of popping pills, I mean – you might find it hard to understand the biting need I felt whenever I was withdrawing. You might wonder why anyone would put themselves through it. But then you haven't experienced what it feels like to be high on heroin. Let me tell you about it.

We'll begin at the beginning, which is where it all went wrong: sticking a needle into myself, or shooting up – everyone knows it's called that. So here's how I did it. And this is what I did to myself almost every day for decades. I'd learned well from that dwarf in Soho. I never had to ask anyone again.

I got my spoon, tipped my heroin in, added a pinch of citric acid, or vitamin C powder, and put water in. Then I heated up the mixture, gently, until all the powder dissolved. Gave it a little stir with the needle. Then I had to filter it with a bit of cotton wool, or a little bit cut off a filter on an unsmoked cigarette. That went into the solution, and through that I drew the liquid into my syringe. I had to be careful when I did that because if I got a tiny bit of dirt into me I'd get what's called a dirty hit, which is the most outrageously horrible thing you could possibly think of. It's like having a year's worth of headaches all in one hit, much worse than migraine or anything like that, along with vomiting and a soaring temperature. I had a dirty hit once that put me in hospital. The very worst way to get a dirty hit was when I was clucking, if when I was cooking my gear up a drop of sweat got into that spoon, because it was poison. That one time I injected the poison, all that bacteria, straight into a vein. I was hallucinating; I was at Alice's and apparently I tried to get into the oven to cook myself. Fucking hell, was I ill. I was really bad. My temperature was 105.

You use ash to smoke crack, unless you've got a gauze pipe, or some wire wool. You can put the crack on the wire wool, or the gauze, and it won't fall through into the pipe. Some people use asthma inhalers; they break the cap out and use a bit of silver paper with a pin to prick holes in the foil. You use the cigarette ash to give the crack something to grip on to, but that's all it's for: it stops the crack – which heats up until it turns into a liquid – from dripping down through the holes in the foil.

Once the heroin was in me, I'd be fine. Sweet.

But what was it like?

It's not that I can't describe it, it's not that the words aren't there, it's just that it's like saying to me, 'What's it like breathing?' or 'What's it like when your heart beats?' To me, taking heroin was like both those things. I couldn't live without breathing or a beating heart, and I didn't think I could live without heroin either. After a while it stopped being something I enjoyed; I just needed it. That probably doesn't make any sense to you – it doesn't really make any sense to me now, any more, now that I've stopped – but eventually I could derive no pleasure from taking heroin, just the feeling that, yes, now I would get through the day, or the night. I will live. I will be able to carry on.

Without it . . . it's hard to describe this. Even thinking about clucking now makes me feel sick. Nothing compares to it.

And what I'm talking about is withdrawing from heroin. Withdrawing from crack wasn't hard. In fact, for me, there was no withdrawal from crack. There's an effect, if you use it regularly, that comes on when you're not using it. You're lethargic. Where I work, people say they're tired all the time, coming off the crack; but is that because they're always lively on the crack? It's not a physical withdrawal on the crack – nothing like the heroin.

It wasn't like you could do anything to stop it, either. It's not like you can plan ahead – I'll be hungry in the morning so I'll make sure I've got some bread in. It doesn't work like that, or at least most times it wouldn't work like that. The first thought in your head when you woke up would be *gear*. If I had gear wrapped round me, I'd make a hit up before going to bed so that as soon as I woke up I'd have one. But if you woke in the night, you were done for, because then you'd do it in the night. Remember, an addict is just about insane, so it's all 'pretzel logic' stuff: 'I can easily get a tenner in the morning so I might as well do that bit now.' It whistles for you during the night – *pheuw-whee*! It's done that to me. I've had it lying on top of the wardrobe and I've heard a voice go, 'Oi, up here!' It had a real voice when it talked to me, the heroin. Always the same voice – a little cartoon voice, a caricature voice, croaky, like the little gremlins in the film. I'd look up, and it'd go, 'What about me? Come and take me.' And I'd answer it, literally: 'Don't be stupid, I've gotta have you for the morning.' But it knew what to say back to me. 'Come on, come and take me. You know you want to.'

You succumb to it. Every single time. There's no will-power on earth that can resist that. If you're an addict, you can't *not* do it; it's impossible not to do it. If you're just a drug user, or you've got a problem with drugs, you might be able to resist; but if you're an addict, you can't. If you wake up in the night, it's going to happen; if you sleep all night, you'll have it in the morning. There's no rhyme or reason to it.

Waking up when there's nothing for you is terrible. The worst of it was you knew it was going to get even more terrible. You'd wake up and you'd have this horrible sweat on you. It wouldn't be leaking out of you, it would be a film on the skin. And the smell; there'd be a strange smell about you. I can't describe it, but it's a bad smell, like a poison, not nice. You know the way you flinch when you stick your nose into your fridge looking for something nice to eat and there's some rotting vegetables in there? That's what I'm talk-ing about here. Not that I smelled like rotten cabbage or anything, it was just the kind of smell you recoiled from. Except, of course, you can't recoil from this smell because it's on you.

You know it's you because you've become acutely aware of your own body odour, your senses having started to heighten. That'd be first. Then your nose starts running, flooding out. You can't stop it; it's like molten candle wax dripping out of your nose. And your feet and legs twitch; you can't sit still. You don't want to drink, but you've got a gooey mouth. Then you start puffing out. You've got to stretch out because it seems you can't get enough air into your lungs. You yawn, but it's not a proper yawn, it's just a noise. A clucking yawn is horrible, a real false thing. You've got to do it because your body's shutting down on you and your brain's telling you to yawn – to get more oxygen inside you – but you can't do it because there's all this garbage like phlegm in your throat, which makes you feel sick. Proper heaving. Your bowels start moving too. This is all taking place the minute you wake up.

You wake up and you go, 'Not another day. Why didn't I die last night? I don't want another day.' This is how heroin makes you feel. I used to wish 'today' would never stop, in jail in Pentonville. I'd sit there looking at my watch, not going to sleep, trying to make time go slower so tomorrow never came, because tomorrow's shit, you don't want it; nothing's worse than tomorrow. The best way of describing it from start to finish is 'I don't want tomorrow to come'. Tomorrow means clucking. You think, 'Oh shit, not another day, not another day of this.'

If you've nothing to wake up to, you get up, you don't worry about washing, you just get dressed. You've just got to get out, you've got to get some heroin, because you know you're running on borrowed time till you can get a bit, and the longer it takes you to get a bit the harder it becomes to get a bit because of all the physical shutdown processes. Everything's a chore. Moving about is a chore, walking is a chore, talking is a chore. You become very Neanderthal: you just grunt or mumble. All right? Yeah. No. You're so knackered all the time. Imagine someone walking along with emphysema; they'd overtake you, because you're dragging yourself along.

The moment often came when I was out and about and I couldn't control my bowels. Imagine having the flu tenfold, and getting up and trying to get past it, only to find yourself stranded somewhere while it gets progressively worse. I can recall one day in particular. I came out of the house and I was in the throes of early withdrawal. I'd just got some money together to get a bit of gear and I had to go to the place of a guy called Duncan in Murray Grove to score. I had the sweats and the yawns and the stretches and the urges, my feet were going, my knees were going, and I was puffing. My skin was crawling too – not itching, a much more horrible feeling. I didn't like to use water on my body when I was clucking because everything ached, even my bones.

I got right to the bottom of Duncan's block of flats and that was it, I had to shit. I went into the bushes outside the flats and squatted down there. It was like, ah, no, how low can I get? But I didn't care. I was beyond caring. I've shat in shop doorways before. People would see me, but I didn't care. You can't do anything about it when you've got to go. You can't shit yourself because you've got to keep walking, and you certainly won't waste even twenty pence on a public toilet. You might need that coin later.

Usually once things have got this far the mental side of things clicks in. You cry, you get very emotional, over nothing. It's what I've always called 'the poor me's'. You just want to get money so you can score, that's all. A tenner, maybe twenty quid – what's that to most people? Not much. But to someone in the middle of clucking it can get to a stage where they're thinking, 'Fuck it, I'm going to kill someone, literally kill someone. I don't care now.' I've certainly reached that don't-care stage.

You're quite spacey as well. Your head's all over the place, you can't function properly, sweat's pouring out of you, you're stinking and you're dirty and you're scruffy, you're just not normal. You know you're going to stand out in a crowd. You're not interested in what anyone's got to say to you, unless they happen to have a bit of gear on them; then you'll listen. You're cocooned from everything around you. You're not aware of anything except the one thing you revolve around: heroin.

Then you come to a point where you become incapable of doing anything. You'll shake, you'll shiver, the gunk in your nose will pour out of you, your eyes will stream, your stomach will heave, you'll be running backwards and forwards to a toilet, heaving again, you won't be able to eat, and you can't drink. Just *existing* – nothing more than that – seems to become so hard. And then your vision starts to go. You get a greasy film on your eyes and everything goes blurred. It's even worse when you've got your money and you know you're going to get your hit because then you're dealing with the anticipation too. Rushing adrenalin makes you even sicker.

If you've got a drug habit, top of the list is to get drugs. And once those drugs are gone, top of the list is to get more drugs. There's no self-actualization; you can't ever reach your goal. It just goes on and on and on. I can remember cooking up gear in a spoon and trying very hard not to spill it while I vomited to one side. Spilling it won't do, so you've got to concentrate hard. Oh, that sound – *hueargh*. I can remember me and fellow users Golly and Pickles all getting a bit of gear and going round Tony Butler's house and all making the same noise while cooking a bit of gear up, all going *hueargh*. It was terrible.

I'll tell you how mad you get when you're clucking. There was usually quite a good supply of drugs in Pentonville; I could easily keep my habit going well in there. Only one time there was a shortage, because there was a shortage out in the real world as well – you get these barren patches sometimes. I decided that, at all costs, I had to get hold of some heroin, or morphine, or diamorphine, *anything* that was going to stop me from clucking. So I feigned appendicitis. I feigned it so well that they took me to the Whittington hospital where I was given some pethidine. I got them to inject me with this pain relief, and I let them take my appendix out in the process. There was nothing wrong with me, but I convinced them.

And that's nothing. I knew a fella who was so strung out, withdrawing, he just didn't know what else to do, so he set fire to his own legs in a hospital car park. Poured petrol over his legs and set them alight, just to get some painkillers. Crazy. This is what addiction to heroin can do to you.

And of course all this was a lot harder if I was working. What I've described so far is what I was like when I was lying about. If I was working with the Old Boy, and he said, 'I'll be round to pick you up at six o'clock,' then, however, I felt I had to be up and ready to go by six o'clock to earn the money to buy drugs.

We'd take our drugs wherever we could – at home, at someone else's home, at a crack house, wherever. It didn't matter where you were, really. If you were in your own home you might make an effort – once, when I was living in a flat on Hackney Road, I had forty-seven ounces of heroin and I wrapped it all up in one-ounce bags (bank cash bags) and put it in the fruit-bowl so it looked nice, with some oranges and things as well – but if you're squatting, or in a shooting gallery, or a crack house, everything was just lying about, because the room's only there for that one reason. In one crack house I remember sticking a needle into myself, drawing some blood and spraying it on the walls, just for a bit of fun.

If I was shooting up at home I'd have all the stuff I needed in a box in the kitchen, for smoking heroin or crack: citric acid in some form, ash, a tin can, a safety pin for making holes in the tin, or cardboard or foil for a pipe – everything except the needles. For those I'd go to the needle exchange. It was an ordinary chemist, but they had a sign on the door that told you they were exchanging needles, so you'd take in your old needles and they'd give back to you a pack of clean needles, barrels, wipes, distilled water and – later, when these things came in – a sharps bin for disposing of your needles. I'd try to get a bag, which would be ten packets of ten syringes, to last me the week. Sometimes you'd get quizzed by some newbie, just started on the job – should you be getting these, that kind of thing – but mostly it was OK, because if you were trying to quit and were on some kind of programme to get you off the heroin it would be the place where you were getting your methadone from anyway. Methadone was what you took to replace the heroin. If I took, say, £100 worth of heroin a day, I'd need 100ml of methadone to stop me withdrawing. In a sadistic way junkies like me got used to, methadone is addictive, so it's harder to come off than the heroin.

Getting needles wasn't easy in the old days. I used to go in and tell the chemist I was a diabetic. AIDS made the difference; it was because of AIDS that addicts like me were able to get free needles. When some friends of mine contracted AIDS, they were given blue polythene bags with syringes and sterile water and wipes plus all sorts of drugs, free. I used to envy them; I used to wish I could catch it too so that I could have all that. And because I didn't care if I lived or died, it didn't matter to me if it was (as it was then) a death sentence. The attraction of the drug was always, *always*, greater than any risk.

Everything is secondary to drugs – money, football, doctors, everything. You get up to piss, then go back to bed, or the sofa. When I used to stay at Lizzie's house, I'd wake up on the sofa, where I slept, I'd have the quilt round me, I'd be clucking and I'd go, 'Got any money?' First thing I said. 'Gissa tenner. Gis. Gis.' And they'd say no, and I'd go, 'All right.' And then I'd start puffing. 'Gissa fuckin' tenner, will ya? What's the matter with you?' I'd drive them so mad that in the end they'd throw twenty quid at me and tell me to fuck off out of the house. I'd promise they'd get it back, 'as true as God built this world', but they never did. I'd think it, but I'd never do it. In the early days I used to look after Lizzie and Fred; if I got a couple of grand, I'd give them three or four hundred quid – there you are, do what you want with it. So in my head it felt like they were paying me back.

I don't know whether anyone can understand this – if you've never suffered from an addiction you probably won't – but nothing matters to you when you're in need. You don't feel the cold or the heat outdoors because you feel crap anyway if you're clucking. You don't feel happy or sad, because you feel crap, and anyway you haven't got time to worry about that when all you want is a hit. So I wouldn't feel guilty about taking money off my relatives, money I had no intention of paying back; or ashamed of squatting down to shit where I could be seen. No. I feel shame for being so drunk in restaurants that I threw up in them, or smashing up the Nag's Head pub. Guilty for damaging the lives of innocents.

By the end of the eighties I was consuming huge amounts of drugs. Every morning when I woke up there'd be the Devil at the end of my bed; he'd be doing press-ups off the bar by my feet. 'Coming out to play?' he'd say, wriggling his eyebrows at me. And I never said no. Well, I couldn't say no, because the Devil had me by the balls.

I was quite successful as a thief, so people wanted to go out with me or buy from me when I had stuff to fence. Being successful meant I had money, and that money got spent on drugs and booze. That is what did it for me: the more successful I was, the more drugs I consumed; and the more drugs I took, the more crimes I needed to commit to pay for them. I could see the way it was going, but at the time I didn't care. Just give me *more*.

And I didn't like to share my drugs. Sometimes I was OK about it for a time, maybe even a few days, but after a while I'd get horrible. 'That's mine, not yours, now give it here.' I just isolated myself and took drugs. I stopped going out. I socialized now and again, I'd go for a drink at lunchtime, but I much preferred staying in with my heroin.

Heroin wasn't my friend, though. No friend had treated me as badly as this – no enemy either. Over the next few years I took more and more until by 1992 I was almost gone. I'd been getting worse and worse, and I'd been getting sicker and sicker. I was bleeding from my arse; I had to wear sanitary towels to stop the blood leaking into my trousers. I couldn't walk. In order to move I had to put my hands on my knees to support myself as I lurched forward like an arthritic crab. I wouldn't go to the doctor's or to hospital because

I couldn't. Any time not spent taking drugs had to be spent making money to buy drugs; there just wasn't time for me to do anything else. I could barely stand but I still thought I could go out and get some money, somehow. Shows you how stupid this addiction disease can make you.

I was round at the flat of a girl called Paula, and Alan, who I was doing a bit of grafting with, came over. Paula said, 'I'm sick of him being like this. Make him go to the doctor's, will you?' Alan had to help me, and it took ages as I could barely move. As soon as we got there the receptionist stared up at me, her eyes wide. She didn't say 'Wait a minute' or anything, she just jumped up and ran and got the doctor. He was in with a patient but he came hurrying out. He just looked at me – didn't examine me, didn't ask me anything, just looked – and then he turned to her and said, 'Call an ambulance, now.'

I was rushed off to Bart's, and into emergency, where they put me in a bed and stuck bags of stuff into me. I had drips everywhere. There were four bags of drips hanging off this trolley by the side of my bed. I suppose my kidneys had given up, and my liver can't have been in great shape anyway, so my blood was probably mostly poison by then. I had to be washed out before they could hope to fix me. So there I was, lying in my bed, in a private room off the side of the ward, with tubes and drips hanging out from everywhere, but the need was still in me. The Devil was still at the foot of my bed, doing push-ups.

After I'd been there a while, a doctor came into my room and said to me, 'I'm going to say this straight, so you'll understand. If you keep smoking crack cocaine, keep injecting heroin and keep drinking, you're going to die. You have to stop. If you don't stop, you will die. Do you understand?'

I nodded. It was all I could do. He left.

The really weird thing about addiction is that it's the one disease that doesn't let on how bad things are. A few short hours earlier I was doubled over in pain, blood leaking out of my rear, every bone and joint screaming at me, my head pounding, unable to keep anything down. So what did I think, now that the doctor had spoken? Did I think, 'Phew, that's lucky, someone's come along at the right moment and told me straight what I must do to get my life back in order'? Did I think, 'I must do what this man says, turn my life around'? Did I fuck. This is what went through my mind: 'What does *he* know? He's only a doctor. Doctors get it wrong all the time. Things aren't that bad.'

The Devil had given up on the push-ups and had moved into my head. He was giving the addict inside me a pep talk. Believe me, I tried to fight him. I lay in bed and argued with the Devil and my addict self. But when there's two of them, there's no chance.

The Devil: Go on, get yourself out of here, let's go have some fun.

Sane Peter: Don't be a fucking idiot. I'm dying here, didn't you hear the man?

Addict Peter: A little fix right now would be good. Something to take the edge off.

Sane Peter: What are you trying to do to me? I will die if I do!

The Devil: Oh, don't be ridiculous. You can handle it; you always have.

Sane Peter: Have you seen the state of me? Look at all these drips and everything.

Addict Peter: Take 'em with you. You can use that trolley to hold on to. Or we can get 'em out. They'll take 'em out if you ask. Then we can get out of here.

The Devil: Come on, let's go . . .

I just didn't have enough answers, because nothing was greater than that need. So, some time the following day, with my actual withdrawal being controlled by methadone, I thought it was OK to confess to the one addiction no one had tried to get me to stop so far.

'Nurse! Nurse!' I called out.

She came over.

'I really need a smoke. Can I go out and have a roll-up somewhere?'

She looked at me like I was mad, which of course I was.

'Peter,' she said, 'you know you can't do that. I can't let you go.'

I begged and pleaded for a while. I was only going to be gone a minute; it would help me sleep; please, pretty please – all the crap. And she bought it.

'All right, I tell you what. I'll turn my head away and you can slip out and go on to the balcony through that door there. But be back in five minutes, mind.' And she wagged a finger at me.

Never, ever trust an addict. An addict is a liar, a thief, a cheat.

I promised the nurse I'd do as she'd asked, and got out of bed.

Oh, the agony of trying to move, pushing that drip stand in front me as I went, holding on to it for dear life, shuffling along slowly towards the lift. I had my hospital gown on, one of those papery things done up at the back, so I must have looked pretty obvious when I wheeled myself out of the main entrance at the front of the hospital and waved down a black cab. But nobody stopped me, and the cabbie didn't even blink when I climbed in, bringing the drip stand and all those bags with me, and said to him, 'Essex Road, please, mate.' As if it were the most normal thing in the world.

Luckily, Paula was at home when the taxi drew up, so she had money to pay for the journey. I dragged myself into the flat and headed for a chair by the table where I could sit down. A tin of lager in my hand, some crack to smoke and heroin to inject, and I was fine.

Until I opened my eyes again and found myself back in the hospital. The same room, the same doctor standing there.

'Are you completely mad?' he half shouted. 'Do you want to die?'

I didn't reply. I couldn't work out if I was dreaming, or had dreamed about going to Paula's.

'Well? Don't you care? Do you want to die?'

And then I said, 'Yeah, well, it gets us all, doesn't it? You're born, you live and you die. It's what you do in between that matters, not the end, and I want to enjoy myself. I want to make the most of it. I don't care if I do die.' And I didn't, I really didn't care if I lived or died, because I knew that no one else did.

He had nothing to say to this, but I could see he was angry with me. 'You,' he said, 'stay there, don't move. Don't even think of moving.' And he walked away.

The rage boiled up. I'd been told off by some young doctor in front of a nurse. I thought, 'Don't you dare talk to me like that.' I mumbled 'you fucking wanker' under my breath, then lay there with a case of the 'poor me's'. I hated him, hated him for speaking to me like that in front of a nurse. I cried. But I did as he said. I stayed for a few days, took their methadone, and then walked out without so much as a thank you or a goodbye. Off I trotted, back to drinking and drugging, back to the madness I called life.

The world I lived in, of drugs and drink, of crime and violence, acted as a mirror to show me what I thought I was, and prevented me from seeing the true horror: the emptiness, the echoing blackness, the desperate need that had driven me for so long, the need that lay within.

Paula was part of this madness. I met her when I was about thirty. I'd just got out of jail and I bumped into somcone I'd known for ages – she was always about – called Sally. Sally was with these two black girls, and I had a drink with them all, and then one of them asked me to come back with them to their place, so off I went. There was a punter upstairs and they were smoking crack and there were these two kids, one of them three and the other no more than eighteen months old. It didn't take me two seconds to work out what was going on, so I went upstairs and interrupted the girls in their work.

'Whose are these two kids?' I asked.

This girl – Paula, though I didn't know her name then – said, 'They're mine.'

'Well, what the fuck are you doing with them here? There's not a stick of furniture in the house. What's going on? Have a bit of respect for your kids at least.'

I slung the punter out – see you later, fuck off. The other girl left in a hurry.

Paula said to me, 'What am I going to do? I've got to go out, I've got to earn money, haven't I?'

I took hold of the two kids and said, 'No. You can't

leave the kids on their own while you go out. That's wrong.'

So I sat with the kids while she went out. I just didn't want to see them children look scared. I knew enough to know that was wrong, irrespective of all the bad things I'd done. If I had any say in it, it wasn't going to happen.

Someone told me this about prostitutes: you either make them fear you, or love you. I didn't want them to fear me so I made them love me. I was with Paula fourteen years, a long time, and I thought I loved her for a while. We worked together. In Soho, we'd work the corner. I'd get punters around Berwick Street, we'd point firmly at a door (which might have led anywhere) and say to them, 'Be here in twenty minutes,' and then we'd bugger off with their money. Sometimes we'd go up a flight of stairs and pretend we were booking a room – which of course would cost the punter an extra fee – then go hide out in Tyler's Court to keep away from them when they showed up.

I still liked working Soho because it was easy to make money there. At night, even if you just whacked a couple of stingers into someone, you got your money. If I wanted gear I'd make a few snide wraps up – wax balls or bags with herbs in them, that kind of thing – wait for someone to come along, sell them, jump into a cab up to King's Cross or wherever, go buy my own gear and go home. Once I wrapped up hailstones in clingfilm and sold them as crack. We had to hurry before they started melting.

It was that simple; you couldn't *not* earn yourself fifty quid in an hour. Then again, you couldn't continue doing that because if the people came back looking for you and found you standing there selling stingers, well, you were done for, weren't you? You couldn't just clip punters every time; you had to vary what you did. You found something you could do, you did it, and then went; you might not go back for a couple of days. But if you were selling bona fide drugs you were there for a couple of days, just selling.

Roy and Alice were still in Soho, in their different ways. Alice worked as a maid in a brothel for a while, and Roy had interests in a restaurant or two in Greek Street. I no longer saw a lot of him, but that was my fault, not his. Right from the word go when I'd decided I didn't want to be a gangster, I'd done things to deliberately piss Roy off. Taking things from him, stuff like that. He'd given me chance after chance after chance, but when I sold a watch that he'd given to Alice, he decided enough was enough. Really and truly all that man did for me was his best, and I repaid him very badly indeed. But I still felt aggrieved about the trick played on me over my grandparents' identity, so I never felt bad about treating Alice or Carol poorly. I got Carol to pawn her jewellery for me. I always promised to pay her back but I'd walk away saying 'silly cunt' to myself as I knew I never would and she shouldn't have done it.

I was always doing things that were horrible, but to me, at the time, they made perfect sense. Like when I came back to the flat one day and found Paula and the kids watching TV. I walked over, unplugged the video, and went out the door to sell it. I told them, 'You can't eat videos,' but that was just my excuse, because of course I wasn't really going to go and buy food with the money, now was I? Another time I came back and no one was in. I had no money and couldn't think of any way to get any that day, so I phoned up a removal company and sold them everything in the flat – beds, saucepans, everything. They came round to clear the place out, I left them with the spare set of keys and told them to post them through the letterbox, then went out and spent the money they'd given me. I don't remember what I said to Paula when she came back. I don't suppose she was too surprised by anything I did any more.

With Paula it had to come to an end some time. I'd been on remand, and had just come out of Southwark Crown Court (they let me go that time), and Alice and Paula were both waiting for me at the court. We jumped in a cab, but halfway home I got out, went into some bar or office, I can't really remember, and got lucky. There was a coat hanging up, I rubbed it down, and there was a wallet in it. I gave it one final check and found an envelope, the kind with a see-through window on the front, and it was thick with twenty-pound notes. Once I was out of there I looked more carefully and found there was £1,800; touch.

I went out with Trevor Jones – Clever Trevor – but all I wanted to do was get home and take my drugs. It had got to the point where I didn't want to be sharing my drugs; it was all right once, but not again. It was all right going out being big-time Charlie Spuds, but I didn't want to keep on doing that. I started resenting Paula, mostly because I had to share things with her, especially drugs. These drugs were my drugs. I'd share with her for a while but after a few days, when she asked again I'd say no, you want drugs you get your own fucking drugs. Why should I give my drugs away? It's like you going to work for a week and someone saying, 'Give us half your wages.' I argued with Paula and she insisted she wanted half. So I sawed the sofa in half. Here, that's your half, Paula, you stay there.

Things between Paula and me really went downhill when I was on the run out of HMP Downview. In the prison there'd been a big problem with hepatitis C and I talked my way into training as a hep C counsellor. So I went to work, did all the right things, while all I was planning was how I was going to use this opportunity to get out. I wanted to take drugs. I could do drugs in prison but I wanted to take more, lots and lots, and although I only had six months left to do, the madness was upon me. I convinced the prison to give me a day's pass to attend some charity event somewhere in Clapham – lots of hep C support groups. Other people were going out of the jail on day release and home leave and other programmes, so I distributed my clothes out to them, one item each, so that as soon as they got out the gate with me I could get changed and hit the road. I went to Croydon, jumped on a train, was in Islington within the hour and had a needle in my arm within an hour and a half.

Now, when I first met Paula she didn't touch heroin. But after we'd been together for a while she started nicking my methadone, to get to sleep with; and then she started nicking a bit out of the big bags (not little wraps) of heroin I used to get, to put in her joint. I didn't realize she was doing this, and by the time I came out of Downview that time she had a full-blown habit. I couldn't work out why, and when she told me I felt terrible about it.

One day not long after that I was in the flat with the two kids and I was looking for money and cigarettes, so I was pulling drawers out, and I found a letter. It was a letter from Paula's doctor to a hospital about her pregnancy. I had to sit down. I didn't even know she was pregnant. I read on. The letter said she needed to have an abortion because I'd been unsupportive and horrible. When she came back, I asked her about it. She'd had the abortion. She'd told me at the time that she had 'a woman's problem' and I didn't need to know anything about it.

I was devastated for a while. Paula and the kids cleared off and it was just me there on my own. All there was in the house was an armchair, a little coffee table with a telephone on it, and a television. That was it; everything else was gone. I just sat there, turned the TV on, got my bit of gear, slept in the armchair, got up in the morning . . . it went on like that for ages.

One day the phone rang. It was Paula.

'Hello,' she said. 'Can I come home?'

'If you want,' I said, and put the phone down.

She'd sold all the stuff in the house and run off to a woman's refuge. She hadn't needed to run off, I never hit her, she was just well fucked up. I turned up one day and she had this woman with her from social services, and she said, 'We're going to this refuge.'

'Why, what's going on?' I asked.

'I can't stand the way you treat me.'

'What? How do I treat you? I don't know what you're talking about.'

The way I saw it, she was very manipulative and it seemed she'd say stuff like that to get what she wanted.

Mind you, I didn't treat her with respect. Paula came to see me a couple of times in prison, though I didn't like her visiting me much. She'd come to Pentonville with some gear, that was it. But when I got out I'd turn up on her doorstep, knock on the door, say 'All right?'

and go on as if nothing had happened, and I'd expect her to do the same. I'd only been in suspended animation, really, my life hadn't changed; and no matter what Paula had been up to I expected her to drop it all and go along with me. Even if I'd been inside for two or three years I'd just go down to the West End, go to a pub and ask around till I found her, then, whoever she was with (she'd remained a prostitute), it was as if all I had to do was click my fingers and say, 'C'mon,' and she'd come with me. It was as if I owned her. That's how it was in my head. I had no respect for her.

It was the same when I decided that was it, that I was going to leave and never come back. We were living in Sidney Street, a flat belonging to someone called Streaksie. Paula was out in the bedroom, I'd got up and wanted to score. I found I had forty quid on me, so I called up the dealer and he came round with a £20 rock of crack and a £20 bag of heroin. I looked at it, thought about Paula, and said to myself, 'Well, you're not having any of this. I don't love you, I don't even like you.' And that was it – I walked off into the sunset. I left her up in that flat, withdrawing; didn't care. Didn't like her any more. I never liked her. I certainly didn't love her. I used to encourage her to go out and get money for me; I was just poncing off her. Her children had been taken off her while I was inside, doing a sentence; she'd taken them round to someone's house, asked them to look after them, and didn't go back. And that's not uncommon in the drug world.

I know all this sounds callous, cold and mean. It was. I was. I didn't want Paula; I didn't even want love. At least, I thought I didn't. I just wanted heroin.

Anyway, you think I was mean to Paula? One time I was eating a meal in the Angus Steak House near Piccadilly and I was reading the *NME*, reviews of bands and listings of who was playing where. I went downstairs to the toilets to take some heroin, came back up, and there were two attractive girls looking at the *NME* I'd left on the table. 'You two in town to go out?' I asked. They were foreign, Danish or something. They wanted a night out. We went to see the Vibrators at the Marquee and then they took me back to their hotel, the Strand Palace Hotel, where we had a threesome. And then, while they were asleep, I robbed them.

I used women. They wanted me, I wanted them to provide me with money and, sometimes, sex. Money bought me drugs, and that counted for more.

Another time I was with Paula, I was nicked for something – can't remember what – and put into Pentonville, on remand, for three weeks. On the day I had to go to court – a summer's day, baking hot – I stole a pair of shorts from the gym in Pentonville and went to court in them, and the judge let me out, miracle upon miracle upon miracle. I ran all the way from Highbury Corner Magistrates' Court to the dealer's house, thinking all the way, 'Give Me Drugs!' Bobby and Kim, it was; they lived on the corner of their estate in Hoxton – a good observation point, with tons of security gates and all that. The problem was, I had no money, so I asked them to give me credit. No, can't do it. I was rattling the gates. 'What do you mean, no? I want it.' They still said no. I was peeved by that because I always paid *him*.

I went off down the stairs, cut off across Myrtle Walk, and saw Sandie walking across. She was a friend's elder sister; I'd rumped her when I was about fourteen or so after a party. She was coming towards the block of flats, and we stopped to chat.

'What you after then?' I asked.

'I'm off to Bobby and Kim's,' she said.

I was really taken aback. 'You don't take that, do you?'

'Yeah,' she said.

I told her my story, and asked her to get me a bit. She disappeared up the stairs while I waited at the bottom, and when she came down she said, 'Here you are,' pressing something into my hand. I looked down and saw that she'd given me forty quid's worth.

'Here, where'd you live, then, Sandie?' I asked, quick as a flash.

She took me to this little bedsit above a chemist on the Kingsland Road, where I took my drugs.

Time was getting on, and I was thinking that perhaps

I should get back to Paula. Sandie started getting dressed up.

'Where are you off to?' I asked.

She told me she was getting ready to go to work; it hadn't dawned on me yet. She could see me looking a bit blank, so she smiled and explained, 'I work up the beat, Commercial Road, Stamford Hill, that way. Wait here. What do you want for your dinner?'

I was a bit dazed by all this generosity, so I just said, 'I'll have a kebab.'

Three to four hours later Sandie returned, and handed me eighty quid, a kebab, a lump of crack and a big bag of heroin. We sat and ate, and smoked the drugs. And that was it; I never rumped her or anything like that. We just went to sleep. The next morning I woke up and went back to Paula's, but that night I returned to Sandie's. Same thing, only this time it went on a little while.

I worked out that she needed to be loved. All prostitutes need to be loved, need to be cared about; they need someone special in their life. I didn't have sex with her, didn't do anything with her.

I was on my way round there one day and I bumped into someone I knew called Alan, a guy I took drugs with. I never knew his surname. He'd just got married to some Page Three bird and he'd moved out to a nice place in Beckenham. He gave me the keys to the flat, told me I could have it; it was fully furnished, all I had to do was keep paying the rent. As it turned out, this was the last time I saw Alan.

I'd been to his place a few times, a nice three-bed-room flat, better than Sandie's poxy one room. I went round to hers and saw water pouring out over the steps. There were people on the street from all these bedsits with all their belongings, crying; Sandie was there too, having a bleedin' fit.

'What's all this?' I said.

'Those fucking brothers of mine. They come round here clucking and they stole the copper pipes to sell for a bag of gear.'

'Well, that's a result, isn't it?'

She looked at me, then at the people all around us and the water pouring out. 'Result? This?'

I told her about the flat, so we got her bag – all she had to her name – and went round. And the same thing happened again: out she went to pay the bills. (Dunno if the rent was paid. There's the rent book, not my job, you sort that out.)

One night she came back and announced, 'I've got a friend, got nowhere to stay, and we've got enough room. Can she stay here?'

'Course she can, as long as she pays her way,' I replied. And I didn't mean anything by that except that she paid for what she used. Don't forget, I wasn't living there, I was still at Paula's.

Trudi moved in, and that night they both went out

together, all tarted up. When they got back Sandie gave me £80 and so did Trudi, and some drugs. I thought, 'This is lovely. I'm getting eighty quid off one, and now eighty quid off the other, and eating whatever they bring home, and taking the drugs they bring back.' Then Denise arrived, and Rowan too. So I now had four lots of £80 a night, and all the drugs I could smoke.

We were all sitting there one day, the girls in their little French knickers and all that, and Sandie said, 'Can we talk?'

'Yeah, if you want.'

'No, I meant in private.'

We went into a bedroom.

'What's happening with this relationship of ours?' she asked.

'What?'

'Well, you don't even give me a kiss.'

So I said, 'All right,' and I gave her a kiss on the cheek.

'No, I want our relationship to be . . . I want you to make love to me.'

'Pffff, do I have to?'

'Well, yeah.'

So I got two condoms, put them on and made love to her. Well, I didn't make love to her, I rumped her. Then Trudi said the same thing to me, a little while later. And I was thinking, 'This ain't good, I don't like this.' So I left the next day and never went back.

Well, I did go back, about three months later. I was passing and I wanted some money, so I decided to get some off the girls, because in my head the flat and the set-up belonged to me. So I knocked on the door and this black guy I knew, Greg, answered. There was another black guy with him.

'Yeah?' he said.

'What do you mean, "yeah"? What you doin' here?'

'This is our Yard.'

'Your Yard? What's all this "Yard" nonsense?'

'Them girls work for us.'

'Listen,' I said, 'this is mine, and they're mine, and I suggest that you go, else I'll get some mates round here and we'll muller you.'

They left, I went in, had a couple of days, got a few quid off the girls, and some drugs, still didn't like it – it was a madhouse – and left again, for good.

Heroin was everywhere, all over London, but its availability did nothing to improve my behaviour towards others. Once I was being held in Finchley police station – the only place they could hold me as all the London jails were full – and I suddenly saw through a window the whole Robbery Squad in another room. Paranoia set in; I convinced myself they were here for me, so I hurriedly got someone to bring in hair dye and overnight I dyed my hair. I went in black and came out ginger, only it was meant to be blond.

I was transferred to Cheshunt police station, and I called a friend when I got there and told him he *had* to come and give me some heroin that night as I was clucking badly. He owed me, so although he grumbled, he said he'd drive over with some gear for before we were locked in. I was taken to my cell. There was an iron gate across the stairs and then three rooms off the corridor. I can remember coming down and looking in one where an extension cable had been run from upstairs; three Indians were sitting watching TV together. They said hello, but I was doing very badly by now and went to lie down on my plastic-covered rubber mattress. After a while one of them wandered over to see me, a packet of Rothmans in his hand.

'You wanna smoke? he asked.

'No thanks,' I said.

Then suddenly – sniff sniff – I'm like the Bisto kid. I smelled something, and it smelled good. I walked over to their cell. They were sitting there smoking heroin.

'What's that?' I said. 'Can I have some?'

'We offered,' they said, 'so of course you can.'

So when my friend turned up in his Triumph I was like, 'Yeah? What d'you want?' even though I'd summoned him and he'd driven over especially. What was I like?

Nowadays I feel naughty if I have an ice-cream, but back in the early nineties, as you can probably tell from these stories, I was just getting worse. The drugs, not to

mention the drinking, were ravaging me. From the outside, and looking only at my behaviour and what I got
up to, you'd say I was heading either to prison for ever,
or death. But down inside me, somewhere, a place I
couldn't have named for you back then, something was
stirring.

Nine

A Shard of Hope

There was no defining moment; it was a slow, progressive thing. It took me a long time to get to the point where I was clean.

I still thought I was good at what I did, but of course over the years things had changed. When I'd first started out I was nicking to pay for drugs, but that had turned into *having* to steal to pay for drugs. For instance, in 1980 I wouldn't have got out of bed for £20. I'd have used a twenty note to light my joint – that's how much it meant to me. By the early to mid nineties I'd have been well satisfied with £20. All I ever wanted, by the end, was twenty quid, twenty quid, twenty quid. It bought you two joeys, two £10 bags. Or, if you were lucky, you got two joeys for £15. Or you bought a couple of beers, phoned up the dealer and told him you wanted two £10 bags but you only had

£18. He'd moan that you were always doing this, but you'd say, 'Fuckin' hell, what d'you want from me?' and he'd sell them to you in the end. Yes, £20 was everything, then.

As I said, the change was a progression, a series of what I call 'yets'. One by one I crossed the boundaries. I can remember, years ago – and I mean all the way back to when I was first in Soho – going through the subway where people scored drugs at Piccadilly Circus Tube station and the hippies were on the floor, and I looked at them and said, 'Look at them fuckin' scumbags, fuckin' state of 'em. You'll never catch me doing that.' I was a user, but I was never going to be like that. But what I should have added was 'yet'.

I started selling things at a young age – I sold my toys to pay for cannabis. So when I started breaking into places I was always good at selling what I'd stolen. In the old days I used to look down on the two-bob shoplifters, the ones doing what we called 'the meat run' – that is, nicking steak from the supermarkets and selling it half price at the cafés. It didn't have to be meat, it could be coffee – anything that could be stolen from the supermarket could be sold. I used to say, 'Mugs. They ought to do it like we did it in the days of going into stores and stealing suitcase-loads, not this petty little small-change shit.' Another 'yet'. By the end I would have been lucky to get what they got for their efforts. For years I'd worked the corner with the Old

Boy so I'd learned to just walk up to people; they can only say no. 'Hello, mate, listen, I've got, you interested?' Trouble was, I no longer looked like the kind of person who had anything worth buying. I looked like what I had become: a drug addict.

Sometimes – not often, but sometimes – I felt bad about what I was doing. Crime was the way I had chosen to earn my money, but there came a point when I encountered a slight problem with the criminal activities I was involved in. And stealing, robbing, thieving and conning don't sit too well when you start to feel guilty about them. Usually nobody but myself was aware of this twinge inside me, but it wasn't long before it became apparent to others.

One night me and the Old Boy had been driving around London for a few hours looking for a bit of work. We were totally skint, the car was almost out of petrol, and I had started to withdraw from heroin. It was getting late and nothing looked like coming together on our usual patches so we drove round to an area that was mostly office blocks. All the occupants had gone home so it was quiet on the streets, which limited our options further. I took an executive decision on what we should do, and said, 'Pull up, mate, and I'll slip in and out of some offices and try and get a laptop or something.' The Old Boy had no problem with this idea because more often than not I'd have a good result trying this out.

I knew from experience that the building wouldn't be empty, that there'd be cleaners about and maybe even a security guard. But I was confident that even though I was feeling the effects of withdrawal I would still be able to bluff my way around the place and get what I had to for the night. If I was confronted by anyone I'd say the usual bollocks about looking for a friend, or for something I'd left behind earlier in the day.

At first I thought I was in luck as there was no one about when I went in, but to my dismay the place was like Fort Knox. I couldn't even get off the ground floor. So after a few minutes of pulling at door handles I turned around and was about to leave when I caught sight of a door marked 'Storage'. Normally I wouldn't waste my time looking inside such a place – I couldn't sell a mop or a broom – but for some reason that night I did. Inside was the usual collection of brooms, buckets and other cleaning equipment, a load of toilet rolls – and, on top of a wooden desk, an old, shabby-looking brown handbag. I opened it and looked in, expecting it to be an empty, discarded one. Instead, I found a purse which had a hundred quid in it, which was a bit of a result, so I stuck it in my pocket along with four bank cards and a diary, which I slipped into the other pocket. I always took the diary or notebook as well, because you'd be amazed how many people write their pin numbers in them.

In the car a few minutes later as we drove away from

the scene of the crime I flipped through the diary, and sure enough, there on the back flap, handily written out with the account numbers above them, were the four pin numbers. I remember the Old Boy saying 'Don't these wankers ever learn?' when I told him, and we both chuckled as he drove us to the nearest cash point.

Back in those days you could only withdraw £200 a day, so we got our £800 and went our separate ways, me to buy some drugs and him to the pub. I kept the cards and diary because we'd discovered that sometimes, if we went back at one minute past midnight, we could draw out another day's money. I never had any expectations when I arrived at the cash machine at a few minutes past twelve, but hey, nothing to lose and nothing else to do, so in went the first card and lo and behold out pops £200. Another £800, and I was well pleased.

I headed back home. I didn't want anyone else to be around as I just wanted to take my drugs by myself, and as it happened that night I was on my own. So I sat down, had my fix, everything was cool – and then it happened.

Something just turned inside me. I thought to myself, 'This is wrong.' I started to feel guilty. I felt like taking this woman her money back and saying sorry. But that would be foolish to do: I would go to prison, and worse than that, I would withdraw. So I didn't do anything about it, just carried on sitting in my chair, getting wasted. But I had genuinely experienced something new to me: remorse.

Because I didn't act on it, I can't make a big deal about it or say that underneath it all I was a good guy who deserved something other than jail – that's rubbish. I was still a robber and a thief; all that happened was that I experienced something I assume just about everyone has experienced as well, only for me it was the very first time in my life. Seeing a pivotal moment for what it is is something we all of us never do. I certainly didn't. I thought about doing the right thing, though. Something, somewhere inside me, was changing, a little bit at a time, like some underground creepy-crawly that takes years to emerge from the ground into something else.

There were other things I did that made me feel different from the Old Boy, and the addicts I hung around with. For instance, I liked learning. London had a lot to offer someone like me – and I don't mean Peter the criminal, I mean someone with time on his hands. This was a period of my life when, during my wanderings around the city looking for things to steal, I would stop for lunch and tea breaks or just take a rest and chill out. My main resting holes were usually inside a church – dry and warm in the winter, cool and shaded in the summer. Sometimes there was a concert in a crypt I would go and check out, usually a bit of classical stuff but sometimes a bit of folk or gospel. I started going primarily for a sit-down and a free cup of tea, however, and I began to enjoy it after a while. I think I felt safe in a church.

I'd grown up knowing one side of London – the dodgy side, the grimy, sleazy side. As I wandered about, driven partly by greed – because where there was culture there was usually someone with a handbag or a camera case – but also by curiosity, I saw another side of the city. I started to go into these places. The art galleries I found blew me away, the museums were really cool, and the architecture in and around the capital was quite awesome. But the thing that properly lit me up was attending lectures.

There's always something going on somewhere where you can hear something interesting for nothing. Again, I usually only went into these places for somewhere warm and quiet to sit, but I found myself increasingly paying attention to these lectures. Half the time I didn't have a clue what the lecturer was talking about, but all the same I sat there and listened. Some of the stuff I found really fascinating, things like globalization, but my favourite lectures were the ones about literature, because many of them covered things I'd read about in prison. All those years of being egged on by Charlie Richardson – 'See this in the paper? What do you think about that?' – meant that I often knew as much as the lecturer, it seemed. Of course it took me ages to realize this, because I assumed that the person up there had Knowledge, that he knew stuff I didn't.

I can't exactly remember where – I think it may have been in Paternoster Square – but I was at this lecture on medicine and the chap was rattling off all these facts and figures when the thought 'I could do that' flashed through my mind. Once again something stirred in me. I'd always liked to hold court in prison, reading to people, and I had a little glimpse of a possible future for me – a future in which I was up on a stage and people were sitting around listening to me. Whereas before I'd never even have considered such a thing, thinking that no one would listen to someone like me, I now realized that I knew a lot of what that man up there knew, and that if I ever stopped being an injecting drug user, an alcoholic and a criminal, well, there was something that wouldn't be impossible for me to do.

A great place for hanging about in was the Tate. I was sitting there one day and I saw this painting, *The Lady of Shalott*, and it blew me away. I loved it. It was, and still is, the most magnificent piece of work I could think of. And then I saw David Hockney's *The Bigger Splash* and I wanted to know more about that too, so I signed up to do a one-day course in how to read a painting, called 'Art and Poetry' or something, and I enjoyed that. I like poetry, and of course I was out of it on heroin, which made it better still. I also liked a painting by Lowry that was shown on the course. I spoke up in the lecture room about it but I can't remember what I said.

I was, of course, hanging around in the Tate looking for tourists to steal from. At that time I still had my schemes and my scams, but none of them worked as well as the ones I used to do when I was younger. Many years ago, when I was only sixteen, I had a great scam at a club called Papillon in Harrington Gardens, off Gloucester Road. Derek the doorman had all the black-cab drivers straightened out. They'd pick up customers who asked 'Where can we go for a good night out?' and bring them down to the club, and Derek would pay the drivers commission. Once they were inside, if they wanted a woman, they'd ask Derek and he'd point them in my direction. The punter would come up to me and ask if I could find them a bird, and I'd say I could sort them out but I'd have to charge them an intro-ductory fee, a tenner. The girls would be lined up over the other side of the club, and I'd go over to one and say, 'I've got a punter over there caked with money. Give us a tenner and I'll introduce you.' Sometimes I earned £300 a night doing this, and at the age of sixteen that was a lot of money.

I had no chance of earning anything like that by the 1990s. I wouldn't have got in the front door of a club, let alone be seen by punters as the man to ask. I was too grubby. But the girls didn't seem to mind as much, they were different. I still had a rapport with the girls. I've always had this . . . gift, I called it, though now I'd call it emotional intelligence. I was quite a respectful person (so long as I didn't get too involved with someone, that is) and I'd discovered that a bit of kindness and courtesy costs nothing. The birds I knew liked that. For a lot of Alice's friends – the married ones – I was their 'bit on the side', so for a while I'd had a lot of work, seeing them all and then trying to avoid them. Some of them would give me money, to take them out. I'd like to think it was because I was great in bed, but that's probably not true. Maybe it was because I seemed like a Bad Boy, whereas they knew I wasn't.

I was the kid mums didn't want their children playing with. Kids got in trouble, but I had got In Trouble. I'd been to approved school, and then to borstal, and then I became a Young Prisoner, and then I went to prison. By the time I turned seventeen I had been to Wormwood Scrubs while the majority of my peers were working in factories, or packing shoes, looking all smart for their mums. I would never understand all that, it wasn't my world, it was something I had no idea about. So to these women I might have seemed naughty, but the way I treated them, I was nice.

Like this woman Mandy. I was in Tony's house in Grosvenor Avenue, taking heroin along with Tony, his wife Ali and my mate Pickles. And there was this bird Mandy there, with her baby in a pushchair, and she had come along to take heroin as well. Well, I wasn't having that going on around the baby so I put him in the other room and told her she should be ashamed of herself.

She must have thought I was nice, showing an interest in her kid and all that, because she came on to me and took me home to her place in Camberwell. We went on the bus. She told me that her husband was out working, so we'd have the place to ourselves. I asked her what her husband did; she said he was 'in security'. As we were about to get off the bus, however, she added, 'You know I said my husband's in security? Well, actually, he's a policeman.' I thought about this for a moment, but it didn't bother me. I still went home with her and shagged her. I went a few more times after that – took some heroin over with me, and we'd shag. To make it more fun, on one or two occasions I even wore his spare uniform while I was doing it, for the kick.

One day we were both sitting there naked, and the house reeked of sex, and suddenly her husband came in. 'What the fuck's going on?' and all that. I didn't really want to get involved in their problems so I got up, said, 'See you later,' got dressed on the balcony and went home.

I didn't think too much about Mandy after that, but a couple of months later I was round at Alice's. She'd had a tip-off that she was going to be raided so I took the house stash, which was just a couple of LSDs and a can of CS spray, and said I'd hide them somewhere else for her so that if the place got turned over they wouldn't be found. I was heading over to Tony's place with the pills and the spray when a van pulled up. Police jumped out and told me they were nicking me for tampering with some parked cars, and named a street nowhere near where we were. I told them it wasn't me and tried to get rid of the stuff I was carrying, but they saw me trying to chuck it and took that too.

They took me to Dalston Lane police station – way out of my patch, as far as I was out of theirs – and who was there waiting to see me but Mandy's ex. I was taken down to the cells where I called the duty sergeant and told him I'd been fitted up for shagging this man's wife. Nothing would come of the complaint, I knew that, but I could get my revenge by making sure that the whole station got to hear about my antics. I even made sure they knew I'd done it in his spare uniform. I went to court and got eighteen months.

Being an addict like I was meant that whenever I was in prison I easily got hooked on things. My usual drug, of course, but training as well. More weights, more reps, more muscle. I've got big legs, but in prison I always had to have the biggest legs. It was my party piece to show the new arrivals my legs. I used to have thirty-six-inch thighs. Massive. I used to pride myself on them, that and my fifty-inch chest. I was a big old lump. And I kept it that way by pumping, lifting and squatting all day every day.

But me being me, I also discovered another way to get that pumped-up look. Inside, someone had discovered 'napos', napolene injections. There were these three big old Welsh boys we used to call the Power Rangers because they had stick legs and thick arms. They said to me, 'You want to get on the roids, boy, they're the thing.' Steroid tablets and napos, they meant. Well, if there was a pill, I was going to take it. So I managed to get some money – I must have sold some drugs or something – bought some roids off them and, bingo!, I turned myself into Popeye. More roids!

I once managed to give myself piles when I was training. I was trying to do my best-ever squat, 180 kilos. That went OK, just, so I thought I'd have a go at 185 kilos, but I couldn't do it. As soon as I went to squat down I knew I'd done myself some damage. The piles came, my back went, I couldn't lift again.

I carried on my scams, even in jail. I used to have pen-pals all round the country – sisters of other inmates' girlfriends, that kind of thing; I'd write to them and they'd give me money. They all wanted to marry me. It started off as a game, to see whether or not I could get a girl to write back to a villain like me; then it became a challenge – how much money could I get out of them? Hello, my name's Peter, I'm having it really hard in jail, please send me some money. Like a charitable donation – the more money you can send, the easier it is to fix something. (Or in my case, the more money you can send, the more heroin I can take.)

Best ever was when a posh bird who lived in Eastbourne came to visit me. She was a stunner. When she walked into the visiting room all conversation died and everyone's eyes went to her. She walked round until she came to my table, and I was sitting there like everyone else, mouth hanging open, eyes wide. No one could believe it when she sat at my table. She was amazing.

I dropped the girls as soon as I got out of jail, almost as quickly as the muscles fell off me once I stopped training, because I simply went back to addiction number one: drugs. I'd moved about a lot over the years, but my choices soon became pretty limited. If I had a lot of money I'd stay at the Cavendish, but when I didn't I went into a bed and breakfast. I used B&Bs a lot. I used to get bored in Hoxton or Islington, I'd fancy a change, and I'd go out and stop at a B&B Finsbury Park way. I had all I needed there, a TV and somewhere to cook me gear up. What I'd do is every day I'd put on my clothes and at the end I'd chuck them rather than get them washed and put a new lot on. This was the time of espadrilles and jogging bottoms, so if I was in a hotel for a week I'd go up the market and buy one of each colour, and some T-shirts. I'd wear them, then I'd throw them away. I still managed to look OK, or at least I thought I did, but washing? Certainly by 1995 washing was a thing of the past. In the early days, when I was out and about a lot of people used to think I was a policeman because of the suits, or slacks and blazers. Even at the very end I still had good-quality clothes on – a Bally jacket, nice shoes, black cords – only my socks could have stood up by themselves. I was a mess on the inside, but I didn't think people could see that.

As always, I was still robbing to make money. The Old Boy came and went in my life; a lot of what I was doing now was too small-scale for him. One thing I did that made me a proper bit of money was working with Pickles and Golly; no one else would work with them. I had somehow got hold of matching keys for the alarm systems in Currys and places like that; I think I'd bought them off a mate called Terry (there was a nice trade in things that might be called 'burglar's tools'). The items on the shelves were alarmed by having wires stuck to the back of them, leading from the alarm box itself. I would simply turn off the alarm, remove the wires from the back of the items we wanted to take, then rewire the alarm back on to the metal shelf and reset the alarm. Then I'd distract the staff by asking lots of questions about cabling and satellites and routers, loads of crap like that. I got quite good at going on about gigabytes, wiggabytes, any old nonsense I could think of to hold the attention of the staff. What about the Panasonic range? Can you build this in? Can it play long-play tapes? And I'd call other people over. ''Scuse me, can you tell me about . . . ?' All this time, of course, Pickles and Golly would be moving things off the shelves nearer to the door, putting them between other displays. At the right moment they'd whisk their coats off, scoop up the video or the TV or whatever it was, and walk off round the corner. In the end we started going a bit crazy, going in with barrows and things. We earned fortunes doing this.

We'd take whatever we'd stolen up to our geezer up Highbury Hill way, divvy up the money and then go off and get our drugs. Don't know what he did with these things once we'd sold them to him; all I wanted was my bit, and then to get away from him. Once it was off my hands, I was safe, I could relax. I'd head off to the B&B. As I said, I liked being on my own. I'd watch the TV I wanted to watch, documentaries and that. I was going through a wildlife programme craze at the time and I watched everything I could that had an animal or a bird or some landscape in it. I didn't want to watch *Coronation Street* or *EastEnders*, which is what everyone else seemed to want to watch. I couldn't stand them. What I did was a bit decadent, or so I thought, and I liked that.

People think committing crime is always the easy option, the lazy way to get things, but while I'm not going to defend my actions, I don't think that's true. From the moment I woke up to the moment I passed out I was living with stress levels I don't think many people could cope with. Lots of people have stress in their jobs, but they can usually tell someone about it.

My job was being a criminal; there wasn't exactly a counselling service available. Quite right too, but still, let me explain.

When you get into hardcore criminal activity, you've got all this going on: you've got to get up and look around, make sure you're not under observation at any time; you've got to get from A to B, to do your bit of work; and you can't know at any time if you're going home that night. On top of that, there came a point when the police were driving around with guns, and they were trigger happy too, so you can add 'didn't know if you were going to live that day' to the list. People might think that sounds melodramatic, but that's really how it was. I knew a chap who'd been busy in the past, but the day they caught him all he was doing was sitting in his car. He was under observation, and the armed policeman leaned over into the parked car – the engine wasn't turned on or anything – and killed him. The policeman came up with some story that David had tried to run him over and all that. Of course he got away with it; they were literally getting away with murder in those days. This was in the days before evidence cameras, so you didn't know when you got pulled in and taken in their van down the station if you were going to get smashed to pieces and all that.

When I had a bit of money and a bit of gear and I didn't have to rush out, it was easy. By 1995 I'd dropped down a level. I was just running on auto-pilot most of the time, and by the time I'd done a few sentences I really didn't care if I got nicked. Once I was a drug addict, it was a case of 'anything goes'. Even then, though, the survival instinct kicks in, because if there's one thing I didn't want to have happen it was to be nicked before I could score. Remember, I'm in full-blown addiction, and when I wake up I've got no gear, so I've got to get some money in order to buy some gear, and once I've got my money I've then got to go to a drug dealer's house and buy my drugs, but he could be being watched by the police, so they might let me buy my drugs and then arrest me, in which case I don't get to put the drugs inside me. I'm withdrawing, and not only have I got to think where I'm going to go to get some money, as I walk along I'm also thinking, almost praying to myself, that I don't get nicked. After I've had my drugs, fine, but not before. Please let me get my bit of gear first, then you can nick me.

Straight away, there's the stress. And no matter how good a thief you are, or how good a desperado you are, sometimes you don't get what you need. Three hours later you're still scouring the streets, and desperation is creeping in like an animal. You're thinking, 'I've got to get twenty quid from somewhere.' When you think about it, in a straight job, after a few hours you've earned twenty quid, but logic doesn't come into it when you're clucking. All you want is that bit of gear, that bit of gear, that bit of gear.

You might get a fiver, and you get a couple of beers to take the edge off it, because something else'll come along. Sometimes I've been out there up to eight hours, and in the end I've done something desperate, really really desperate: walked into a shop, pushed people out of the way and taken money straight out of the till, or smashed a window and not cared. One time I was in north London with a Turkish fella and we walked past this gold shop with all these Omega watches. I went over to the railway line, where I found a big lump of metal. On the way back I went into some shop and nicked an umbrella. I said to Kem, 'You stand here and hold this open.' All these people were walking past, and he said, panicking, 'What you gonna do?' and I said, 'I'm having all them watches cos there's no one in the shop.' And I smashed this window – which is how I got the scar on my wrist, reaching through the broken glass to get the watches out, although I didn't care; I'd gone beyond caring – and I thought the umbrella Kem was holding up would hide me from all these people. If the umbrella's in front of me, no one will know what I'm doing.

I'm gone. I'm a lunatic at this stage. But the rewards seemed to justify it.

I was on the floor. I'd woken up in dustbin shelters with frozen urine on me too many times. I'd walked round picking up bottles of beer left behind by Friday-night drinkers and discovered, too late, that one of the bottles didn't contain beer but piss. I even tipped a copper off once, telling him where some guys had their heroin stashed, but only because he promised he'd give me half of what he confiscated when he nicked them.

I hated the world. No one cared what happened to me. I had visions of my own funeral. Even though I wanted to be burned, the vision was always of me being lowered into a grave and all these people swooning over me – like that was going to happen. It's so sad that I still entertained this when the reality was I wouldn't have made it into a pauper's grave.

In my desperation I even scammed Roy and Alice. They'd found out about this clinic in Switzerland where the doctors took out your blood, washed it and supposedly helped you get clean of the heroin addiction that way. Alice and Roy were going to pay for me to fly over there, but I manipulated the situation. I told them I'd found a place that did this for five thousand, a bargain, but the place had to have the fee in advance, in cash. I was to take the train from Waterloo and blah-de-blah . . . I promise to go, and if you really love me you'll do this for me . . . I got on the train, got off at Guildford, which was the first stop, and spent that five thousand as fast as I could. I had gone too far, even with my own family. I went back with my tail between my legs and said my sorries, but it was too late.

The real world – the world of salaries, and kids, and

time off when you were sick – was further away from me than ever. One of the last times I went out with the Old Boy was when we went up to north Finchley, near the arcade, looking for something to do. We were driving along when he looked out of the window at a bloke in the car next to us and said, 'Mug.' I looked out of my window at a bloke walking past, briefcase in hand, hurrying towards the office, and went, 'Mug.' Then we both looked at the people scurrying about and said, simultaneously, 'Mugs.' But here was the thing: we'd had to borrow a fiver off someone to get enough petrol in the car to get up there to find someone to rob in the first place, while they had houses, jobs, families, holidays and weekends. So who were the mugs?

Ten

The End – or Was It?

The relationships I had – with the Old Boy, One-Thumb Norman, even Pickles and Golly – lasted over some years, but we weren't a team of any description. We just used to enjoy each other's company or take the same sort of drugs and stuff.

Pickles and Golly were from Hoxton. They were not friends in the sense that you could count on them or trust them, and probably not one person on this planet liked them, except for me. I thought they were all right. We evolved in sort of the same way, because I'd known them since we were all kids together. The relationship I had with them settled into some kind of routine: we'd go out and do business, the three of us, for a couple of weeks, part when the novelty of the situation wore off, then meet up again three or four months later. The Currys jobs we did were our chief earners.

We'd meet up at a particular pub, all us crooks, where everyone we knew was a crook, and we'd pass on what we'd learned. Like the old Rolls Royce scam. You used to be able to put your fingers under the rim of the boot, knee the number plate, and open the boot, though this only worked on some models. You could do the same sort of trick with some Transit vans: hit them under the lock, on the back, and the lock would pop out, and you could open it up. People would pass this sort of information on. When central locking first came out – one of us learned this, I suppose either from hearing it from someone else or just by giving it a go, and after a while told the others – all you needed to open a centrally locked car in those days was half a tennis ball. You put it over one of the locks where you would normally put the key, whack it in hard, and the locks would all pop up, forced up by the air. You can't do it now.

My mate Terry also told me about the Cruncher, said he'd get me one made up but I mustn't tell anyone about it. A Cruncher was a tool that could open any car. There was a locksmith in south London who made up Terry's Cruncher, and he made one for me too. All it was was a big thick Allen key ground down to a regulation key shape, but a certain shape; you put it in the lock and went crunch, and it just did the job. I earned fortunes with my Cruncher. I'd go over to Hampstead, wait till I saw a few cars parked up when the owners went out dog walking or playing tennis, and then go round, open the boots up and take whatever gear they'd left behind. With my Cruncher, I was quite popular as someone to take out for an afternoon's robbing. Loads of people asked me to get them one, but I told them I couldn't. I didn't even know the name of the man who'd made mine.

You'd learn these things because that was the life we lived, the places we knew, even the women we associated with. Everyone was criminal. I didn't know any straight people. Who was straight, then, anyway? In the criminal world, no one's straight. The people who bought the things you'd stolen, they weren't straight; nor were their customers. In the drugs world it was the same. The people who bought drugs off you, they weren't straight, though they might appear to be, with proper jobs and all that.

I never envied anyone for being straight, I enjoyed my drugs too much for that; but at the same time I did wish that I could give them up and be clean. Funny, isn't it? The thing that was killing me was the thing I enjoyed most in life. The thing I most craved, every minute of every fucking day, was the thing I most wanted to be able to put down and walk away from. I did try, God knows I tried.

I was conscious even in the early days of the feeling that maybe, just maybe, I should stop taking heroin. At the age of twenty-one I had a go at stopping that got me nowhere. Over the following years I'd made sporadic efforts at giving up, but always – without fail – I'd be back on it within hours, never mind days. Prison, in terms of my drug taking, was like some kind of rest. Leading a chaotic, lunatic lifestyle, I'd burn out, and if I presented as a chaotic lunatic at a prison I'd get a rest, mostly because in prison I'd smoke rather than inject heroin. Necessity, you see, the law of supply and demand: syringes and the like couldn't be supplied no matter how much I fucking demanded them. So it was back to the Kit-Kats and the tin foil. Vein rejuvenation, I called it. Outside, I used to slaughter my veins. They became so hard to find that eventually – and this always makes people squeamish – I'd inject the drugs into my neck.

People I knew either died or got cleaned up. I used to have a doctor who tried to get me to give up. Victoria was her name; she really put some time into me. In an effort to help me she'd write me these outrageous methadone prescriptions. I'd pretend I'd lost them and she'd write some more, so I always had plenty of methadone, even if I couldn't get the heroin. She only did it to try to get me to quit; and she was always look-ing for a treatment centre for me. It was she who managed to get the funding for me to go to a place called Clouds, down in the country. I agreed to go when she first put it to me but I couldn't afford it, and no one would lend me the money because they knew what I'd do with it if they gave it to me. So when she called me into the surgery to say that she'd managed to get local-authority funding for me, well, that was a real breakthrough.

I'd been prepared to try a rehab place since my mate Buzzer had gone into one for treatment; he'd come out straight and never looked back. Buzzer was always badgering me to go in and get sorted. It was he who took me to my first Narcotics Anonymous (the junkie's version of Alcoholics Anonymous) meeting.

The two of us had been attacked by some policemen and we were going to court about it. One December evening in 1987 he came round to get me to sign some legal papers, and said, 'Come on, I'll take you to a meeting.' He was due to pick me up at seven p.m. to go to this meeting, so I injected a quarter gram of heroin and sat waiting for him. What a shock I had when he arrived. He looked well, fit and healthy, not out of his head on drugs, but most of all he smelled clean. I'd forgotten what that was like.

We went to this meeting at St Leonard's – NA meet-ings are held wherever they can be, often in church halls as they are available and cheap – and this is where my long journey really began, though of course I didn't know that then. As far as I was concerned, the meeting was a load of crap. I only managed to stay the course because I went up to the toilets halfway through and injected myself with heroin. The meeting kicked off with some readings, then some geezer told us his story. There was a lot of talk about God and 'a higher power', none of which I knew anything about, or wanted to know anything about, then it ended with the 'serenity prayer'. At that first meeting there were all these prize guys, and they were giving it large, putting cash ostentatiously into the pot (we all had to make a contribution to pay for the rent of the room and the tea and biscuits), but although they'd stopped drinking and taking drugs they hadn't quite got it right yet as they were still robbing banks. I had a tenner on me, two five-pound notes, and I was saving that money for a £10 joey later, but when all these chaps were throwing in their money it came to my turn and I had to be accepted by this group and so I had to put something in. So in went a fiver. I resented having to do that so much.

To be honest, I really thought that Buzzer had taken me to the Salvation Army. I sat there and thought, 'What on earth's all this about?' I went back to Carol's after and goofed about on the sofa; Buzzer had gone home as he had to get up early next day to return to the treatment centre.

'What was this meeting all about?' my aunt asked me.

'Who knows? Right lot of old bollocks if you ask me,' was my reply.

I suppose that somewhere in the depths of my mind I

had heard that there was another way, a life without drink, drugs and crime. The trouble was, I never had the faintest idea how to find it or where to look for it. But at that meeting, despite my attitude, the seed was planted. Things were never the same again.

A week later I was back at Carol's, having a shave and cleaning myself up a bit, and she said, 'Where are you off to then?'

'I'm going to that meeting I went to last week.'

She looked puzzled. 'I thought you said it was a load of old bollocks?'

'It was,' I said, 'but I've just got to go again to make sure.'

And that was how it started, for me. Even in my maddest moments I went to meetings. I'd go in off my nut, I wouldn't know nothing about nothing, I'd fall asleep and people would wake me up, and off I'd trundle into the sunset. So God knows just how many of these meetings I went to. Often as not I'd go off and shoot up in the toilet, and most times I'd arrive stinking of booze as more than likely I would have been pouring cans of strong lager down my throat all day. Still, something made me go, though I can't explain it. I used to kid myself it was for the cup of tea and biscuit, but that wouldn't have been enough in the madness. It was the only place I never stole anything from. The pot would go round, all the people there would put some money in, and in any other circumstances I'd have

nicked it, but I never stole anything from those meetings. Never realized that till just now.

Like they say in the fellowship, 'If nothing changes
then nothing changes,' so I still went out committing
crime after crime and buying bag after bag of heroin,
and I continued to sit on park benches with all the other
addicts and drunks and down-and-outs, drinking can
after can of super-duper gut-rot lager. One of the
reasons I went to the meetings was because I missed my
friends. I wanted to stay in touch with them, but
I also wanted to know, a little, how it was they could
come off the drugs.

I saw a lot of Buzzer around that time. It had become
fashionable among a lot of the people I knew to clean
up, and some of those I was closest to – Buzzer,
Clifford, people like that – had gone away and come
back different, spiritual, which I didn't understand but
thought seemed quite nice. Even though I carried on living the way I'd always done, they never blanked me. I
remember one day walking down the road in Hoxton,
East Road, near St John's Church, and a car pulled up
and Buzzer and Clifford were in it. I was limping
because I'd been missing the veins when shooting up
while pissed and my leg was all swollen. They gave me
a right lecture – you're going to die and all that. And I
went, 'No, I'm all right.' But I wasn't.

Clifford in particular had been almost as bad as me.
Once, Buzzer, Clifford and I were at Norman's – black

Norman, that is, not One-Thumb Norman. I'd stolen two suitcases full of little glass 30ml ampoules of diamorphine hydrochloride; this geezer in south London was trying to sell them and I'd just nicked them off him. We were injecting them, three of these ampoules at a time into our works, and I can picture black Clifford ... nice as you like, but he's got a sausage on him, that boy, and I'll never forget that moment in time when I looked across and he had his sausage in his hand and he was trying to inject into it because he couldn't get a vein anywhere else, and he had tears rolling down his cheeks. I'll never forget that. We were supposed to be chaps, but we really weren't. It was all an illusion, all a front.

That afternoon I went out to sell a chequebook and card I'd also taken from this geezer and I got nicked, in Dalston. I went to the snooker hall to sell it to black Leroy, and all of a sudden it got raided and I was standing there with the chequebook and card in my hand. Marvellous.

Buzzer and Clifford are both still clean today, twenty years on. Miracle.

Probably the best place for someone like me at that time was that treatment centre out in the country called Clouds, and thanks to my GP, Victoria, I got the chance to go. I hitched down there. I'd been given money for the trip, but they made the mistake of giving me the train fare the week before so of course I went right out and spent it.

I'd been told to get there early, but when I arrived it turned out I was half a day early – Sunday evening instead of Monday morning. They told me, 'We don't want you here tonight, come back tomorrow morning.' I said, 'I've just hitched down, I'm here now, I've got nowhere to go, so, see those bushes over there? That's where you'll find me in the morning. When you're ready for me, wake me up and tell me it's Monday morning.' So they found somewhere for me to sleep indoors. I suppose all the dormitory spaces had been filled. When you're an alcoholic and you're detoxing, you've got to be in a dormitory room, because you can start to fit. You need some people around to help out if you go that way.

I soon found out I was the only one there on funding; everyone else was paying for their treatment. It wasn't cheap, so I bore in mind what my doctor had told me before I went – 'You'd better do this, and do it properly, blah blah blah.' I just can't think how I didn't take that chance. I mean, the place was beautiful. I'd never been anywhere like it before. It also seemed other-worldly to me. Things happened there that could never have happened back where I came from. One morning, for instance, we were sitting on the veranda, there was a mist all round the grounds, and this great big stag came out of the woods, stood there as if to say 'Yeah, who wants a bit?' then trotted back off into the mist. It was lovely.

As I'd not paid to be in there I did get some grief from

one or two pricks. One bloke called me a guttersnipe, so I tricked him into coming outside with me, got him into the shrubbery, gave him a right-hander and told him to stop treating me badly. He started blubbing and offered me his Rolex. I told him to keep it; if I wanted a Rolex, I'd go out and buy myself a Rolex.

Most of the other people were OK, and I got on well with them. There was a woman in there we called Mother Badger, and me and a few others were the Badger gang. I was the last one in so I was Baby Badger. We used to play tricks on people. There was a magistrate in there, Albert, a raging alcoholic, and they put him in our group. The day after he came was the day they dished out TDs, 'Therapeutic Duties', and when you're new they don't give you one. So everyone was standing in this big room while the list was read out, and Albert piped up, 'I say, I say, you haven't mentioned me. What do I have to do?'

'Nothing, Albert,' I told him, 'you'll not be doing anything till later on. I'll tell you later on.'

That evening I told him he was on badger watch through the night. There was a hand-bell for ringing for group time and meal times, and I said to Albert, 'You've got to sit out on the veranda looking over the croquet lawn, and you have to get up every hour to check, and if any badgers appear you have to ring that bell, loud and long, and go round waking everyone up, shouting, "Badger, badger!" OK?'

'Yes, yes, got it,' he said.

Now coming off the booze is no mean feat – you're hallucinating and all that. So at quarter to four in the morning I got a black bin-liner, wrapped some white paper round it, went out on to the croquet lawn and stuffed it under a croquet hoop. At four o'clock in the morning everyone was woken up by Albert the magistrate running manically round the building, ringing this bell and yelling, 'Badger! Badger!' Clang clang. 'Badger! Badger!'

I was in hysterics, but I did get in big trouble.

Then I got into an improper relationship with a French girl called Valerie and was asked to leave Clouds. I went to catch my train back to London, and needed to buy some cigarettes. I went into the café on the station platform and in one sentence undid all the good work of the last few days: I went to ask for two packets of tabs but instead said, 'Two tins of Tennants, please.' I thought for one second about saying, 'No, sorry, I didn't mean that,' and handing the cans of lager back, but my inner prick said to me, 'You can handle it, it's only two tins, come on, show the beer who's boss.' I drank them both, spent the train journey back to London propping up the bar drinking everything they had, and by the time I fell out at the other end I was well back on the piss again.

I went on to get more treatment at other centres, such as Barley Wood and the Brighton Housing Trust, because I was desperately looking for a bit of help. And I was already desperate, even though it hadn't got that bad yet – not as bad as at the end anyway. I never thought it was that bad, but that's the trick addiction plays on you: it always lets you think you control it, not that it controls you. Now that I know about recovery and addiction, I'm wise to every trick this disease plays. As I said, it's the only disease that makes you think you're OK when in fact you're fucked.

In all these places I went to, I didn't do rehab properly, but that's because I couldn't quite understand what it was I was supposed to be doing. I didn't trust the simplicity of the process. I went to all these treatments, all these NA meetings and all that, but I never realized that I literally had to stop. I thought someone else would do that bit for me.

But every time I went to a treatment centre, I learned a little bit more about what I was supposed to be doing to get myself straight. I call it my metaphoric toolbox. This is how I describe it to people now, how I explain what it was like for me during those years, even though I wouldn't have known what I was talking about then. When I left Clouds, I picked up a saw and a hammer, and for the next few years I stumbled around trying to undo screws with this saw and hammer. It didn't work, and I didn't know why. I went to Barley Wood in Bristol, same thing happened: twelve-step programme, again I left prematurely, after two to three weeks, and on the way out the toolbox was flipped open and this time I picked up a drill and a T-square. Still couldn't undo those screws. The pattern repeated itself in Brighton. I was asked to leave again with yet more tools in my hands that I couldn't (wouldn't) use.

Eventually I had all the tools, but I just didn't know what to do with them because I hadn't really studied what they were for. I hadn't paid attention, I never really listened. It wasn't until I reached the very end, when I knew I could go no further – when it was literally either turn back or die – that I suddenly realized that all these tools I had were the things that were going to make it OK for me; all I had to do was work out how to use them properly. That's when things became serious.

I attended Alcoholics Anonymous meetings as well as NA ones. My first was in Bournemouth, which used to be called Recovery City. It was known for being a quiet place, and maybe that's why it worked. I was taken by a man I called Pete the Guru. He's been thirty years clean, even longer. I knew him as the Guru because he was so switched on.

I had had some kind of crisis again – there were so many I can't really pinpoint anything – which made me think I really had to do something about it, that I had to turn to someone who could help me. At this stage, as I said, I didn't know how to go about this for myself, but I did know that the meetings I'd been going to in the past were the best thing for me, so I turned to those organizations for help. I phoned someone and was put in touch with Pete the Guru. I said to him, 'I really need to try coming off the drugs again,' and he asked me where I was. I explained that I was in London.

'Do you know the King's Road?' he asked.

'Yeah, of course,' I replied.

'Well, there's a Cocaine Anonymous meeting starting up, it's the first meeting, the first one of its kind. If you get there I'll meet you there, then take you to Bournemouth.'

So I trundled off to this meeting. He turned up with this geezer Alan, and afterwards he took me back to Bournemouth and stuck me in a hotel. We went out to the pub once I'd put my stuff in the room. After watching me drink, Pete said, 'You know, Peter, perhaps you need to go to AA as well. Come to this meeting tomorrow night.' He then explained what would happen when we got there.

Now clearly, one special thing about Narcotics Anonymous, and Alcoholics Anonymous, is the anonymous part. I've chosen to talk about my experiences so I've blown my anonymity, but I respect the right of others who go through NA and AA not to do that. At all AA meetings, the position of chair is not fixed; someone is asked to take it, and someone always does. It's how it's done. That night it was an old boy. He was Canadian, he was on holiday, and he'd just come to a meeting. He was seventy years old and – I'll never forget this – thirty-three years sober. The meeting began as they all do, then the chair told us his name, told us he was an alcoholic, that he was really grateful to be here, and then, 'I'd like to share my experience with everyone.'

I looked over at this old boy and thought to myself, 'Him? What on earth am I going to have in common with him? How's he going to help me?' But he stood there and basically told me my life story. My criminal behaviour, my family, my drinking, everything, everything, everything. And the bits that didn't fit into my life then have since come true. I thought, 'Wow!' It didn't transform me overnight, but it certainly laid the foundations. That old boy's story showed that it wasn't kosher by that time for me to be a drug-addicted-alcoholic lunatic, but I still didn't realize I was bang in trouble. He talked about desolation, about being destitute. I didn't recognize that yet, but it happened to me, it came true. I look back in awe at that man. I'll always remember him.

Part of my problem was that I knew I was a drug addict, and that the drugs were killing me, but I didn't think I was an alcoholic. I thought I just liked a drink, like everyone else. So when all these people said, 'My name's blah-de-blah and I'm an alcoholic,' it meant nothing to me. This was the first time I had an inkling that this might – just might – be a problem for me. And like all the other problems I had, it was one I didn't confront, but it sat there and worked away at the back of my brain, letting me know it was there.

I hadn't yet had the kick in the guts I needed – that came later. But that kick in the guts ignited all these images that had been in my brain all those years, like those clichés hung up on posters around rooms: 'Keep It Simple' was one; another was 'Think Think Think', turned upside down. I remember saying to the Guru in a meeting, 'Why do they always put that "Think Think Think" upside down?' and he said, 'Why do you think?' and I went, 'Eh? Oh. Ahhh.'

It's all about acceptance. This recovery lark, it isn't rocket science, but you need someone to guide you, and some people need explanation. I needed both. This is a downpipe, this leads to a soakaway. And I'd say, 'How? Show me the principle, then I can relate to it.' Because I hadn't yet had it explained to me exactly what it was I needed to understand, every time I was shown the path I had to follow I stepped off it and went my own merry way. So I'd come out of rehab centres or meetings and head straight off to score or get a drink. I used to fall asleep in meetings; it was the only place I felt comfortable enough to fall asleep.

As the number of meetings I attended went up and up, while I came and went without them appearing to have any effect upon me, some of my clean friends got fed up and gave up on me. You can only tell someone so many times to stop using. I wanted to start doing the right thing, and I wanted my friends, because I was lonely, but soon I had no one left to talk to. Everyone dropped me, one by one. No one liked me; I never liked no one. I had nothing to give but I wanted to take everything. My need to be loved was immense. I longed for a special friend but I had none, I wanted respect but had none for anything or anyone. I wanted to die. Suicide looked quite attractive.

I did try it – killing myself, I mean. I thought that if I took a really big hit, if I OD'd, then no one would miss me and all my problems would be over. Trouble was, I had a go – took a massive dose a couple of times – but woke up some time afterwards thinking to myself, 'Wow, that was fantastic, what a trip.' I'm the only person I know who enjoyed trying to kill himself. You see, here was my problem: I had got to the point where I didn't care if I lived or I died. It made no difference to me because I couldn't see that it made any difference to anyone else. So taking a massive amount of heroin and surviving it wasn't a proper attempt at suicide, nor was it a cry for help; it was just another sign of the power the drug had over me. Heroin could do what it wanted with me. I would have done anything – I *did* do anything – for heroin. I was both the lover and the slave of the drug, and it never, ever loved me back.

This lack of control is something that is addressed in NA and AA. As part of the process you have to admit you are powerless over your addiction, your predicament, and that life has become unmanageable. When I was first confronted with this, they were only words; they meant nothing to me. I couldn't even say 'predicament' let alone write it or discuss it. I couldn't say 'powerlessness' either. No matter how well read I was, when I got to this point I realized I didn't know the words at all. No wonder it took me so long to understand it at all. And then you're told you have to surrender and admit your defeat, and no human being wants to do that. Keep It Simple. Once it was simplified, it all made sense, but only because I'd worked it, read it and lived it, been with it for years.

It was years before I could stand up and say I was an alcoholic. I had no problem admitting I was an addict, but I couldn't say I was an alcoholic. I quite enjoyed being an addict – it was glamorous, it made me feel more of an outlaw, people I admired like Lou Reed and Hendrix were junkies – but there was no glamour in being an alcoholic so I didn't recognize it. Of course now I know there's no glamour in either of them. If criminality in itself is selfish, and addiction is very selfish, then alcoholism is even more selfish than that. More bad stuff happens with people who are drunk than with those who are drugged up. The majority of domestic violence is fuelled by alcohol. I think that's horrible.

After a while I started to take part in the meetings. I'd

get up and talk, because I liked talking. I'd say things like 'You're doing this all wrong'; but saying it about myself took ages. You have to be honest, and I lied for years – quite good lies, because I thought I was there to impress people, that I was there to be respected. Until I accepted that I needed the help of these people, until I accepted that this was how it was, I remained in trouble, with no way forward. I offered my opinions freely at the meetings without really bothering to listen to anyone else's, which is why the suggestion I eventually got was 'Take that cotton wool out from between your ears and stick it in your mouth for once.' (The person who said that is one of my best friends now.) And then I was given more advice by another person I actually listened to, to start looking for similarities not differences. You know, that bloke Albert in Clouds might have been a magistrate, and I might have been a crook, but we'd both been lying drunk in a gutter, pissing ourselves. There's a similarity.

All my life I'd wondered how to get respect for myself, and from all the evidence I'd ever had laid out in front of me it seemed the best way was to be the most cruel, the most violent, the most intimidating person alive. Now, for the first time in my life, I began to see that there might be another way.

I was trying, but I still felt I could run the show, that I could do parts of the twelve-step programme but not all of it, only the bits I wanted to do. Drink and drugs were the things I thought were the solution for my problems – the abuse I'd suffered, the rape, the loneliness. I told myself that's why I took the drugs and the drink. But the truth was that those problems were still there for me when I went clean. Nothing was solved by being smothered under an ocean of booze and heroin, and that was a tough one for me to realize.

One of the problems I had with going to meetings and trying to quit was that it all seemed to take so long; worse still, you'd start to get help from someone and then they'd say, 'Good, that's going well, see you Monday, then.' It drove me mad, because addiction doesn't take a day off. I used to look forward to going to a meeting, but there was nothing at the weekends to help someone like me, someone who was still stuck with the disease of More, More, More.

And my life at this time was one of chaotic desperation. I'd stumble out of bed, look for something to make some money from so that I could get some drugs and get through the day, and maybe at some point get myself to a meeting. Gone was Peter the clever bastard con artist; the days of me walking into an office to nick things – once, I even got the office manager to help me load up the computers I was nicking from him – were all over. I no longer looked the part, I was too obviously an addict.

I could still be nice to people on the streets, though, that still worked, and because people in general are so naive that they tend to trust easily it wasn't too hard for me to be successful. Like the time one hot summer's day I was scouting about along Marylebone Road, looking for a way to make some decent cash, and I walked past Madame Tussaud's and saw a good-looking dark-haired girl. As we approached each other our eyes met and we smiled.

'Hello,' I said. 'Off to see the waxworks, are you?'

'No,' she replied, in an accent that turned out to be German.

We started talking and I found out she was a law student who really wanted to visit the Old Bailey to see it in action. I offered to be her guide, although I neglected to mention that I knew more than was good for me about Her Majesty's courts.

When we got to the Bailey we made to go through the entrance to the public gallery but the security geezer stopped us, pointing at the things hanging off this girl's shoulders.

'Sorry, no bags or cameras,' he said.

She looked dismayed, so I said to her, 'No problem, give me your stuff and I'll wait here while you go and have a look.'

Thanking me, she handed over her bag and camera and set off to the public gallery.

After a few moments I said to the security bloke, who I'd been chatting with so as to seem as natural as possible, 'Listen, mate, tell my girlfriend that I'm over at the restaurant on the corner opposite waiting for her,' and I walked off with my day's money.

I sank further and further. One time I bought a load of crack, and to smoke it I needed cigarette ash (the crack liquefies when it's heated up and I, like most crack smokers, put a bit of ash into the pipe to hold the liquid to prevent it running down into the pipe when I was smoking it). I had quite a lot of crack that night and I wanted to smoke it all, so I collected the dog-ends from around the flat to put in my pipe to smoke, clearing all the ashtrays of dirt. Only that wasn't nearly enough, so I went outside the flat, into the stairwells, picking up the dog-ends to stuff into my pipe. Still there wasn't enough; I had a big parcel of crack cocaine to get through. I was completely manic by this stage. I went out into the street and swept up dog-ends – I lived on the cleanest street in Islington that night – and then, because that still wasn't enough, I broke into the cars parked on the street and stole their ashtrays. Nothing else, mind, no matter what was lying around, just the ashtrays. I must have smashed the windows of about twenty cars in all. That's what addiction does to you. Madness.

Going mad meant I lost that flat, probably others after it – I can't remember, really. I do know I tried to go back home, only my own mother refused to come to the door. That night, and for quite a few after it, I ended up living in a car. I don't know whose car it was, but it was near the Angel, parked up opposite the Lord Wollesley pub on White Lion Street. I kept all my stuff in it and slept there at night. Oh, it was cold. I went into the Alcohol Recovery Project on City Road for a cup of tea and to read a paper, and I'd go to Carol's house for a wash and to get some clean clothes. I didn't need to wash much in those days: I always had short hair, I don't grow a beard, and as long as my face and hands were clean I thought I looked OK, so I could leave it a while before doing anything about it. In the mornings I'd change my socks. I'd chuck the ones from the day before on the back seat and rummage around for a pair that weren't as smelly, the ones you could bang on a table because they were so crusty and dirty. The pair I put on were as bad, but they'd had time to air out, so they were good enough to me. But what I was really trying to do during the day was get into a treatment centre because I knew I was dying. I'd recently had pneumonia, and I couldn't live out on the street.

One afternoon I came back from the ARP and saw that the car was being towed away. Now this to me was my house, all my possessions were in there. Now they were gone, just like that. Everything I owned. I stood in that street and cried. It just couldn't get any worse, I thought. It was the most devastating moment of my life.

My madness deepened, and I started seeing things. I

once saw an albino baby orang-utan. I was living in Victoria for a while, in the flat of a prostitute called Mara. She was killed a few months later by her lover. I suppose he was jealous of seeing her with other men, but he didn't need to worry about me as I didn't want to sleep with her; her flat was just a place I used to go to take drugs. I went to her place on the number 38 bus, and one day I found cocaine on the seat. I was bad by this stage, not too far from the end, and I was hallucinating. When I got to her place I took all that cocaine in one go. I never really liked the stuff so it hit me hard, and that's when I saw the animal in the corner of the room. It didn't bother me or anything – I knew it was a hallucination – but it was there.

Later that week Paula came over and was smoking with Mara when I walked in and took their drugs – when I saw something I liked, it was mine. I smoked them all in one go. I must have looked a sight as I was naked and covered in blood: I'd had trouble finding a vein so the blood from all my mistakes was trickling down all over me.

I left a little for the morning, and when I woke up I decided to go to Bournemouth. I didn't know where else to go. I had to find someone who could help me, and I thought I could make a go of it there. So off I went, although the Old Boy told me not to go. He said that there was only one road in and out of town, and that's a bad thing because if they want to get you they know exactly where you're going to go – and sure enough I was nicked three days after I arrived, for burglary. (I used to wander down the backs of the houses, where they had long gardens. I'd chuck stones over and see if anyone came out to investigate. If there was no one in, I'd break in.) I was found to be wanted in Brighton and Chelsea too, so the judge in Dorchester Crown Court called me 'the AwayDay Burglar'. The screws called me the InterCity Burglar. When they passed me on the landing they'd make train noises as they walked past – *bee-bah*. Hilarious.

They brought the other cases down from London, I got four and a half years, and as soon as I got into prison I went through a detox and managed to stay clean for the rest of my sentence. But this was a bad thing, because it meant I was deemed something of a prison success and they put me out on parole when I didn't want to go. I was sent back to Bournemouth and put by my probation officer into a hostel.

I managed only a few weeks, that was all. I didn't want to go out, I knew I wasn't ready, but out I was sent. I didn't talk to anyone, didn't let them know how I felt. I was lonely, sad, scared, unhappy, but me being me I couldn't admit to it. I'd go to my meetings and say 'Fine' if anyone asked how I was. I phoned a mate, Chris. He asked, 'How are you?' I'd only been out a couple of days, and I told him, 'Chris, mate, life's never been so good. I'm in the gym every night, down on the sea front, going to me meetings. Life's never been so great.' I was in a phone box at the end of the road. I came out of that box, walked back to the hostel and up to my room, sat down on my bed and cried, because I was so unhappy. I couldn't admit to him that I was like this, because I couldn't say that to anyone.

There was one person I wanted to talk to, a bird who'd been watching me training in the gym, but I didn't know how to say hello to her. I was walking along the sea front one afternoon and saw her walking towards me. I could tell from the body language – she was slowing down, her pace matching mine, that kind of thing – that she was going to say hello to me. I wanted to say hello badly but I didn't have any money to say, 'Do you want to come and have a cup of tea?', and because I couldn't do that I couldn't speak to her at all. I looked away, so she went past me.

After about three months in the hostel I did end up meeting a bird. My bail conditions were ambiguous – 'You must reside at blah-de-blah in this road and report to your parole officer, blah-de-blah' – and one night I met this girl who took me home with her (I didn't do anything, because I'd never done the dirty deed straight). The following morning I returned to the hostel only to find a little welcoming committee. My probation officer had been there and found me absent, so I was in big trouble.

'Your licence says you have to be here every night,' I was told.

'Oh, no, it doesn't,' I pointed out, 'it simply says I have to reside here.'

I went to look for my probation officer but she wouldn't even listen to me. She told me straight away that she'd revoked me, and that I would be taken back to prison. 'You hang on here and I'll phone the police,' she added.

'Fuck off,' I replied.

I walked out of that hostel, went back up to London, and that was it – I was immediately back at it. I stole something, sold it, went for a drink – just the one, of course – gave someone some money to go and find Paula, she turned up, we had a drink, and I told her I was clean.

'Nice one,' she said.

'Have another?' I said. 'Shall we have a rock? Only one, mind. And a bit of brown just to come down with?'

Even though she was still using she tried to stop me, but then, 'Oh, go on, one won't hurt.' And a couple of months and loads of money later . . .

We just didn't move for all that time. We'd lie about and take drugs. Not only did we get our food delivered, we also got the drugs sent in. When the money finally came to an end, I walked out and went back to the craziness.

That's when I ended up at that flat over in east London, the one Phil and Sophie lived in. The place may have been disgusting, but it was safe, and I trusted Sophie and Phil. I relied on them. We had this un-written pact that we'd help one another ... but my deterioration was too rapid. The theory is that when you start using again you pick up from where you last left off; well, I'd burned all my bridges, so I was a lost cause. I tried overdosing again, but just as before I woke up four hours later and thought, 'Phwoar, that was a nice one,' double pleased that my number wasn't up. This fatalism was in me all the time now. Because I'd left Bournemouth rather than go back to prison simply because I'd stayed out for one night, I knew I was going back to jail – if, that is, they got me in time.

So there I was, living in shit, smoking, drinking and injecting, stealing and lying. I told so many lies, I ended up believing them myself. Like me and the Gambia. When I was younger I used to end up on a landing with all the prize guys in the jail. We'd sit about playing cards and they'd all swap stories about 'when I was in Marbella', that kind of thing. One day I came across a newspaper carrying a piece about the Gambia. It looked like a nice place so I got hold of books and read all about it so that I could tell people, 'Yeah, when I was in the Gambia ...' But as I said, the fucking strange thing was I wound up believing it. First time I met my wife Louise I was telling her the story when halfway through I paused and said, 'I'm lying to you. I ain't never been there in my life.' For probably twenty years I'd been telling that story, about being on holiday and swimming across the river to Senegal. I needed to be accepted, I couldn't be a second-class citizen, so I'd tell lies like this, hoping to seem – to feel – the same as everyone else. That was me, always wanting to take shortcuts to get somewhere. Recognizing that what I'd said was a lie, and telling Louise this, was a real break-through for me.

Every day living with Phil and Sophie was a struggle, waiting to die or to get caught and be sent back to prison, and every day was the same. Until the time I pushed my way into a house on Canonbury Square and had a fight with a man I'd come to know was called Will.

Eleven

Conference and Confidence

After breaking into Will's in 2002 I was taken to Pentonville for breaking my parole conditions in Bournemouth, and I was held there while awaiting sentencing. There was no one left to support me any more, now that I was going back to jail. I needed money to get by, to pay for tobacco and things, and I had to think about where that was going to come from. I'd burned all my bridges with my family, so I knew there was no chance I was going to manipulate them to get them up on visits, and I had no friends, so I was going to have to survive on what the prison gave me, and that was about £2.50 a week. I needed to make some fucking drastic decisions. Not buying drugs and booze would be the best start, so I went on a detoxification programme.

Nowadays there's little or no help with anything like

that. You go in with a habit, you come out with a habit; they've just maintained it for you. When I went into jail, the usual form was that I went to see the doctor and said, 'I've got a habit, can you give me a bit of juice?' He'd tell me to report sick in the morning, saying there was nothing he could do for me now, so if I was clucking when I arrived I had to wait until the following day. Come morning, I'd go on the sicklist and tell the doc loads of lies about using this-that-this-that, because I'd want as much as possible from him. And he would give me methadone.

Whenever I went back to jail I never used to think I'd detox. You always think you want to stop, but you never do anything about it, because you're always too scared. This might sound strange, but it's what you've done all your life. I took stock of my life. I'd had kidney problems, liver problems, pneumonia, and some of the muscles around my heart were poisoned. This was a consequence not just of the drugs I'd taken but also of not looking after myself properly, like that time I discharged myself from hospital because they wouldn't give me enough methadone. It was time I started to look after myself, and this time when I went into Pentonville, when my licence was revoked, I knew as soon as I got in there that I was going to detox.

At first I went through all the usual bollocks, but it was nothing more than a little bit of bravado in front of the chaps. I was, in truth, mightily relieved to be in there. I finished the detox programme a little prematurely, because I was just knocking back the medicine. I was near the end so I just knocked it back. It usually takes two weeks, but I completed it in ten days. I wanted to go on to the drug-free wing, although there's no such thing in prison; the proper name for it should be the not-quite-as-many-drugs wing. It was just a little easier to stop on that wing, that's all. I'd made my mind up. Once I'd accepted I couldn't go on any more, it was easy to stop.

There was a screw in the Ville and me and him had had fights in the past, proper fights. When I was a lot younger I went to the chapel in Pentonville to pick some drugs up which had been hidden there for me, only I got caught, and got the life beaten out of me by the prison officers. Handcuffs behind my back, booted all around the place. This man was one of the screws who attacked me that day, right in front of the vicar.

He came to my cell one morning when I'd just finished my detox, opened the door, saw the state of me and said, 'Fuck me, how are you?'

'I'm fucked,' I said. 'I can't do this no more.'

'What?'

'I'm fucked, I can't do this no more,' I repeated. I had tears coming down my face.

He said, 'What do you want?'

'I want to go up on the drug-free wing.'

'Pack your kit, I'll go and sort it now.'

And he did. Me and him, we didn't see eye to eye, never had, but on this particular day he must have looked into my eyes and just known – much like Will when Will looked into my eyes – that I had reached the end point and could go no further.

I felt old in prison this time round. I felt that my time was passing and that I no longer had the right to expect help from other inmates. I couldn't bribe anyone to help me as I had no money, and I couldn't strong-arm them into helping me out because I was no longer as fit as I used to be. Most importantly, I no longer had the will to intimidate people into helping me. This change was nothing to do with the fact that I hadn't managed to get away from Will, because I could have got away from him, but to have done so would have meant doing something quite drastic, and I just wasn't prepared to do that any more. I could have grabbed a knife in Will's kitchen, but I didn't. Probably when I was younger I would have, but not any more. I'd hit people with iron bars before, shot people with crossbows, done all sorts to people, but those times were all in my past. I had reached the point where I couldn't do it any more.

The same thing happened to so many people I knew who'd been regulars in jail, who'd been in and out all their lives: all of a sudden you're the old lag, you're the geezer who's been going there for years; you turn up to a reception, and the screws call you by your first name. 'Hello, Peter, ain't seen you in a while, how you been?'

I didn't realize how frightening it was when that started happening to me, at least not at first. I was part of the furniture. I'd become a professional prisoner.

I decided to live, to stop being an alcoholic and a drug addict and get my health back, but beyond that I had no ambitions and no idea. I was prepared to live in jail; if they'd said they'd keep me in jail for the rest of my life, at that point that would have done me fine. I was perfectly happy with being the geezer who runs up and down the stairs with a cup of tea for the screws, odd chores like that. If they'd sent me to a nice little prison miles away and given me life, I wouldn't have given two fucks, because that would have been all right. If the judge had said, 'Right, you're going to prison and you're never coming out,' I'd have said, 'Righty-o, judge, thank you.' And I could have made that happen, easily, by knifing Will, but I didn't. Self-preservation kicked in. There was no time for weighing up the pros and cons; the cognitive process was so rapid it was instantaneous, and the decision was made. I was in Will's house for ages, longer than I'd ever been anywhere, and I think my subconscious brain was saying, 'Stay here and get nicked, cos it's your last chance.'

I was always comfortable in prison; it was home to me. Over the total of eighteen years I spent inside I adapted to prison living, so much so that when I first started living on the outside I even walked differently from the people around me, shuffling along while they strode. Prison shaped me in other ways, too. In the old days, this would have been a good thing, in the days when inmates were taught a trade. The system had the right idea then: they would get the scallywags off the street, lock them up in a nick and teach them something practical, something they could use to earn an honest living once they were released. Somewhere along the line, though, the powers-that-be lost their way. Nowadays people leave prison with as much hope as when they came in – none. Prison routine, a numbing day-to-day routine, became all I knew and all I wished for. I was fast becoming the thing I used to laugh at when I was younger, and which I'd fleetingly wanted to be: the shambling, aimless figure who lived in prison because it was a safer place to be.

I can remember my first time on heroin so well, but I can't remember my last. My last didn't strike me as that because I never knew it would be my last fix, so I don't have any memories of 'giving up' heroin like I have for starting it. The 'giving up' took place over weeks rather than minutes.

Detoxing is a two-stage process, physical and mental. The physical part's the easy part, although uncomfortable, because the drug comes out of you in just a few days; with booze, it takes a little longer. The object is to control the physical symptoms, to stop the addict being sick and make sure he isn't clucking too severely. The most common detox method is a gradual methadone reduction. Obviously the starting amount varies from person to person depending on how much of a habit the individual had, but let's say I was using 40ml per day. The reduction would go something like this: day one, 40ml; day two, 40ml; days three and four, 35ml; day five, 30ml; day six, 25ml; day seven, 20ml; day eight, 10ml; day nine, 5ml; day ten, 2ml. There may be a need to prescribe Valium or some sort of sleeping draught for a couple of days at the end of this process, but again, this will depend on the needs of the individual, and exactly where he is, i.e. in prison or in rehab.

It's not great, but it's a lot easier than what's going on in your mind. Even if I was feeling OK with the amount of methadone physically, and those amounts let you know it was a struggle, my mind would tell me, 'It's not enough, I need more; this ain't enough, I need a bit of gear.' Addiction is insanity. It plays tricks on you and tells you things that only another addict could possibly understand. Once the detox process is complete and the clucking stops and you start to look physically well, that's when the addict part of the brain really tries to take charge, saying, 'You're looking really well, you can handle it now, you won't get a habit, you can use or booze and control it.' No matter how bad it all was in the madness, the addict in my brain would try to push it from my mind while a voice in my head chiselled away: 'Go on, go on, have some.'

I'd spend days on a rollercoaster of emotions, feeling

happy then sad, scared and confused, suddenly tearful, and any feelings I'd suppressed for however long the addiction had had me in its grip would join in. It really was a bit scary, this 'life on life's terms', and the fact that I didn't know how to handle all the emotional stuff that was going on made my fears worse. I felt inadequate because I just didn't know what to do with it all. In the past I'd have gone where it was safe, where all the emotional stuff was blotted out – that is, I'd have retreated back into addiction. But now I wasn't going to, so every day was a constant struggle. I had to be on my guard 24/7.

There were many other things that had to change, now that I had decided to get clean and stay clean; chief among them was keeping away from people. I could do my time in prison, but I couldn't be around people. What I wanted, more than anything, was to go into solitary confinement and not see people, for ever. Once I'd started the process of quitting drugs, straight away that meant people began to wander off when I walked into someone's cell; after a while I was asked to keep clear of them at certain times. If they were going to have a party and get right out of it, I wasn't welcome; me being straight made them feel uncomfortable. It was very odd, being asked to stay away from people who were doing what I'd been doing happily for years, but then, to be honest, it had started to become easier for me, that kind of thing, as I didn't want to be like that any more. I was becoming a different person, although slowly, and keeping away from the drug addicts in prison – which basically meant everyone else in there – was a step on that path.

But when I started to think about it, I realized that something wasn't quite right with me if my dream was to be locked away on my own for ever. I'd lost interest in everything. I didn't want to communicate with anyone, didn't want to do anything with anyone, all I wanted was to be left alone. But there was another part of me that was frightened by this desire for isolation, a part that knew that going that way led to one thing and one thing only: madness.

I'd done being mad in prison, and I'd done being around mad people. When I was first sent down I was a hard bastard. I'd wanted to be harder still, so I'd done brutal, crazy things. I had looked the part too, with my shaved head and little beard. I even wore sunglasses all the time. They were so much a part of my look that I even used to go to bed in them. How mad is that? And the mad people I've seen and heard in prison: someone flattening another guy's head while he was writing a letter, bashing his brains out; hearing someone scream- ing from his bed after the bloke whose nose he broke that afternoon had shoved a knife up into his heart from his hiding place under the bed.

I think I must have just grown tired of the foulness, the violence, the hatred that seeped out of the walls. For years I'd believed that this misery acted as a mirror, that what I saw reflected back at me was *from* me, that the grimness of my surroundings showed me what I thought I looked like, and so I felt it fitted right in. But as I changed and stopped taking drugs I realized that I was wrong. This was no mirror but a cloak, enveloping me, preventing me from seeing what I was really like – what the world was really like – and what was there to be changed.

I can only say these things looking back on it now, of course; I wouldn't have had a clue what you were talking about if you'd tried to discuss it with me then. I can see now that I was ready to change; I was ripe for it, in fact. I'd changed my mindset, slowly, in the long months leading up to this time in jail, and I'd started to deal with my addictions. Things were slotting into place for me, like a car on an assembly line, but I wasn't the finished article. Something needed to turn the key, to start me up, if you like. And the key turned up one day, only it was a policeman, and he was called Kim Smith.

Kim came to see me in prison. He explained that he worked on a programme that tried to restore the victim of a crime to the centre of the criminal justice system by giving him or her the chance to meet the person who'd committed the offence and then by allowing the victim and his or her family to explain to the offender what effects the crime had had on their lives. Kim explained

that if I took part in this 'Restorative Justice' programme it would be to the benefit of the victim, not to
me, specifically; he also made it clear that taking part
would have no bearing whatsoever on my case, that
it wouldn't even be mentioned in court as part of my
sentencing. I didn't have any trouble with any of this,
so I agreed. I thought that taking part sounded like the
right thing to do, and as I was trying to put the rest of
my life together I couldn't see any reason why I should
choose not to take part. So when Kim first put it to me,
I thought, 'Yeah, maybe it would be nice to say sorry.' It
wasn't as if it was going to do me any harm. In fact, I
thought maybe I'd learn something for myself as well.
I certainly didn't expect to be changed by it.

There was another, less noble reason I was prepared
to go along with Kim on this. You're always looking for
a change in prison, for something to break the
monotonous routine, and this Restorative Justice programme would get me out of my cell for an hour.

But as the weeks went by – it was two months before
we had our conference date – I found I didn't feel quite
so interested after all. Perhaps I even began to worry
about it a little. Kim came to visit regularly to see that
I was getting ready for the conference. He explained to
me that each of the two people I'd stolen from or
attacked who'd agreed to take part would be bringing
some of their family, as they wanted to involve them in
what was going to happen, and he said that I should try

to get my family's support as I might end up feeling a bit isolated on the day if it was just me on my own.

My family laughed at me when I rang them up and asked them. 'Fuck off,' came the response. 'You'll have us on fuckin' *Jerry Springer* next.'

One thing I was lucky with was my reading. All those years of being stuck next to Charlie Richardson meant that, among other subjects, I had read loads of psychiatry and psychoanalysis. So I thought I could cope easily enough with the conference because I'd have everything planned out in my head beforehand – what to say, what emphasis to give it, that kind of thing. So as soon as I knew the date the RJ (as Kim referred to Restorative Justice) conference was to take place, I got myself ready with all the talk, all the language, made sure I knew what buttons to press to make it sound like I was taking part rather than just turning up. I expected it to go the right way for me. After a few decades of manipulating people, this was all second nature to me.

It was a Tuesday, about two o'clock. I'd had my lunch – it was baked beans and sausages; I think I ate less than usual – and the screw came to collect me. I walked down out of my cell, along the landing, down the stairs, and out over the floor to leave the block. As we walked down a long corridor, this meeting, which had seemed like a good idea only a few minutes earlier, something to break up my day, really started to get to me. I hadn't ever felt like this before. I was getting tense, feeling sick, and I suddenly knew that I didn't want to go through with it.

The screw stopped halfway down the corridor, turned to me and pointed to the door. I stepped up to look into the room through the glass panel at the top. There seemed to be a lot of people in there, and apart from Kim I didn't recognize a single one of them. They were looking at one another, laughing and talking. I was on the verge of turning to the screw and asking to be taken back to my cell, but Kim must have seen something out of the corner of his eye because at that moment he jumped out of his chair and opened the door. His face had a serious look on it, and all the trust and certainty I'd felt in his company over the last couple of months evaporated on the spot. That was my future, in there, and I didn't want any part of it.

I stood stock-still, thinking I could never cross that threshold. Then Kim reached out, took hold of my upper arm, said 'All right, matey?' as he always did, and pulled me in. I fell into the room, which had fallen silent, and, not looking around at all, headed for the nearest empty chair.

Kim's hand pressed down on my shoulder, and that gesture relaxed me a little, enough to encourage me to lift my head and look around. On my right was a space and then an empty chair, Kim's chair. Next to that was a woman, and I knew from what Kim had told me before the meeting that she was Will's wife. Opposite me and after her was Will, the man I'd fought with. Not that I recognized him; I suppose the adrenalin and the fact I was so far gone at the time meant I didn't take much notice of what he actually looked like. Will was a big man, strong-looking, and he sat bolt upright, his large hands resting on his knees, looking keenly at me. Next to him, in a grey suit, his head hanging almost as low as mine, was another man who I knew was a doctor I'd nicked a laptop from earlier on the same day I'd broken into Will's home. His house wasn't far from Will's. The man sitting next to him was his partner, then there was another gap, and then it was back to me. I'd never felt so exposed, so isolated, in my whole life. I wished someone was there from my family. I wished anyone cared enough about me to want to be there.

Around the edges of the room were other people, people from the RJ organization and others, but I was so dazed to be in there I didn't even notice them. It was months later when I learned by accident who they were, and how many of them had been there.

Kim sat in the empty chair next to me and started things going, all according to the plans he'd laid out with me. First off he introduced everyone in the circle, then he laid out how the session would go. Ground rules were established. There was to be no finger-pointing, but no lying or pretence either. Emotions were good; no one, especially me, was to be protected from the truth. We all nodded at his points, and while he spoke I felt slowly lulled into a sense of security. I could do this, after all. I knew what to say; I'd read all the books; I'd talked it through with Kim. I trusted Kim. I knew he wouldn't let anything bad happen to me here today, so I began to settle back into my seat. This was going to be OK.

And things were, for a while. Kim finished speaking, one or two of the people in the circle commented, I said the right things – no problems. As soon as I'd spoken out loud I realized that I was comfortable with all this, I could handle it. I explained why I'd done what I'd done, what had driven me to break into their homes and threaten them and attack them. At one point I started to address Will. I gestured at him and said something like, 'When we met—'

'Met? Met?' Will exploded, and nearly stood up out of his chair.

Kim looked alert, ready to help if necessary.

'We didn't meet, you know, at some bloody cocktail party, you broke into my house and attacked me!'

Will had gone red with fury, and his veins were standing out on his neck. The emotions – anger, fear, whatever – were pouring off him in waves. He let me know how he felt when he got up to his room and found me there, and what fighting me had done to him, not just the physical pain but also the anguish and anger he'd experienced for days afterwards. He then explained to the group how his anger and frustration stemmed from his feelings of failure. He'd failed to protect his wife, and their home, and that was why he wanted to see me, to see who it was who had done this to him.

Everyone else remained silent during Will's tirade against me. As he wound things up, I realized that I couldn't think of a thing to say in response; but that didn't matter because as soon as Will fell silent the doctor spoke. He could barely lift his head off the floor. He told us about how he didn't like to return home, how he felt unsafe doing so; how the laptop I'd stolen – which I'd almost immediately sold for no more than £20, so that I could buy a wrap or two – represented to him his life's work; that his research materials, his papers, all the notes he'd taken on all his patients had vanished overnight; that I'd taken away everything that meant something to him, and had treated it as worth-less. He'd found it very hard to come in today to confront me and . . .

And then he leaned forward in his chair and cried.

I'd taken it all from him, in a moment, his work and his dignity, and it had come to this, a professional man sitting in a room in a prison, sobbing.

Kim turned to me and asked me to respond to what had been said. The silence in the room pulled tightly around me. Everyone stared at me. All of a sudden the ground seemed to shift underneath me. My throat closed. I couldn't speak; I felt I couldn't breathe. It was like I was being squashed into a tiny space.

'I . . . I . . .'

I felt suddenly very hot, and then very cold. Tears rushed into my eyes. And something else happened, too. There was no longer a devil taunting me, tempting me; instead, someone invisible stepped forward and slid a sharp cold blade deep between my ribs and into my heart.

I had no answers for how I had ruined these people's lives. God, what had I done? What had happened to me? I had lived my whole life cut adrift from people, living in my own little bubble, and suddenly the anger and pain of two men forced its way into me and I knew, perhaps for the very first time in my life, not only how someone else actually felt but also what that felt like for myself. I'd done this to them, me. It was me that hurt them, me that had brought them here. I can only explain to anyone reading this that I'd *known* this before, but now, for the very first time in my life, I *felt* it. And it hurt.

Will had not just forgotten about me, as I had him, once the door to the police van had closed. His whole life was different, including his relationship with his wife. And the doctor . . . if it were possible, after what Will had said, I felt even worse. This doctor saved lives, he was working on saving even more, and I'd come along and destroyed that in seconds. His tears were the single slice of pain that penetrated and changed me. Nothing I'd ever gone through before compared to that moment. It was more powerful than the death of people I'd known for ever, like Fred, who'd died in my arms. It was the most powerful moment I'd ever experienced.

I didn't want to go away, I didn't want to vanish or anything, I wanted to face what I'd done, but I also wanted to stay sitting there while all that was bad in me leaked slowly on to the floor, to be washed away down the drain. The shame of what I'd done ran up and down inside me, and once again I felt hot and then cold and couldn't look at anyone. I was responsible for this, and things could never be the same again.

I don't want anyone to think I want people to feel sorry for me. I don't deserve that. I just want them to know that I was no longer pretending, that what Will and the doctor said cut right through the fierce exterior I'd always shown to the world, to slice up my heart underneath.

I had no one beside me, unlike Will and the doctor, who I could lean into for comfort as I sat there. Tears came to my eyes and I felt like crying, and they watched me, waited for me to finish, waited for me to speak. Somehow I did manage to tell them how I felt, or at least what I thought I was feeling: that I wanted to say sorry for what I'd done; that I had decided that I was not going to do it again;, that I was no longer taking drugs, or drinking; that I was going to stop being a thief. I managed to croak this all out and then I stopped, because it was too hard for me to say much more. Instead I sat there and – me, the tough guy – shook.

All my life I'd been hard, like some kind of statue, stone on the inside as well as the outside. Nothing could reach me because there was nothing to reach. Now, suddenly, these men had poked the statue and realized that it was just made of sand, which crumbled under their fingers. I came apart in that room; all that I knew as me, as Peter Woolf, the bad man, the alcoholic, the addict, the rebel without a clue, fell away. Someone else, buried deep down, was slowly revealed in the process, though I didn't know who that was. I didn't even know how to recognize him.

Kim spoke. He said that he could see that what had been said had truly affected me, and that he hoped this meant I would be changed. He reminded us all that part of the agreement of the conference was that I should express my remorse to these people by writing to them, and I nodded. But that wasn't the end of it. Both Will and the doctor asked me to write not just about my expressions of remorse, but to hear that I was conquering my addictions and problems. They wanted me to tell them that I was putting my life in order.

I felt humiliated, but not by these men. No, I felt humiliated by myself. I felt humbled by them. I'd done this to them, and for what? For drugs, and drink, for something that nearly destroyed me. And now these men, men I'd done great harm to, were reaching out their hands to me and saying, 'We would like to see you do well, we would like for you to address your addiction problems, we would like to hear from you by letter, telling us of your progress.' Somehow they had found the humanity to extend their hand and care. No one, ever, in my whole life, had cared about me like that. Sure, people had looked after me, but only so that I could be more useful to them, that I could fit in with them, do what they wanted. No one had ever expressed concern for me and my feelings, and a desire for me to be a better person. Will and the doctor cared about me, and they had no reason to; if anything, the contrary should have been true: they shouldn't have cared about me at all. And because of that, it counted. It mattered. I badly wanted Will and the doctor to be proud of me. I now had a purpose in life. Someone had shown an interest in me, and more than anything in the world I was determined not to let them down. I was going to achieve the goals we had all set.

When the conference ended, everyone stood up and went to help themselves to a cup of tea. I just sat there in a daze. Kim put a cup in my hand and someone – I've no idea who – put their hand on my shoulder. Only for a moment, mind, but that touch, a warm touch, went right through me to my heart again. And then a screw came along to tell everyone it was time to go as I needed to get back to my cell before my tea. I'd no idea I'd been in the room that long.

Everyone got up and went towards the door. I was closest, but instead of walking through I stood still and gestured everyone else ahead of me. They walked up the corridor as I stood in the doorway, watching them go. Will turned his head to look back at me as they disappeared around a corner. I didn't want them to go, I wanted them to stay, I wanted to escape, I wanted never to see them again – I didn't know how I felt any more. Reality had left me, or at least what I'd always known as reality.

'Come on, then,' said the screw. 'Time to get back then.'

And I walked back with him into the main block, down the corridors, along the landing, up the stairs, and into my cell. I sat down on the bed, and Mr Terry, the officer on my landing, stuck his head round the door.

'So how'd it go, then?'

I suddenly realized that I had no earthly idea how it had gone.

'I dunno, I couldn't tell you,' I said.

'Well, did it go well, at least?'

'I really don't know. I can't say.'

He stared at me for a bit, as if I was hiding something from him, then said, in a disappointed sort of way,

'You'll be wanting this anyway.' He handed me my food tray before moving on.

I stood up and put my tray on the table in front of me; but I was on auto-pilot, and sat back on the bed again. I didn't want to eat. What I really wanted to do was cry, but I couldn't – not here, not now.

'How'd it go, then?' asked another voice. This time it was Fat Gerald, who was in the cell next to me.

I said the same thing to him. I couldn't say what had happened; I couldn't figure it out at all. Had it gone well? Was it a 'success'? What was a successful conference? How was that measured? What happened next? What was I going to do, stuck here in this cell with no one to ask, no one to help me understand what had just happened to me, what I was going through?

'Aren't you hungry?' Mr Terry was back.

'No, no, not at all, mate. Take it if you want it.'

I barely had time to gesture at the tray before it was whisked away.

This time I was left alone, just me and the thoughts boiling in my head. I had to hold on to the things around me – the bed, the chair, the table – just to be sure I was really there, that the world wasn't tipping over and I wasn't about to fall off, because I wasn't sure about anything any more. I'd been out of it on drugs before, had amazing trips on LSD and all sorts, but nothing like this. This was frightening, because it was real. I couldn't wake up from this one.

That night I had a dream, one I had every night after the meeting for several weeks. I had a picture in my head of a circle of people, and in that circle were Kim, Will, the doctor and me. Several other people were there, not always the same 'other people', but always there were the four of us. It was a painful dream, filled with sadness. The doctor always cried, and I hated that I'd made that happen, though when I woke up I was filled with gladness, not over his suffering but glad that I could see the vision, that I could now feel someone else's pain and suffer myself as a result. It was his torment that kept reminding me how easy it was to cause pain and harm to another human being, and that was like a splinter under my skin, reminding me again and again what it was exactly that I'd done.

It was up to me to stop that from happening again.

I tried telling everyone in prison about my experience. I tried explaining to them that when we broke into people's houses, when we robbed them, when we punched them and ran off with what they were carrying, that this mess of anger and frustration and guilt and rage and fear is what we did to those people. And no one cared. They'd say 'They can afford it' or 'Who cares?', all the usual crap.

Being a good guy really doesn't sit too well with other prisoners. I had a reputation from my past of being violent, deceitful, crazy and dishonest; now the new labels came fast and furious. 'Grass' and

'Bible-basher' were the first of them, even though I had never picked up a bible or even gone to church – well, not since I was beaten up that time. Then it was the turn of the prison officers, most of whom thought I was up to something or had finally gone stir crazy. It required a lot of effort on my part to convince people I meant it, that I was no longer biding my time till I could get out and rob and score again.

These early days of change really were tough times. I was a bit of an outcast. It hurt when I was called names and saw people nudging each other and laughing at me, but I was determined to live up to the promise I'd made at the RJ conference, and I stuck to it, no matter how hard other people seemed to want to make that for me. I knew I had to make a commitment, to take a risk. The RJ conference was like jumping on a train and having to get off at all sorts of stops on the way to experience different things. At every stop I encountered a new fear.

Part of my rehab was going to a therapy group in prison run by an organization called RAPT (the Rehabilitation of Addicted Prisoners Trust). I don't think I'd have managed to do everything I did if it weren't for RAPT. In the past, as I said, I had made half-hearted efforts to get off the booze and drugs but they'd always ended in failure, so I had a 'failure' mindset. But what motivation had I had in the past? I had no prospects, or so I thought. I was a crook who expected to spend the rest of my life in jails; not only did I expect that, so too did everyone who knew me. I was a professional prisoner. I always took the easy option and returned to what I knew best. It was safe, it was easy, and I knew how to do it, so I'd give up on giving up and go back to heroin and stealing. It's hard to do anything when everyone, including me, has no faith. Now, though, I had the motivation, and I had people trusting and believing in me. I owed it to Will, the doctor, to Kim and to all the people I had done damage to over the years, myself included. Taking part in the RJ conference changed my life because it gave me a purpose in life. It was the beginning, the thing that really gave me the determination to succeed.

So I joined the RAPT programme and went straight into group work and one-to-one stuff with my counsellor. At first I tried to be the aloof intellectual and put myself on a pedestal, but really it was a mask, a defence to hide my fears. When it came to getting honest I would put my parts on and holler and shout and pack my kit and threaten to leave, but the staff had seen it all before and they knew. It was all fear. Everything I did was generated by fear – fear of failure, fear of success, fear of rejection, fear of love. My counsellor Val had me sussed. She told me what fear meant to me – Fuck Everything And Run – but that there was another meaning that I could choose to follow: Face Everything And Recover.

Part of my treatment with Val that has stayed with

me was when she gave me a bag of Lego. I thought, 'What's this?' But she was insistent that I make something with it. So I started making a house, only it was a jail, and in the smallest room inside the house I stuck a figure up against the wall, his face turned towards the bricks. 'Who's that?' asked Val. 'Well, me, of course,' I told her. And it struck me, then, what I had been doing to myself all these years, shutting myself away because of the fear. That Lego was a real eye-opener, I tell you. Next I made a parrot, and as soon as I'd made it I burst into tears.

The trickiest bit of our therapy, for me at least, was when we were asked to discuss our feelings on a daily basis. Now, for years I had been masking or burying any such emotions; feelings were things to be kept repressed. When Val first asked me 'How are you?' I replied, 'Sweet,' which wasn't exactly the answer she was looking for. But it was all I could come up with; I didn't know what else to say. 'Happy' and 'sad' were just words, 'confused' and 'angry' were from another language. Having spent a large chunk of my adult life in prison I had become even more adept at hiding my feelings. I suppose that fear was the feeling I most frequently experienced, along with anger. They seemed to go hand in hand when I was in prison.

To help me understand, Val gave me an exercise to do to try and draw out my feelings. I was given a sheet of A4 paper with all these different cartoon-style faces showing types of emotion by way of facial expression, and I was supposed to sit in front of the mirror and make these expressions on my face so that I could identify the feelings and work out what it was I was supposed to feel inside as I was expressing it on the outside. I would glance at the chart of facial expressions, then look in the mirror and practise an 'angry' look, or whatever I felt was right. What a crazy time I had then. I used to be in the mirror for about an hour every morning trying to get an 'expression' just so I could go into that morning's 'feelings check group' and be able to say, 'Today, I am feeling happy,' or whatever. Often I would be asked to explain why I was happy, or whatever, so I'd have to make up some bollocks to go along with the face I'd taught myself to pull that morning. I thought it was a test I had to pass; if I got it right then something better would happen to me. I'd go into, say, a major rant about why I was angry but it would all be over some imaginary incident. I had no idea of what it meant to have those feelings. I guess I never had. As I said, feelings were things that betrayed you so you didn't let yourself have them.

Over time I went through all the feelings that were so comically illustrated on my 'feelings chart', perfecting each individual look for each individual feeling, progressing from angry, happy, sad and scared to confused, frustrated, alarmed – but then I hit a stumbling block. I just could not master 'exasperated'. I got more and more exasperated in my failed attempts to copy the facial expression on my chart that was supposed to show the look of a person who was exasperated. Now, if that ain't complete lunacy I really don't know what is.

A big part of my rehabilitation was feeling the shame, and I have felt it a lot. I still do, and I don't like it. No human being likes to feel shame. I've had to accept accountability and responsibility for a lot of things in my life. There's a scale of feelings, I think: ashamed, shame, bad. Most of the things I did were bad, and I had to learn to accept that. I'd done what I'd done. The only thing I couldn't stop wishing was that I hadn't hurt so many people. If all I'd done all my life had just affected me, not other people, it would have been all right. In my book there's a distinct difference between shame and feeling ashamed – shame is making a mistake and feeling bad about it afterwards, but if you're ashamed of something, not only do you deeply regret it, you wish it had never happened – and there are a few things I still feel ashamed of today. I once stole some money off an old lady with a Zimmer frame. I picked some money out of her purse and got nicked for it immediately. I was clucking my nuts off, she'd come out of a post office, I saw a plastic bag with £20 notes sticking out of it and I went for it. And I feel ashamed about the man from Texas whose cameras I nicked. He was a visitor, and I sucked him in, chewed him up and spat him out.

Those episodes in my life seem a long time ago now, and some years have passed since my rehabilitation. I am very lucky in the fact that I have remained friends with the woman who was my counsellor at the time. Val and I often meet and laugh about those early days of rehabilitation. I kept in touch with Will and the doctor, too. I wrote and told them that I realized I had harmed them. I thanked them for attending that conference, and I explained how it had affected me every day since. I told them about the various rehabilitation programmes I'd completed while serving out the sentence I'd received, that I was doing the right thing, and that, lo and behold, it felt OK. No, it felt bloody good.

Will passed a message back through Kim, saying that he was pleased to hear of my progress and hoped that I'd keep it up. He also asked me to write to him again. He wanted to hear more from me about my rehabilitation and what plans I had for the future now that I was going to live a crime-, drink- and drug-free life. And he wanted to know how I felt now that I'd made these momentous changes in my life. I could have cried when I read his letter. No one had ever said anything like that to me before. No one had ever asked me how I felt, or wanted to hear a truthful answer.

I'd never made plans; I had always lived from day to day. I didn't know how to go about planning a life. Every decision had always been taken by other people, or so it seemed to me. I mean, I'm not saying I didn't decide to rob and hurt people, of course I did. But planning further ahead than that night's escapades and entertainment? I'd never had to do that. In jail I knew where I'd be the day after next, and the day after that. But now? Where was I going to live when I got out? What was I going to do?

Some decisions were easier to make than others. For instance, sitting alone in my cell I made more promises about making amends to the anonymous victims of the thousands of crimes I had committed. But saying sorry to nameless, faceless people was going to be hard, if not impossible. I thought long and hard about how I should go about the task, but I couldn't solve the problem. In the end I came to the conclusion that I couldn't fix all the problems I'd caused, I could only do my best to fix some. I also decided that I wouldn't go back home. I couldn't go back to Hoxton, because that place made me feel a certain way, and I didn't like feeling like that. And I decided something else, too: I would learn to help other people, and that the best people to help would be those like me. If I could stop just one person breaking into someone's house, if I could stop just one person lifting up that needle and injecting themselves, well, that'd be a good deed indeed.

Once the system realized I was no longer a threat and in fact would perhaps be better in a different prison, I was transferred. Hollesley Bay was my last prison, an open prison – the first one I'd ever been to. You may have heard of it as Jeffrey Archer went there. Initially I was quite worried about going there as everyone told me I wouldn't like it because I was too institutionalized. I didn't know what to expect. I thought perhaps it would be awash with drink and drugs, and as I'd been to some low-risk places I didn't like – the freedoms had spooked me a bit and I'd asked to go back to a more secure prison – I was worried that Hollesley Bay would be even worse for me.

The first afternoon I was there an announcement came over the Tannoy. 'Free time,' the voice said. I didn't know what that was, so I said to this fella, 'What's that mean?'

'Well, you can do what you like, can't you?'

'Do what I like? How's that? What can I do?'

He looked at me, a bit puzzled. 'Well, you could go for a walk.'

'What do you mean, go for a walk?' I couldn't understand him. We were in jail.

He paused, then said he'd show me, and we set off out of the prison for a walk, as he'd promised. We walked along the edges of fields and through gates in the hedges and up a steep slope until, after what seemed miles to a city boy like me, we came out up on the top of the slope and there was the sea. Running down in front of us was this vast stretch of shingle, and all the way out into the distance was the blue sea littered with ships of all kinds and sizes. I stood and stared at the scene. I thought that this was what it was like on holiday, because I'd never been on holiday. Going down to Clacton wasn't a holiday, it was just me tagging along with all my problems in a bag with me. Suddenly, on top of this blowy spot, I felt released from the chains of my life. All the things that had pulled me down over the years were mine to let go of, at last. I felt true freedom, a glorious impulse, for the first time. This was not the freedom of the outdoors, of being away from my four walls and a bed inside the jail, not even of being free of the crippling addictions that had led me inside in the first place and held me down, tightly, for so long. This was the freedom from fear that before that moment I'd never known. I'd nothing to be fearful of now, and no one to fear. Most of all, I had nothing to fear from myself. If I'd been on my own I'd have laughed and shouted till my throat was raw.

HMP Holleslcy Bay had an education department, a gym, and food the like of which I'd never tasted; we once had roast pheasant for dinner. We weren't locked up or anything like that, we were treated very much as adults. In the past, as I said, that would have put me right off the place. The old Peter wanted order and routine and would have hated it in an open prison; the new Peter liked being given responsibility for himself, knowing that there was someone there watching out for him.

I put my time there to good use and applied to do an HNC course in counselling. The nearest one to Hollesley Bay was in Norwich. I was late on my first day. I thought Norwich was a small place, I thought I only had to leave about fifteen minutes to get there from the station, that the place would be only a short walk away. But when I asked at the information desk in the station, as soon as the woman behind the counter began to explain about buses and whatnot, I knew I was going to be late. So I ran up there.

It was a hot day, and I arrived at the venue sweating and panting to find that the other students were sitting in a circle and had already been through all the preliminaries. Ian the tutor said, 'We've just done the introductions, perhaps you could introduce yourself at break-time?'

I said, 'No, I want to be part of this right from the start. Can't we do this all again, starting with you?' I pointed at the woman opposite me. 'What's your name?'

'Louise,' she said.

'Right, hello, Louise, my name's Peter and I'm a serving prisoner.'

Might as well get it out in the open, I thought, see how everyone reacts. Nobody said a thing; no one even blinked. Louise told me later that she thought I was brave coming out with it like that, but if you're going to open up to a group, what's better than a group training to be counsellors?

At break-time, Louise stood up and went to the machine in the corridor to get a coffee and to smoke a cigarette, and as I needed one too I found myself talking to her.

Cigarette smoking is my last habit, and I'm not ready to quit it yet. When you're in early recovery, you feel like giving up everything, including smoking. You see a doctor to get help to give up, but the doctor tells you not to. Don't try to do everything at once, they tell you, because the physical side of withdrawing from nicotine is very similar to that from heroin. Of course I know it's as detrimental to me as the drugs and drink were, but it causes less harm than the violence associated with drinking and the criminal behaviour associated with heroin.

One day I plucked up the courage to ask Louise if I could ring her about some of the things that were coming up on the course, and she said yes. I wrote to her, then called her up, and she wrote back.

Soon the time came for me to be released. I was very nervous about this, in a way I'd never been before. I'd coped with all the changes in prison because I had the support I needed inside – AA meetings, NA meetings, room and board – but how would I cope with life on the outside? It wasn't like before when I'd never had any ambitions: now I wanted to go out and stay straight, but I had no idea what it meant to be normal, I'd never done it. I had been doing voluntary work out

Ipswich way on day-release, initially teaching numeracy and literacy to people with learning difficulties – people with Asperger's or Down's, and people who'd been in really bad accidents and had to re-learn some basics – and I'd taken to it. I'd also gone to college. But I'd always come back to go to bed in the prison. Simple things really baffled me, things that other people take for granted but which I knew nothing about. You might laugh, but I had no idea that you had to pay for water, for instance. I thought water rates were what posh people had to pay, that water was free for everyone else. You turned on a tap and water came out. It was the same with bars of soap: I thought they just magically appeared, because wherever I'd been there was always soap. I'd never had to buy it, not once.

Of course, when I got out, that's when the struggle began. I was doing the voluntary work in Ipswich, and I had a flat there, but with no gas, no electrics, no curtains, nothing, and it was winter. All I had was Louise. She came to the flat and couldn't believe it – no lighting or heating, no furniture, just the floorboards. I needed help to get set up, so I went to a benefit agency, but it was a nightmare. They said they couldn't do anything for me. They'd sent a cheque to me to help me get started to HMP Hollesley Bay, but I left before the cheque arrived, and as the claims process took ten weeks they couldn't issue a new one until that process was complete. I got annoyed and said, 'I'd be better off in jail.' They said, 'Well, go off and get yourself arrested then.' I was really shocked when they said that. There I was, trying to get on the straight and narrow, and there they were encouraging me to stay off it. I couldn't believe it, and I decided never to go to a benefit agency again. I wasn't going to let another human being treat me like that.

It's easy to give up; it's hard to stay that way. If you can do it without support, you just get yourself locked up in a cell with a bucket and a box of tissues and you can come off heroin, simple as that. Alcohol's a little bit more difficult, because you'll probably be having fits and all that. But you can do it. Staying off it when you face setbacks, though, that's the tough one. But I have something up my sleeve to help me stay off drugs: I know I've got another relapse in me, but I also know I haven't got another recovery in me. Remembering that keeps me safe and sane.

There's always a mass of emotions going on inside an addict – a rage of angels, I call it. You want to stay off, and the longer you do the happier and more proud you become, but you also know this pride is something you have to be careful of. In the past when I felt bad, I'd go out and do something to feel better; but when the euphoria wore off I'd feel a little bit worse than I did before. Now I had the opposite problem: if I was feeling good about my achievements, I had to watch the temptation to say to myself, 'I've got this licked'; or, worse, decide to treat myself – I've got so far, I deserve something as a reward. That's why NA and AA were so vital for me, because the people I met there knew exactly how I was feeling and what I was going through, because it was happening to them too. Louise used to resent me going off to meetings a bit. We'd be doing something and then I'd suddenly stop and say, 'I've got to go to a meeting,' and she'd think it was just me mucking about. But gradually she came to understand it was because of the meetings that I could be there in the first place.

Take my first Christmas out of prison. Louise had already introduced me to her parents. I'd been very nervous, in case they served me peas – I didn't know how to eat them with anything other than a spoon and I didn't want to go back to my old ways now that I was no longer the person I'd been. I needn't have worried: they were, and they remain, very good to me. That Christmas, which we spent with Louise's family, I was finding it hard. All this stuff we'd never done when I was a child, this frenzy over presents and dinner and all that, started to get to me. I was thinking that everyone else was enjoying themselves the way they wanted to, so why shouldn't I? I realized that I needed to talk about it, so I said to Louise, 'I need to go to a meeting, but it's Christmas. What can we do?' Louise thought about it for a moment, then got the key to her dad's shed out in the garden. We went out there, sat down on some stools, and Louise said, 'Right, let's have a meeting.'

'My name's Peter and I'm an alcoholic,' I said, and immediately I felt better.

When I came out of prison, I was prescribed these blockers, which were supposed to prevent you taking drugs and drink, because I felt vulnerable and feared I might turn to the booze in a panic. I went to the chemist to get them, but I never took them. I kept them in a bottle in the bathroom, and simply knowing they were there was reassurance enough. I don't take many pills now, certainly nothing that has anything in it that might trigger something inside me.

Slowly I started to put my life back together, and part of that meant treating my family normally. When I went down to London I went to see my aunt Carol. We sat in her kitchen and I told her what was going on for me up in Ipswich and how I was getting along. Suddenly she reached out a hand and rested it on my arm, to indicate that I should stop talking for a moment.

'Do you know,' she said, 'this is the first time in thirty years you've spoken to me.'

I was taken aback. All the years I'd seen Carol, stayed over at hers sometimes . . . 'What do you mean?' I said. 'I always talked to you.'

'No,' she replied, 'I don't mean that. What I mean is, this is the first time you've ever strung sentences together. All you used to say, for thirty years, was "Lend us a tenner. Gissa? Gotta? Can I?" That's all I ever heard from you.'

What could I have talked about, to anyone? I didn't care what they were thinking or feeling, all I cared about was what I wanted to do, and fuck everyone else. They didn't matter to me; they were an inconvenience that I had to put up with. But I'd learned that I couldn't live like that, that no one can. The life I had found again was a precious one, and I should use the time I had in a better way.

But I found it harder to change my relationship with my family than I thought. Obviously they were pleased to have me sane and sober, but they don't really understand what it is I do now, or how I live the way I do, so although I still see them I don't go down very often.

I'd also learned that with drugs, one's too many, a thousand's never enough; and that help must be offered to you all the time, twenty-four hours a day, seven days a week. After all, addiction ain't a nine-to-five thing, so why should recovery be? Being a recovering alcoholic and drug addict has its problems and pitfalls as well as its bonuses. One of them is that I was always eager to say yes to everything; saying no felt like a return to the bad old days, when I was selfish and thought of me, me, me first. You have to learn so many things over again, though it's not so much like a child learning them for the first time as someone who's had an accident and has to re-learn skills. Recently, I've learned to say no, which is a fucking great thing.

Louise and I got married. I asked my family to come; they made humming and hawing noises, but I wasn't having any of that. Kim, who in the past would have been my mortal enemy – a policeman, for heaven's sake – was my best man. Alice said to Kim at our wedding, 'I never thought I'd be at his wedding, I always thought it'd be his funeral.' Kim and I talk on the phone, often, and lately he's started asking me for advice. I can't begin to describe how that makes me feel.

The day I got married, everything changed, because I felt that I had a future. The change was every bit as great as at the RJ conference, but in a different kind of way; different knowing where I'd be next week, and the week after, and who I'd be with, for the very first time in my life. Kim retired not long back and I took Louise down to his retirement dinner in the Tower of London. We sat at a table with Will and his wife, eating and talking normally. I still find that amazing.

Louise told me later that initially she found living with me presented her with one or two problems. I was still like a child, so she said: I had to go round the house shutting all the doors before I could get into bed, and I had to sleep with a light on. The habits I'd had in prison followed me out. I didn't like the night in the country one bit, I wasn't used to it being so dark. One time I came out of our GP's surgery and had to feel my way home, couldn't see a thing. Another day Louise said to me, 'You know, Peter, you don't have to ask permission all the time.' And I realized that even when I had a cup of tea I was saying, 'Is it all right . . . ?' I hadn't noticed. There was so much that I had to learn, things that everybody else takes for granted. Washing towels was another – clean ones had always just appeared in my life until then.

If this makes it sound like Louise was letting me sink or swim, it wasn't like that at all. She was right behind me in everything I did or tried to do, only she was trying to get me to stand on my own two feet. She was also determined to help me fit in with people, like when she said to me that I had to learn to do 'small talk'. Louise had noticed that I tended to clam up when people spoke to me, because I didn't know what to say to them. I felt I couldn't talk like I used to in the pubs, and I didn't want to launch into a discussion of the rehabilitation of prisoners with someone who'd just asked me the time at the bus stop. 'Small talk,' said Louise, 'that's what you've got to learn.'

Now, when Louise said things like that to me I felt I should agree, and then find out what she meant afterwards. I didn't want to lose face by asking her what she meant (some of my bad old habits hadn't left me yet). I'd internalize everything rather than ask. So when she said 'small talk' I thought she meant talk about small things – matches, baby carrots, stuff like that. I don't even want to think about the first time I tried it, and the look on Louise's face.

Sometimes my feelings of inadequacy would kick in and I'd keep my thoughts to myself. When Louise suggested we have a Hallowe'en party for the kids, I agreed, only I didn't know what a Hallowe'en party was. She'd said we'd have hot food, pumpkins carved out, and some apple dunking. Mr Obliging said yes, and carried on saying yes for the next few days while inwardly he panicked. What the hell was apple dunking? The day grew closer and I got more and more anxious. I couldn't let on that I didn't know what she was talking about, but before I threw down my keys and said, 'That's it, I can't do this no more,' I thought I'd give Kim a ring.

I told him the problem, and he laughed. I slammed the phone down on the table and stormed round the house, swearing and kicking out. Then I went back to the phone and picked it up. 'Don't you fuckin' laugh at me!' I said. 'Don't you know what's going on here?' Kim apologized, calmed me down and explained what was going on. Not about the apple dunking – I soon picked that up – but about keeping things from people, especially Louise. I realized that I had to totally open up and stop worrying about losing face, which was just a hangover from my old world.

Some of the hangovers from my past were funnier, even to me. Living in the country was a bit of a surprise for a city boy like me. I thought the pigs out in the fields were chunky-looking Staffordshire bull terriers when I first saw them; I thought pigs lived in pig sties. And when I was first working I was helping to clear drains and we were sitting about eating our sandwiches and I said, 'Those are funny-looking ducks.'

'Ducks? Where?' said my co-worker.

'There.'

'Where?'

'There! Right in front of us!'

'Those aren't ducks, you idiot, they're geese.'

'Geese? But geese don't swim, do they?'

Louise's kids tease me about my speaking – the 'Olly and the Ivy was one of mine they enjoyed that first Christmas. Once one of them was doing some speech therapy, learning to say his 'f's properly, so to help him we were going round the table coming up with words so that he could hear the difference between them and 'th' sounds. Fish, find, field, and then it was my turn – fink.

In this process of adjusting to 'normal' life, I can't stress enough how important it was to me to have Louise tell me when things were OK or, occasionally, when I'd misinterpreted people and their reactions. I had always seen things as black or white; Louise helped me to see that there were such things as shades of grey. I was so, so lucky to have Louise; everyone in my position should be lucky enough to have support like that. It doesn't have to be a husband-and-wife thing, it can be a support team, but rehabilitation is very hard – too hard, I believe – to cope with in isolation.

It's been far from easy, changing my life. In fact, everything's been really, really hard. People were very cynical. Some of my family are waiting for me to fall from grace, are hoping for me to fall, so they can say, 'I told you it was all bollocks.' But I've stopped wanting to be the best at everything, even the best recovering addict. Now I just want to be me. I get up at half five in the morning, put the kettle on, have two cups of coffee, feed the dog, feed the cats, and make the boys' lunches for school – I'd be lost if I didn't have that to do. As I said, I've had to learn so many things for the first time – small talk, bedtimes, walking in the country, cutting the grass, shopping, family games – but for the first time ever I can say that my life's all right. I'm content.

I don't miss any of it, not the drugs, not the booze. For the last five years alcohol has not been in my life. Nowadays I even get special Christmas puddings with no brandy in them, on account of what Louise's mum calls my 'problem'. And when I go to hospital I feel nicely singled out because all my files carry a skull and crossbones on them. I'm potentially contagious, you see, having contracted hepatitis from a needle some time back. My liver's fucked, I have these pains that sometimes mean I can hardly walk upstairs, and because of all the injecting I did I've got no visible veins. When I go to hospital it's a day's work to get a blood sample. After they've stabbed me for a while, causing me pain, I make them stop. In the old days I would have taken the syringe out of their hands and put the needle in myself, simply to avoid the pain. I was always good at finding a vein in the old days. I used to call myself Dr Death at one point because if people couldn't get a hit, couldn't find a vein, they'd say, 'Help us out,' and I'd say, 'Never fear, Dr Death's here,' and do it straight away. That's because I had always taken heroin by injection, right from the start, rather than smoke it first and then try to inject.

I see people from the old days every now and again. Hoxton . . . I've never yet gone back, and I don't want to. It's a shit hole. It's only smartened up at one end; the other end, up near the canal, is where the scag is. *Scag City* was made there; the heroin plague took off in Haggerston. I don't have any desire to go there or even to think about it. The majority of people I knew in Hoxton are dead anyway, or they've moved or cleaned up.

I chose to go to work with the people who'd helped me, and I now do a lot of work with Restorative Justice programmes, attending conferences, speaking at meetings and the like. Amazingly, Will does it with me. We stayed in touch, and he feels as strongly as I do that it could make a difference to so many people, as it has done to him and to me. We both firmly believe that it should be a regular tool of the justice system and we're happy to give up our time – and in Will's case that's pretty valuable time, so he's doing a great job because, like me, he believes in it – to try to make a difference.

A lot of what we do involves me going back over my life and telling people what exactly I've done, so that they can see how far gone I was, and how far Kim, Will and the others had to reach to pull me back. I find it very hard to do this at times. I can see my story in sections, but it's in abstract; sometimes the sections don't marry up. That's the result of all those decades of alcohol and drug abuse. One thing I do know is what effect my crimes had on people, and I can't hide from that any more. So none of it's easy; there's no one particular thing that's hardest to talk about. I try not to let it affect me, but it builds up, and sometimes I think . . . *fucking hell*. I half-wish I hadn't done all the things I did, but I'm glad I experienced what I experienced because I want to do something about the future to stop young people going down the same route. I went with Sir Charles Pollard (see Afterword) to speak at his old school, Oundle, and although I found it a very tough experience talking to the pupils there I also enjoyed it very much.

As I said, I'm a firm believer in RJ and what it can do for you; we use it at home with the kids all the time. I'm now starting work with the Metropolitan Police, trying to change the lives of prolific offenders, the ones who are halfway down my road. So I believe I've found my purpose. I believe God got hold of me, shook me up and said, 'Liven yourself up, boy, for the future.'

I had to experience the dark in order to appreciate the light. Back in 1974 at the Old Bailey, Judge Donaldson, giving me my first three years, for GBH, said to me, 'Young man, there's a tunnel, a mighty long tunnel for you, but there's a light at the end of it, but in your case it's a mighty dim light.' Today, I'd like to tell him I wear sunglasses.

The other day I was at a meeting at Number 11 Downing Street, talking about restorative solutions with Sir Charles Pollard, Will and loads of others. On my way out, on the street outside, I stopped to ask Charles something when I heard a voice.

'Excuse me, can I have a word?'

I looked round and there was a copper advancing on me, his hand pulling a notebook out of his back pocket. Now, I knew I was in Downing Street and that no one was going to muck about there, but I did reel back for an instant. It had been a while since a policeman advanced on me brandishing a book, but it was never good news in the past.

'Do you mind?' the officer said, pushing the book towards me. 'I saw you on Trevor McDonald the other night. I really admire you for what you're doing. Can I have your autograph?'

* * *

Louise said to me, on my fiftieth birthday in 2007, 'How do you feel, then, turning fifty?'

I was mindful of one of the key ideas from the twelve-step programme: it's today I'm not drinking or taking drugs; I have no control over tomorrow, and I take life one day at a time.

'Well,' I replied, 'fifty, clean, sober and free can't be bad.'

And do you know, it's not. Not bad at all.

Afterword

Sir Charles Pollard on Restorative Justice

Sir Charles Pollard joined the Metropolitan Police as a constable at the age of nineteen. His first beats included Soho and, later, Islington and Hoxton. For eleven years he was Chief Constable of Thames Valley Police, the largest non-metropolitan force in the country, where he pioneered the routine use of Restorative Justice for tackling youth offending.

On leaving Thames Valley, Sir Charles took up the position of chairman of the Justice Research Consortium, working with the eminent criminologist Professor Lawrence Sherman (now Wolfson Professor of Criminology at Cambridge University). Sir Charles was also a board member of the Youth Justice Board for England and Wales for eight years until 2006, leading on Restorative Justice and chairing the board in 2003. He also chairs the Winchester Restorative Justice Group, a

*network of RJ organizations that works to promote RJ;
and he is a trustee of the Restorative Justice Consortium.*

*In autumn 2004, Sir Charles set up the not-for-profit
organization Restorative Solutions Community Interest
Company with Nigel Whiskin, formerly chief executive of
the crime prevention charity Crime Concern, providing
advice, support and training to organizations that are intro-
ducing RJ into their working practices. Peter Woolf works
as an associate trainer for Restorative Solutions CIC.*

Peter Woolf's story poses two questions. One, what
made Peter into the criminal he was? And two,
what changed him? What caused him to turn his back
on everything he'd known?

Policing and the Justice System
These are the issues that most people with an interest in
the justice system in this country would like to understand. In my roles as a former policeman, someone who
dealt with people like Peter all my life; as an advocate
and implementer of restorative justice; as a witness to
Peter's remarkable transformation; and, I'm proud
to say, as a friend of Peter's – as someone in all these
roles, I think perhaps I know some part of the answers
to these questions.

In 1967 I was a young Police Constable in Islington,
with a beat not very far from Peter's home in Hoxton.

One afternoon I responded to a call where a ten-year-old lad had been firing an airgun from the balcony of a block of flats into a school playground, injuring some of the children. They all knew who the shooter was, and where he lived: a boy called Eddie.

So I went to his flat and knocked on the door. There was no answer, but I heard a movement inside. I shouted through the letterbox, 'Eddie, this is the police, I know you're in there, can I have a word with you?' Eventually the door opened and I looked down to see a sandy-haired, surly boy glaring up at me. 'Yeah?' he snarled. It quickly turned out that Eddie's mum and her partner – both regular visitors to the police station where I was based – were out. Eddie denied knowing anything about the airgun, but I decided to go in and search the flat, empowered as I was by the Firearms Act.

As I tried to walk in, Eddie stood in the doorway, blocking the way, arms folded, ferociously staring at me. 'You ain't comin' in 'ere without a warrant.' Though only ten years old, he had clearly learned some things from his mum about how to respond to the police.

Police assistance arrived, and Eddie was arrested. We never did find the gun, although Eddie was subsequently prosecuted and convicted on the evidence of the children who had seen him doing it. After his arrest Eddie's mum came to the police station to take him home and to make a formal complaint, which alleged that in searching the flat my colleagues and I had trashed it and, among other things, had put chairs into the bath and turned the taps on them. When the duty inspector visited the flat that is indeed how he found them – placed there, as I know, by the family themselves.

Here was my introduction to criminal families in London: a boy absent from school, left alone in the home, causing criminal mischief, with no respect for normal values, and already an arrogant liar – while his mother tried to cover up for him, supported everything he did, made malicious and false allegations against the police, and was prepared to damage her own property to do so. As a young man from a 'nice' middle-class family of caring, loving and public-spirited parents, blessed with the privilege of a private education, and a naivety derived from all these things, there could not have been a greater contrast between my own up-bringing and that of Eddie.

Eddie could easily have been Peter Woolf, who was then about that age. Though Peter's family seem to have had different ways of dealing with the police, Peter was just like Eddie: out of control, a liar, violent, selfish and arrogant, challenging authority, all promoted and supported by his 'parents'; a walking disaster destined to tear society apart and to spend much of his life in prison.

That early encounter with Eddie has always made me wonder: what can the police, the justice system and society do to sort out people like Peter and Eddie, brought up in a criminal world in which dishonesty, violence and selfishness are handed on from one generation to another? During the forty-plus years of my career in the police and with the Youth Justice Board, I grappled constantly with that problem. I came to think that, with most criminals from whatever background, there was always some hope of reform; that, given the right motivation and support – such as drug treatment programmes, help with getting a job, having friends or family to rely on – there was a chance that most offenders could be turned into honest, straight citizens.

But I also thought there were a very few criminal people out there who seemed beyond any hope at all, people brought up to commit crime, who live without any moral code, and without the slightest likelihood of reform or change. Had I known Peter at any time during his criminal heyday, I am sure I would have concluded that he was someone like this; I would have said he was just plain 'evil'. He would certainly have seemed to me to be someone beyond redemption, someone with whom it was not possible to reason.

It was the possibility of redemption, and the hope of reason, that had dictated my career. I joined the police because I wanted to make a difference to society. This may sound idealistic but it was my genuine motivation, as it is for many police officers. I also joined on the basis that in this country we had one of the best legal systems in the world. My mother, a historian educated at Cambridge, had always told me of the pride we should have in this; how, over the centuries, our legal system had developed and adapted to become a real beacon of freedom and democracy in the world, particularly in the way it dealt with offenders and through the rights it gave them, unique to Britain.

During my thirty-six years in the police, I came to see that both of these assumptions were wrong. Quite simply, the justice system didn't work then and it doesn't work now. Any chance of making a real difference to society through policing and the traditional legal system was, and still is, doomed to failure.

Our trial system fails because it is wedded to the past, not to the present or future. A New Zealand judge who visited England recently observed that 'the adversary model is largely unchanged in its essentials since the end of the eighteenth century. Lawyers from the year 1800 could walk into our criminal courts today and recognize most of what they see and hear. The same could never be said of the practice of medicine, or most other professions.' He is right. Despite attempts at reform by Governments of all political persuasions, and the judges themselves, our justice system is still in a time-warp.

It has merits in the way jurists have carved out proper

rights for defendants and laid down the principles of fairness. But it has one fundamental flaw: it is only the legal injury done to the State, not the physical, social and emotional hurt suffered by the victim, that is properly addressed. Victims of crime are hardly involved in the justice system at all. Surely they, too, have a right to be involved, not just as givers of evidence or as jurors? (Incidentally, juries were originally made up of people selected precisely because they knew the offender or something about the case, including the victim.) Why would you expect victims and citizens to have confidence in a system where they are excluded from it in any meaningful way; do not have their needs considered, let alone met; and often see themselves as mistreated (for example, while being cross-examined) by it?

Justice in the courts has become too much like a game, one in which victims, the public and society are losing. It should be about getting to the truth, not about red tape, or point-scoring, or antiquated rules and rituals. Despite the valiant attempts of many judges and magistrates, too many court hearings are still like an adventure playground for lawyers. The adversarial nature of the trial, the bureaucracy and technicalities, all of them contribute to the unreal, artificial drama of the courtroom disconnected from the real world outside.

Put another way, the courts do not seem to have a

moral purpose. Surely justice should be about *right* and *wrong*, not what you can get away with. The offender should be held to account for the wrong he has done – the wrong to another person, the harm he has caused, quite apart from the technical, legal offence against 'the State'. The old maxim 'Don't do to others what you would not want done to yourself' is pretty basic, but it is an important principle of a civilized society.

Is it, then, any surprise that the courts, to a criminal such as Peter once was, were an irrelevance? The games played in court seem to have reinforced his view of the world, not the other way round. Peter went to court numerous times during his criminal career, resulting in him spending eighteen years of his life in prison. Why is it that none of these experiences had the slightest impact on his attitudes, beliefs or behaviour – worse, they actually reinforced them?

I would turn the question around: if the objective of the justice system is to hold someone like Peter to account for what he has done and stop him committing more crime in the future, why would you actually expect our traditional justice system to work? Given the 'games-playing' culture and the fact that it largely excludes from its deliberations the impact crime has had on the victim, there is no reason why it should work at all.

The key is *conscience*. Our court processes have evolved so as to keep conscience – that is, emphasizing the difference between right and wrong – out of the reckoning. The system is designed to concentrate on facts and logic, to keep emotion out of the deliberations, so that a trial is as fair and unbiased as possible. This is highly laudable. No one wants to see people wrongly convicted; however, neither do they wish to see criminals wrongly acquitted. An impartial search for the truth is the best way to try to achieve this.

But this historical obsession with keeping emotions and feelings out of the system, of ignoring the power of conscience, has been taken too far. Courts have two roles, not one: first, to determine whether a suspected person is guilty or innocent, or at least deemed to be innocent. The principle of keeping emotion out of the trial system is absolutely right when applied to this function because it needs to be about analysing the facts and weighing the evidence. The second, however, is of a different order. Once a person has been found guilty, the role of the court is to sentence him. Role one is to determine whether the defendant did it or not; role two is, now that we have concluded he did do it, what we do with him.

What society demands is that the offender be held to account for what he has done, with fair punishment where needed; that he makes amends for the harm caused to his victim; and that action be taken to try to stop him committing more crimes in the future. An important way to achieve these things is to engage the offender's conscience, or at least to try to do so. It is to get the offender to understand what he has done; that what he has done is wrong; that he has harmed someone else, or the community, or society in general; that he needs to make amends for it; and that he must do none of these things again.

You would have thought this was pretty obvious. Surely this should be the starting point if we want to stop offending and reduce crime? But sentencing in our courts has little or nothing to do with people's consciences; in fact, as I said, our legal system goes out of its way to exclude any emotions, feelings or conscience from being considered as part of the sentencing process. It is the principle of punishment and retribution that overshadows everything else.

To motivate people to change their ways, to appeal to the human qualities most people intrinsically have in one way or another, and to engage their consciences in as powerful a way as it is possible to do – well, of course this is not always going to work. There are some crimes where this may be inappropriate, and some offenders with whom it is most unlikely to work. But taking the whole gamut of crime and wrongdoing, there is a massive area where this is something that is likely to work wholly or partially with a lot of people.

Of course, most of us expect punishment to be a major response to crime and criminals. Most people feel that criminals should be punished either on the basis that they should be punished, rather like 'an eye for an eye, a tooth for a tooth' from the Old Testament; or that this will deter them from doing it again (a theory that is very questionable); or that this should also deter others (a theory which is probably correct in some cases); or several of these.

Some of these assumptions are wrong. They hold that people who commit crime and appear before the courts *know* they are doing wrong, and therefore must be punished in order to deter them and others from doing such wrongs. Do offenders who consistently commit crime, who have been brought up to believe crime is a natural way of life, think they are doing wrong? Did Peter Woolf think he was doing wrong when he committed his thousands of crimes, until he met Will and the doctor at their Restorative Justice conference?

Obsessed with this, our courts hold that conscience, emotions and feelings can have no part to play in determining sentences, and the most obvious implication here is that victims of crime have no role in contributing to the sentencing decision. But why would anyone expect a sentencing process to be effective, and to have the confidence of those it is there to serve, if it excludes from its workings the very people most affected by the harm it is supposed to tackle or prevent?

Of course the reason put forward is that victims of crime will be so angry at what has happened that they will be out for blood; they will be out for naked revenge and want excessive and unfair punishment. Like many other assumptions in the law, that is simply wrong; it is one of the many myths on which our justice system runs. Yes, victims of crime probably *will* be out for revenge if they have been excluded from the court process, which heightens their feelings of isolation and anger – who would not be? But the research now over-whelmingly shows that one of the impacts of restorative conferencing – when victims meet their offender – is to *reduce* the victim's desire for revenge. Far from putting pressure on judges to hand down an excessive punishment, victims who have been through RJ are more likely to press for a constructive, sensible, balanced punishment – probably, if anything, too *low* a tariff – rather than the other way around!

It is no coincidence that both these features – engaging offenders' consciences and giving their victims a place within the system – are largely missing from our court processes. The one small exception is in very serious crimes such as murder, where 'victim personal statements' – a written statement by the victim's next of kin outlining the harm and distress felt, read out by a lawyer – are now allowed. Though a welcome, pragmatic attempt to improve the justice system, these are nevertheless very impersonal and miss out the key element of RJ – giving victims a *real* place in the system. It is only by *involving* and *engaging* those affected by the crime that the important things – emotion, feelings and conscience – can be brought to bear on the problem society is trying to tackle.

If it is these two things that are the key to Restorative Justice, how do we need to re-fashion the sentencing system in our courts? The answer is to routinely use RJ as an alternative, or as an add-on, to our traditional sentencing process. In fact, RJ should be the usual default mechanism to be considered or attempted first.

Peter Woolf and Restorative Justice

How was it that Peter, who was among the most prolific and serious of London criminals, changed? The person who attacked, robbed, deceived and trampled over almost everyone he met is now a reformed character. Will, one of his victims, remarked to me recently, 'Charles, I have been thinking about Peter and, do you know, he is one of the most decent people I have ever met?' I thought about this myself and concluded that, yes, the Peter I know – the person I have met since the restorative conference – is in fact someone with charm, kindness, integrity, honesty and unselfishness.

How can such a thing happen? How is it that this thing called Restorative Justice has changed his life? And not just his life; it has also changed the lives of those who spoke in his conference, such as Will. We can speculate that if Peter had continued with his life of crime many others, too, would have become his victims. It is thanks to the change Peter undertook that this did not – will not – happen.

Peter's life had never been affected by his going to court, by being tried and sentenced, by spending half his life in prison for stealing to fund his drug habit. He didn't like going to court, but not because it was tough or challenged his behaviour; he didn't like it because it was an irrelevance. Court interfered with the normal progress of his life. Since he was going to prison anyway, and he was comfortable there, he might as well just get on with it. He would much rather just be told how many years he had got, then he could start his sentence and get on with his life.

At the RJ conference, however, Peter was affected by coming face to face with Will and the doctor, the men who came to represent to Peter all those he'd beaten, robbed and generally mistreated. Affected to the extent that when he got back to his cell afterwards and people asked how he had got on, he couldn't put the experience into words. He was stunned. All he knew was that what he had been through was so demanding, so emotionally tough, that he was traumatized by it. Peter has told me subsequently that he still thinks of that experience almost every day, years later, and still remembers new things about it that make him think really hard.

For the first time in his life he had to think of other people; he discovered the terrible harm he had done to them. He had hardly ever felt anything like that before. He couldn't think why, but now that was the only thing he wanted to do. All he wanted was to be able, in some way, to put right what he had done to Will and the doctor and their families.

But it's not enough to engage someone's conscience, to make him feel deeply ashamed at what he has done, without doing something to help and support him too, so for Peter a further surprise came from Will and the doctor. Far from wanting to criticize and attack him after he had already expressed genuine remorse and apology, they expressed a wish that he sort his life out and never do what he'd done to them to anyone else ever again. They didn't want blood. They didn't want revenge. All they wanted was that from now on, regardless of what sentence he received at court later on, he went straight; that he came off drugs; that he sorted his life out; that when he got out of prison he would get a job. In short, that he would become a decent person.

Peter had hardly ever before come across anyone who had cared about him, let alone like that, and all this from two strangers, two people whose lives he had made a misery and who owed no obligations of any sort to him. This meant there was now one big thing in his life that Peter simply had to do. If he did not do this one thing, he would not be able to live with himself.

He could not, and will not, ever let Will and the doctor down.

People have said to me in the past that Restorative Justice is 'pink and fluffy', that it is soft. We need to be tough on crime, don't we, people say; we have to be tough on criminals, put them into court, let them face the majesty of the law and the courts, let them be punished, let them be sent to prison for a long time.

But this is nonsense, as we know from Peter's experiences. In court a criminal doesn't have to say anything, or answer any questions. He doesn't have to account for anything he's done. Even better, he has a mouthpiece – a lawyer – to put forward his side of the story. A mouthpiece protects him from having to answer for himself, and when it comes to 'giving mitigation', after pleading guilty or being found guilty, the mouthpiece usually tells the judge his client is full of remorse and won't do it again, even if everyone in the courtroom knows that's a lie. It is all part of the game. Lawyers are not expected to make judgements about whether what they are told by their client is true or false, they are just paid to present the case as best they can. Coupled with this is the fact that the criminal hardly ever has to meet, or even see, the person he's stolen from or attacked. It is as if that person doesn't exist.

Is this tough? Does this make offenders think about what they did? Do they feel held to account for the harm they have caused to others? Are their consciences engaged at all? Do they feel remorseful for what they did, or are they just sorry for themselves that they got caught? Or is it all just water off a duck's back?

What is undeniable is that RJ challenges offenders to think about what they have done; it requires them to take responsibility for it and, if they genuinely feel remorse, to be able to express this remorse and say sorry.

Saying sorry *is* a very important feature of human behaviour, despite the cynicism it sometimes attracts. If you doubt this, check your reaction next time someone accidentally bumps into you. Are you more inclined to react positively to someone who marches on without a backwards glance or someone who stops, smiles and says sorry? If genuinely said and meant, saying sorry not only helps victims of crime get over the trauma of the crime against them, it is also a major factor in the offender's mindset that leads to stopping or reducing re-offending.

Of course, saying sorry on its own is often insufficient, although the research shows that, if genuine, it is usually the single thing victims value most. Making amends by other means is also important, for example by paying financial compensation, carrying out agreed tasks for the victim, or 'paying back' by doing voluntary work for the community.

Still, it is surely a complete travesty to talk of the courts as 'tough' and to talk of Restorative Justice as being 'soft'; if anything, it should be the other way round. In any event, it should really be about whether it actually works or not – that is the important thing to know. Peter's experiences during the many trials he attended and the sentences handed down to him are cast in sharp relief with what happened to him at his restorative conference.

We know that it was RJ that stopped Peter's re-offending, in conjunction with the support he received afterwards. We also know from research that this is commonplace with RJ. It very often reduces re-offending, particularly in crimes involving a personal victim, for example assault, robbery or burglary, as opposed to shop theft or fraud against the State. In some RJ schemes these reductions in re-offending have been as high as a third or a half. So RJ reduces crime, sometimes significantly. Less crime means fewer crime victims in the future. Surely that is more important than whether RJ seems 'tough' or 'soft'?

Primarily, Restorative Justice is about the victim and the wider community, rather than the offender. All the evidence from hundreds of RJ schemes across the world shows that victims of crime who agree to attend conferences and meet 'their' offender are 'satisfied' with what happened to a far greater extent, both more often and more fully, than in the traditional court process. This was certainly the experience of Will after meeting Peter at the conference.

Over 90 per cent of victims are 'satisfied' with Restorative Justice; contrast this with court, where less than one third of crime victims are satisfied with how they are treated. And 85 per cent would recommend RJ to others in the same situation. We also know that RJ often helps victims get over post-traumatic stress disorder (PTSD), not only improving their lives and the lives of their families but also saving us all, the tax payers, medical and social welfare costs.

Through RJ, victims are able to find out about the crime and ask questions such as 'Why me?' They usually receive an apology and reparation, sometimes including monetary compensation when the offender has money or a job to earn money. They are reassured, their confidence is returned and their fear of crime is assuaged. They also usually feel less angry and retributive and want – more than anything else, more even than a heavy punishment – an assurance that the offender will never do this to anyone else again and will be held to account for this undertaking. None of these gains is usually possible through the court system.

How Does Restorative Justice Work?

That the amazing outcome for Peter and Will has come from a restorative conference is not simply down to luck or good fortune. Restorative Justice is designed precisely to have that effect; it is not just a question of throwing some people together in a room and hoping for the best. It required considerable training, experience and skill from Kim to ensure that all the parties involved approached the conference in the right way.

This he did by first obtaining their consent to meet, and then by preparing them properly for the encounter they would be taking part in. As well as having to follow a particular route to staging an RJ conference, a trained facilitator such as Kim has what is called a 'script' to follow, a process by which the facilitator takes the group through the RJ process, tackling a number of simple questions asked of each of them. There is no magic to it, it is simply a common-sense way of using discussion, feelings and emotions as a way of resolving conflict and of re-establishing a relationship between the parties that can be honoured by them both.

Peter and Will's conference was not unusual. Many conferences are similar, but each one is unique to the circumstances of the particular case, to particular crimes, offenders, victims and others who attend. In the trials of RJ conferences carried out throughout London, of which Peter and Will's was one, virtually all brought substantial benefits to the victims, families and friends who attended – which is the prime aim of the conference – and many brought benefits as well to offenders and their families.

This is because modern RJ follows two simple principles of psychology. The first is that it is the people involved in the conflict who should be the ones to resolve it, rather than strangers in a courtroom. This is so that the solution the two parties – wrongdoer and victim – come up with is a binding one, because it is a solution both have agreed after their deliberations; it is not imposed upon them from outside. In the RJ conference, this is called the 'outcome agreement'.

The second principle is called 're-integrative shaming', which loosely means the shame an offender feels in front of his friends and family at having committed a crime. This idea comes from the work of the Australian criminologist Professor John Braithwaite, who says that most people ask the wrong question when it comes to crime: instead of asking 'Why do some people commit crime?', the right question to ask is 'Why do most people not commit crime?' His answer is that most people don't commit crime because they are worried that if they did, and they were caught, and they were confronted directly with how they had harmed the victim in the presence of someone close to them such as their family or friends, they would feel desperate shame. They would be devastated at how they had let down those close to them. So they decide not to commit crime. That is why most of us don't think of crime, or about committing crime, in the first place!

Interestingly, at his conference Peter did not have any supporters, family or friends, although this didn't make any difference to the outcome. The sheer impact on Peter of hearing, for the first time in his life, of the harm he was causing – such extreme harm, leading to such extreme shame – was so great that not having family or friends with him altered nothing. The terrible harm he had caused, regardless of who else was there, was what caused him to feel such massive remorse.

Restorative Justice and the Justice System

Of course these things don't work all the time, with everyone, with every case; but if RJ works a lot of the time with a lot of people in a lot of cases, then why is it the one thing our conventional justice system doesn't do? We all recognize that there are no panaceas when it comes to tackling crime; but it is common sense that our system should deal not only with the crime as something 'against the State' but also as something that causes harm to others and to the local community.

Restorative Justice should normally be the first thing to be considered when a crime is solved and the offender caught, not the last. The court should be considered as the long-stop, the safety net, the process that deals with the wider public interest when RJ can't. But, expensive, legalistic and remote from the real world, it should not be the automatic default mechanism for dealing with crime, the first port of call, as it is often seen now. It is RJ that should be considered first. As they were originally intended to be, the courts would then be the fail-safe mechanism for the justice system, not the front line.

Put another way, the courts should be the goalkeeper and full backs for our 'team' that tackles crime, but nothing more. Can you imagine a football team where the whole side is made up of goalkeepers and full backs playing out of position? The right analogy is that the forwards are the various elements designed to help people stop committing crime and make amends, such as reparation to the victim, drug and alcohol programmes, schemes to help offenders find accommodation and jobs, support to offenders to educate and train themselves, and so on.

Where does Restorative Justice fit in this team? RJ consists of the midfield players, the dynamos who provide energy and purpose to the side, probing away, trying to set up and involve the forwards, linking with the full backs and goalkeeper, sometimes falling back to help the defence, at other times going forward and scoring goals themselves. The RJ midfield players are the motivators and animators of the team.

Restorative Justice works. It provides the motivation – the missing ingredient – in our justice system that could improve it hugely. It reduces re-offending and therefore reduces crime. It helps victims get over what has happened to them, so that they can renew a normal life and not walk around forever frightened. It reduces crime victims' desire for violent revenge against their offender. It would make our justice much more humane and effective.

Not only that, Restorative Justice is also far less costly than the traditional system. Take Peter and Will's case. The cost to the public of holding the restorative conference – police time, visiting and preparing those to be involved, administrative costs, the time of prison staff, etc. – was about £800. On the other hand, the saving from Peter's change of behaviour from that of a prolific criminal and addict to a law-abiding member of the community was £1,690,000 from the same public purse. This saving, worked out with reference to Home Office documents on the real costs of crime, is made up of the monetary value of the crimes that, on a modest assumption, Peter would have committed but for the conference and the rehabilitation that followed; and the cost of prison where he would undoubtedly have found himself for much of the rest of his life had he not changed his mindset. In fact, this cost-saving has been worked out on the basis only of the five years after the conference – Peter was so ill after his life of drugs and booze that his life expectancy was short if he had carried on as he was – but he has now already exceeded that and looks set for a much longer life! The figures show that if RJ only worked fully once in a hundred cases with offenders like Peter (and research shows it would do much, much better than that), there would still be a cost-saving ratio of 1:21. So every £1 spent on

RJ would bring savings of £21 elsewhere in society.

In conclusion, we now need to get Government policy changed so that people's consciences and emotions become recognized as a legitimate, important part of the process for tackling crime, and victims of crime are genuinely given their place in the justice system. To do that, RJ needs to be mainstreamed across the whole country, as a proper part of the criminal justice system working alongside the courts, prisons and community sanctions to bring improved justice for all.

And Restorative Justice principles work equally well in schools and other environments. In schools, where they are called 'restorative approaches', they improve behaviour across the school, tackle bullying at root, make schools happier places in which to learn and reduce the number of children tipped on to the scrap heap through exclusion. RJ can also work in the community setting, in neighbourhood policing or where local people adopt it as their way of resolving problems, in resolving conflicts at work, or as part of workplace disciplinary processes.

Peter and Will feel the same as I do, and together we have been to many parts of the country to talk about the benefits of RJ, including two conferences at 11 Downing Street. To sit there with these two men, who willingly share their experiences, is always fascinating and sometimes humbling, and I believe it is something that gives hope and inspiration to all of us seeking a better society.

For the Downing Street conferences, I prepared a paper, one part of which stated:

> Restorative Justice is particularly effective when linked with other interventions to stop or reduce re-offending, and to help victims. It can be used at different points within the CJS [criminal justice system]: as a diversion from court in youth justice (e.g. final warnings) or adult justice (Home Office conditional caution trials); as part of the Youth Court process with, for example, referral orders and youth offender panels; as part of the Adult Court sentencing process where restorative conferences can be held between plea and sentence or after sentence (Home Office trials nearing completion); and as an important part of Prison and Community sentences prior to completion and as a driver for successful rehabilitation.

Now, imagine if that were to come into the justice system, that instead of simply punishing people we were able to deal with them in a manner that reinforced society's disapproval of their behaviour, allowed the victims to express themselves freely on the matter, yet didn't condemn them to a system where most re-offend very quickly. How much more effective would our sentencing be, how much better would be the outcomes, not just for those offended against but for all of society?

I hope Peter's case can, through this book, inspire the accomplishment of the vision of a much more effective, less expensive, more humane system of justice in our country. We all want a justice system that works.

There are many organizations and individuals working across the UK to provide Restorative Justice services. If you would like to find out more about what is available or how you can get involved, please contact:

Restorative Solutions Community Interest Company
Restorative Solutions CIC is a not-for-profit organization working for the public good. It was registered with Companies House on 16 February 2007.

Company number: 6110507
Address: 12 Nolan Close, St Andrews Ridge, Swindon, Wilts SN25 4GP
Chairman: Sir Charles Pollard, QPM
Business Director: Nigel Whiskin, MBE
Associate Trainer: Peter Woolf
http://www.restorativesolutions.org.uk

or

Restorative Justice Consortium
The Restorative Justice Consortium is the independent membership organization for Restorative Justice in

England and Wales. It exists to promote the development of RJ; to provide information about RJ to the public; and to support their members, many of whom are RJ practitioners. The RJC is a registered charity.

Charity number: 1097969
Address: Albert Buildings, 49 Queen Victoria Street, London EC4N 4SA
Tel: (020) 7 653 1992
Chairman: Peter Patrick
Chief Executive: Harriet Bailey
http://www.restorativejustice.org.uk

If you have been a victim of crime and went through a restorative process as part of the outcome of that crime, you may like to join or support Victims for Restorative Justice. It is a new organization set up by victims of crime who have benefited from their experience of Restorative Justice, and who want others to be afforded the same opportunity. Victims for Restorative Justice can be contacted through the Restorative Justice Consortium.

Glossary

charlie — cocaine

chasing the dragon — smoking heroin

china white / white Thai — types of heroin

(to) clip — to receive payment for the promise of sex, for example, but not deliver the goods

diamorphine hydrochloride — pharmaceutical heroin

DF118 — an opiate-based tablet that can be used as a heroin substitute

downers — generic name for sleeping pills, tranquillizers, etc.

draw / bush — marijuana

Driminyl / blues / bombers / Purple Hearts / Dexys (Dexedrine) — types of amphetamine (synthetic mood-altering stimulants)

fence	someone who buys stolen goods
fraggles	prison term for the mentally ill in the hospital wing
getter	someone who gets drugs for people
grunting	preying on the elderly
hanging out / clucking	withdrawing
joey	a wrap of heroin
Largactil / Mellaril	anti-psychotic medicines meant for schizophrenics
Mandrax	a downer
methadone	heroin substitute
Mogadon	sleeping pills
mong	past the mellow stage to non-communicative; a trance-like state
napolene ('napo')	a steroid
Nembutal	a downer
nonce	someone arrested for a sexual offence (the word comes from what was written above the prisoner's door: 'Not Of Normal Criminal Element')

Pethidine	opiate-based drug (as used during labour)
puff	cannabis
scag / henry / horse	generic names for brown heroin
screwing	burglary
screws	prison officers
smack / tackle	generic names for heroin
stingers	fake drugs, to sell
trips	LSD
Tuinal	a downer
uppers	generic name for amphetamines
wraps	a £10 wrap is £10 of heroin in paper